COLONIA

Written and Illustrated by Jeff Nicholson

COLONIA : ISLANDS & ANOMALIES
Published by AiT/PlanetLar
2034 47th Avenue, San Francisco, CA 94116

Originally published in serial form as
COLONIA # 1-5 by COLONIA PRESS,
P.O. Box 193681 San Francisco, CA
94119. Colonia is © 1998-2001 Jeff
Nicholson. All rights reserved.
This edition is © 2001 AiT / PlanetLar

http: // www.ait-planetlar.com
http: // www.coloniapress.com
Printed in CANADA by Quebecor

FOR ROXANNE

Why a man made of fish?

Why, so I could do a series called Colonia, of course.

Why Colonia?

Why, so I could keep making comics, of course.

Why keep making comics?

Oh, now that's a difficult question.

I was one of those comics guys from the eighties who were determined, tooth and nail, to make a living from comics. Yes, I loved comics and have since I was a tot, but I also dreamed about being a comics publisher; creator; an entrepreneur; to live the life! (whatever that was) and this went back to childhood as well. It was all rolled up into one, and after making a marginal and perilous living at it, off and on, through the eighties and nineties, the two loves kind of died together when the whole bubble burst.

No, you will not make a living from this, Jeff . . .

That bubble burst for different people at different times, but for me it was 1997. Coincidentally, that was also the year I had wrapped everything up artistically. All the ideas I had come up with and cultivated for the last 20 years were DONE. Everything I had come up with in my teens or twenties was either based on people I knew from life, or was a parody of other artists' characters, or was semi-autobiographical. Finally all those projects that I thought would never be finished were actually finished. I had an opportunity to do something completely fresh, and not have the obsession of self-employment to possibly pollute it or ruin it entirely.

That year two of the comics series I was enjoying the most were *Bone* and *Castle Waiting*. These books offered fun, straightforward storytelling, yet had a fully realized epic below the surface that kept you wanting more. I had used that "simple episodes that build a complex tale" approach, more or less, with *Ultra Klutz* and *Through the Habitrails*, but visually and thematically my past work had been going the way most comics went over the last few decades: with obscure camera angles, dark abstraction, and mindless psychedelia.

Apparently I wasn't the only one getting tired of the state of comics. In addition to *Bone* and *Castle Waiting*, a stable of other books (*Akiko, Replacement God, Age of Bronze*) were establishing themselves, suggesting there was a small but important audience out there that enjoyed some good ol' fashioned comics.

That industry buzz inspired me to use my "clean slate" on a comic that both kids and older comics fans could enjoy. I also hoped to bring in some of the elements from my childhood favorites (*Kamandi the Last Boy on Earth, The Wizard of Oz* novels, television's *Lost in Space*) that I felt had universal appeal. The only obstacle was that I wasn't attracted to working in a quasi-medieval reality, as most of the current "fantasy-adventure" comics were set in. My fascinations growing up were with the ages of discovery and of colonization. I loved looking at old maps of North America, inaccurately rendered, with encroaching empires all scattered around. The moment I thought to have this new series take place in the new world rather than the old world was the moment Colonia was born.

I made a conscious decision to never sit down at a keyboard and roll up my sleeves, demanding I come up with a script. I let Colonia inhabit my head all of its own will, and I refused to even take any notes for several months. Early mental versions didn't even have Jack as a character. Finally, late in 1997, after seeing a reproduction of an old Greek (?) deity with fish head – fish hands – fish feet, I was ready to get cracking. Since then all of the scripts just wandered into my head while out hiking. Everything in this volume had wandered in by Summer of 1998, before the first issue was even released. Only when it was time to do the thumbnails would I type out the script from memory.

Visually Colonia was also a complete back-to-the-drawing-board. I was starting to get in a rut of drawing from how I used to draw, instead of drawing form observation. This results in something like a bad copy of a copy of a copy, and I'm sure you can think of a few comics artists who've fallen into that trap. I started to embrace the use of reference and made a little hobby out of building a reference library, both of print and of video tape (History Channel on freeze frame is a must). That self-copying rut proved hard to get out of, too, when I started the thumbnails for page one. I laid it out the way I always would have, with oblique overhead angles, and was getting all grumpy and not knowing why. Then I realized what I was after. In a film from the forties, you wouldn't see a pirate movie open with oblique angles, it would go establishing shot, middle shot, close up. For page one of Colonia I re-did it just like that, and it was exactly the way I want to communicate this story.

I admit I became seduced by the self-employment bug (again) after the second issue. I quit my job for a bi-monthly jag on Colonia 3-5, which was only possible because I saved up a pile of money from the day job. I was hoping to go bi-monthly for a year, but an old debt from a previous round of overextended self-employment came calling and swept the war chest away. After only four months I was back at my day-job and just burned out enough to put off working on Colonia 6 for about six months. So it's slow and steady from here on out. With a good day job, I will never get derailed by any crackpot side projects or overblown "Tours."

I hope you will stick around for this slow and steady saga. One nice thing about the internet; you can always check in and see if I'm still at it.

Jeff Nicholson
August, 2001
Coloniapress.com

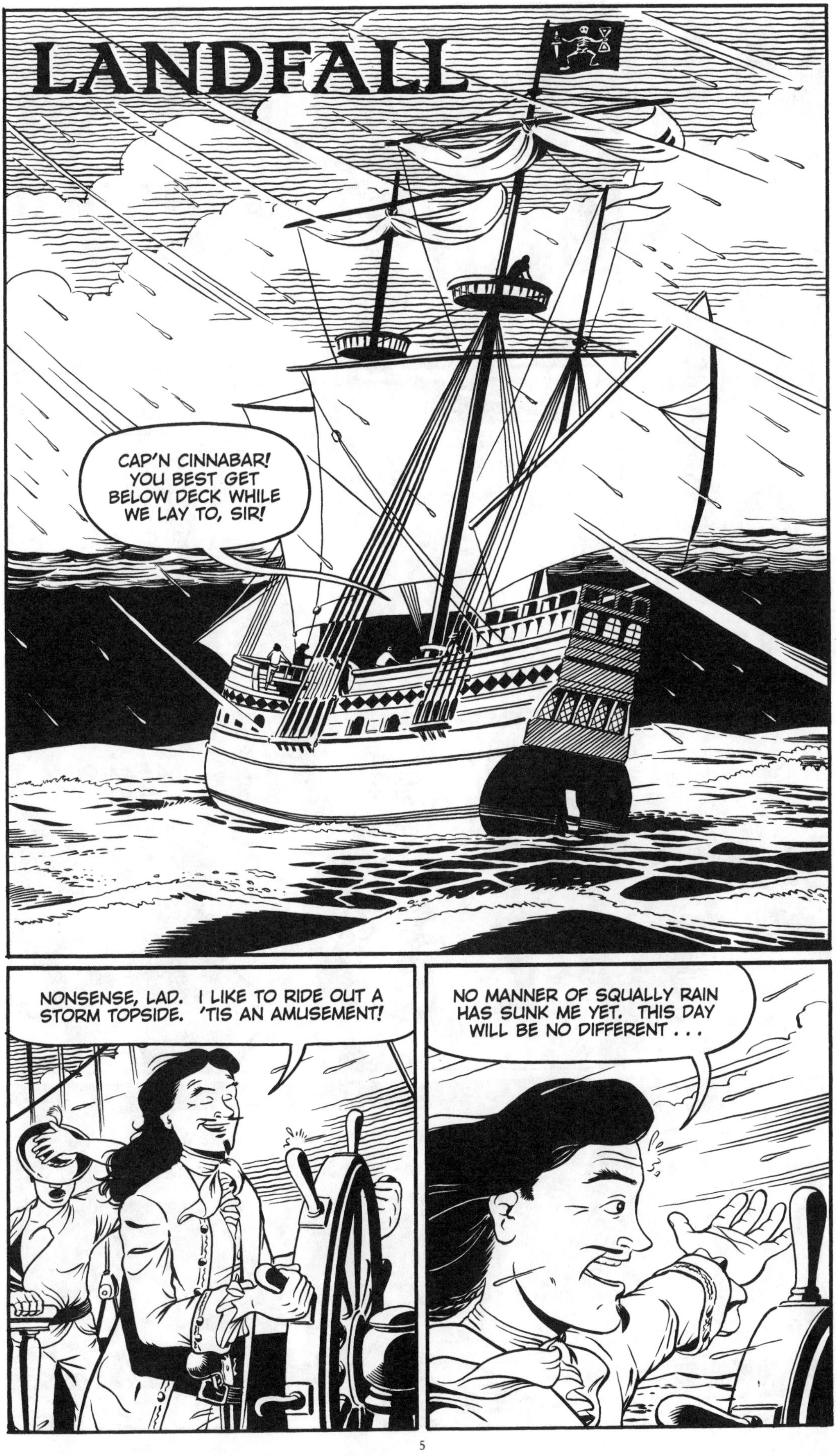
LANDFALL
CAP'N CINNABAR! YOU BEST GET BELOW DECK WHILE WE LAY TO, SIR!
NONSENSE, LAD. I LIKE TO RIDE OUT A STORM TOPSIDE. 'TIS AN AMUSEMENT!
NO MANNER OF SQUALLY RAIN HAS SUNK ME YET. THIS DAY WILL BE NO DIFFERENT . . .

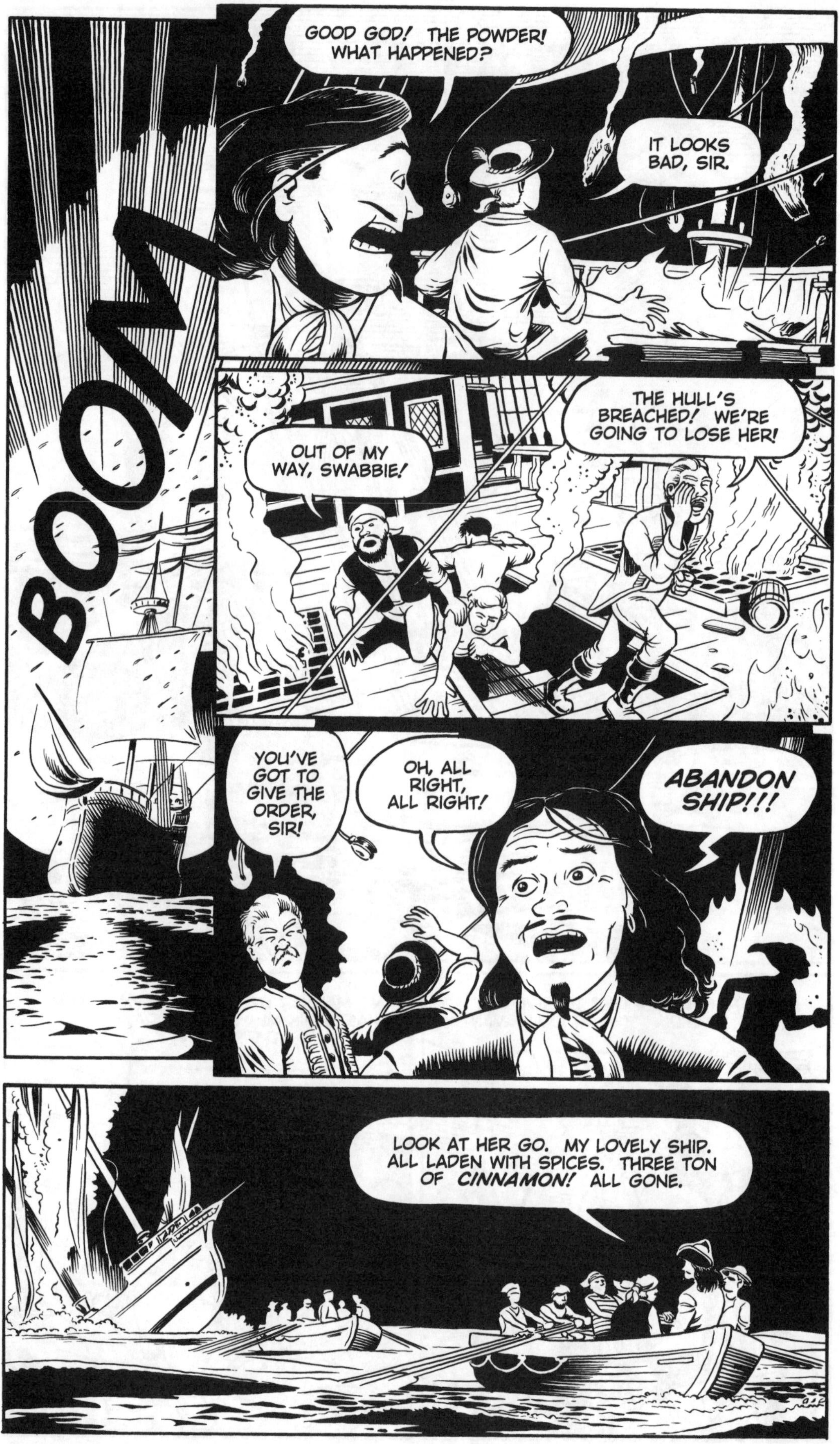
BOOM
GOOD GOD! THE POWDER! WHAT HAPPENED?
IT LOOKS BAD, SIR.
OUT OF MY WAY, SWABBIE!
THE HULL'S BREACHED! WE'RE GOING TO LOSE HER!
YOU'VE GOT TO GIVE THE ORDER, SIR!
OH, ALL RIGHT, ALL RIGHT!
ABANDON SHIP!!!
LOOK AT HER GO. MY LOVELY SHIP. ALL LADEN WITH SPICES. THREE TON OF CINNAMON! ALL GONE.

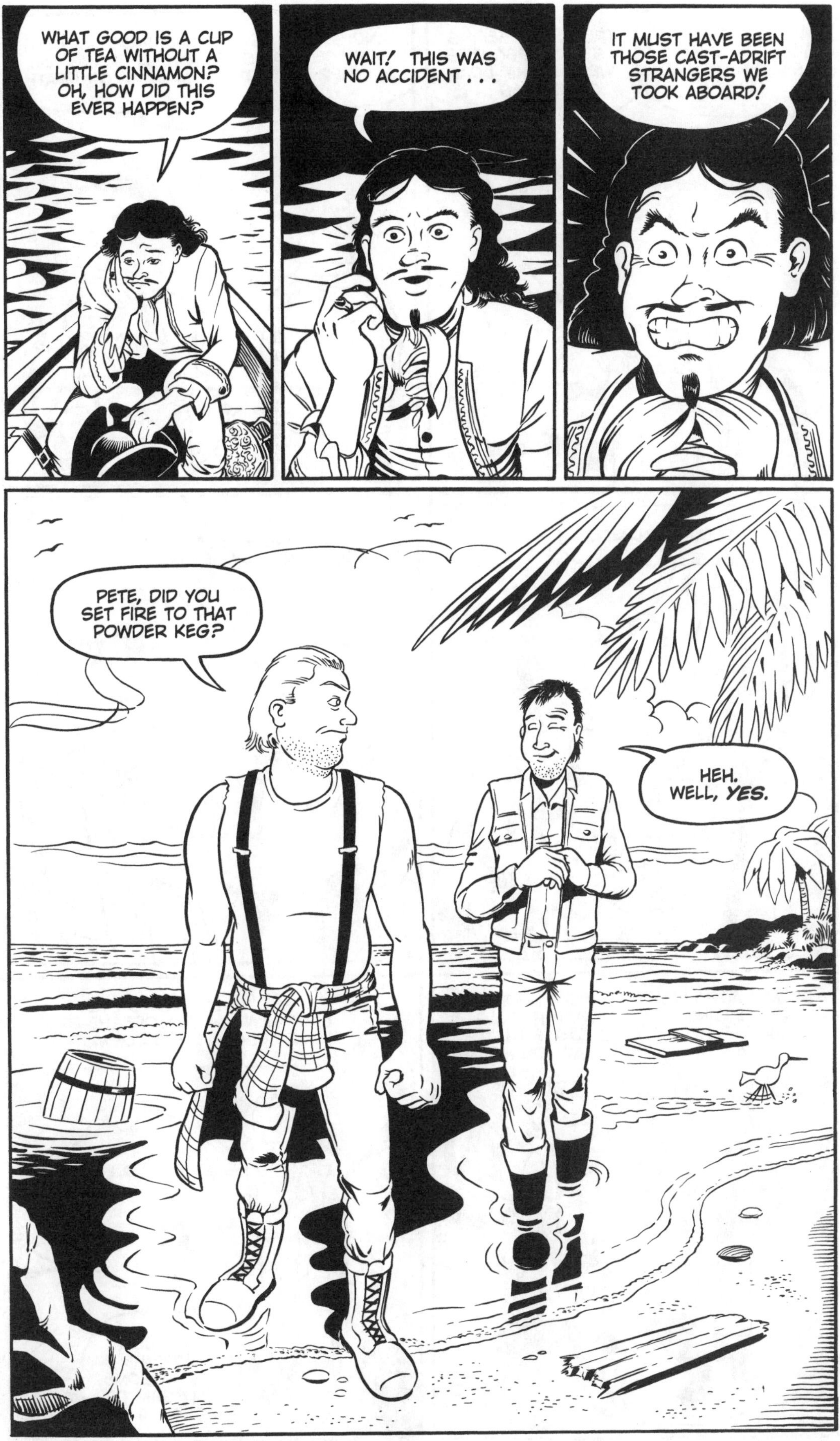
WHAT GOOD IS A CUP OF TEA WITHOUT A LITTLE CINNAMON? OH, HOW DID THIS EVER HAPPEN?
WAIT! THIS WAS NO ACCIDENT . . .
IT MUST HAVE BEEN THOSE CAST-ADRIFT STRANGERS WE TOOK ABOARD!
PETE, DID YOU SET FIRE TO THAT POWDER KEG?
HEH. WELL, *YES*.

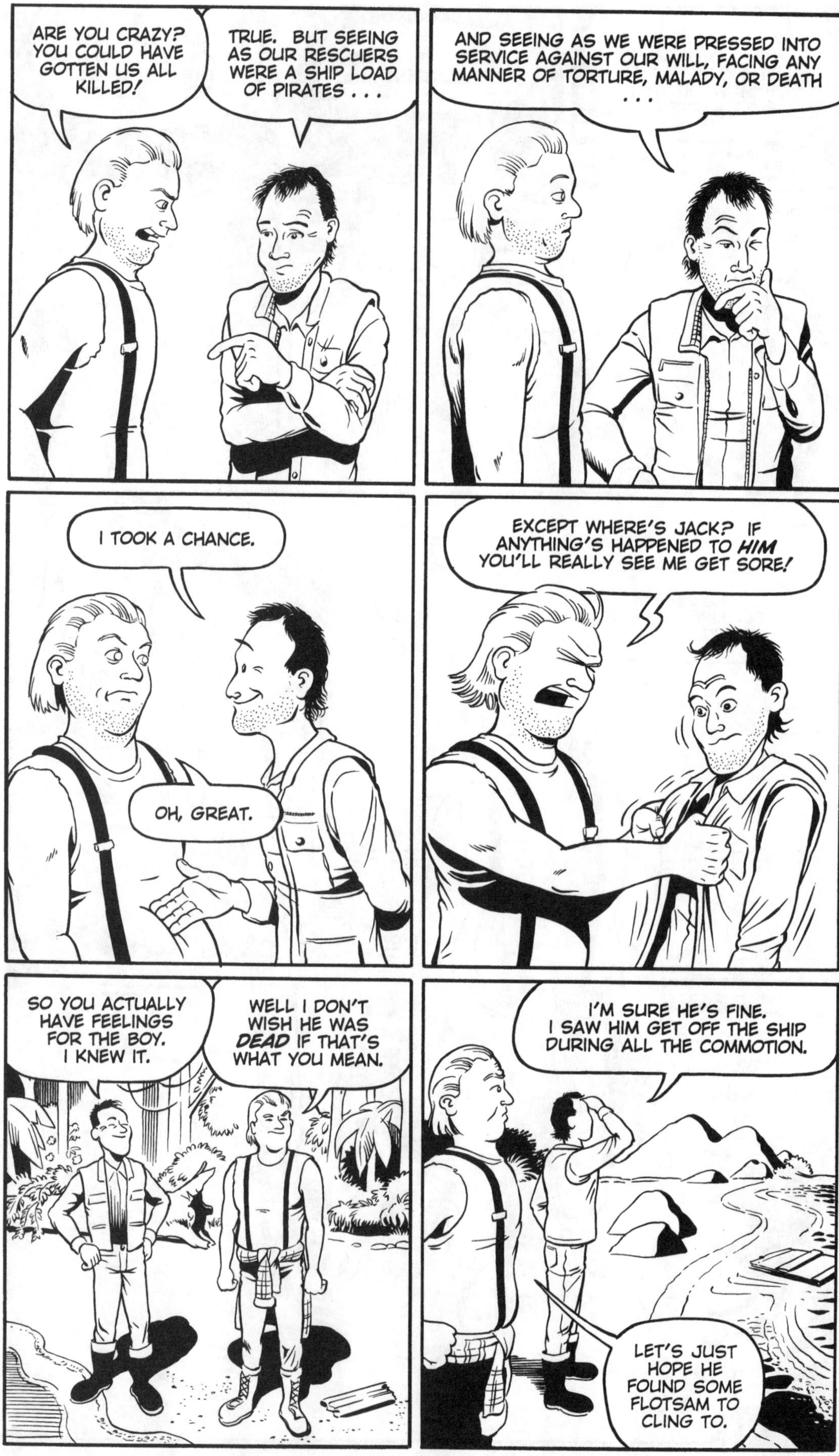
ARE YOU CRAZY? YOU COULD HAVE GOTTEN US ALL KILLED!
TRUE. BUT SEEING AS OUR RESCUERS WERE A SHIP LOAD OF PIRATES . . .
AND SEEING AS WE WERE PRESSED INTO SERVICE AGAINST OUR WILL, FACING ANY MANNER OF TORTURE, MALADY, OR DEATH . . .
I TOOK A CHANCE.
OH, GREAT.
EXCEPT WHERE'S JACK? IF ANYTHING'S HAPPENED TO *HIM* YOU'LL REALLY SEE ME GET SORE!
SO YOU ACTUALLY HAVE FEELINGS FOR THE BOY. I KNEW IT.
WELL I DON'T WISH HE WAS *DEAD* IF THAT'S WHAT YOU MEAN.
I'M SURE HE'S FINE. I SAW HIM GET OFF THE SHIP DURING ALL THE COMMOTION.
LET'S JUST HOPE HE FOUND SOME FLOTSAM TO CLING TO.

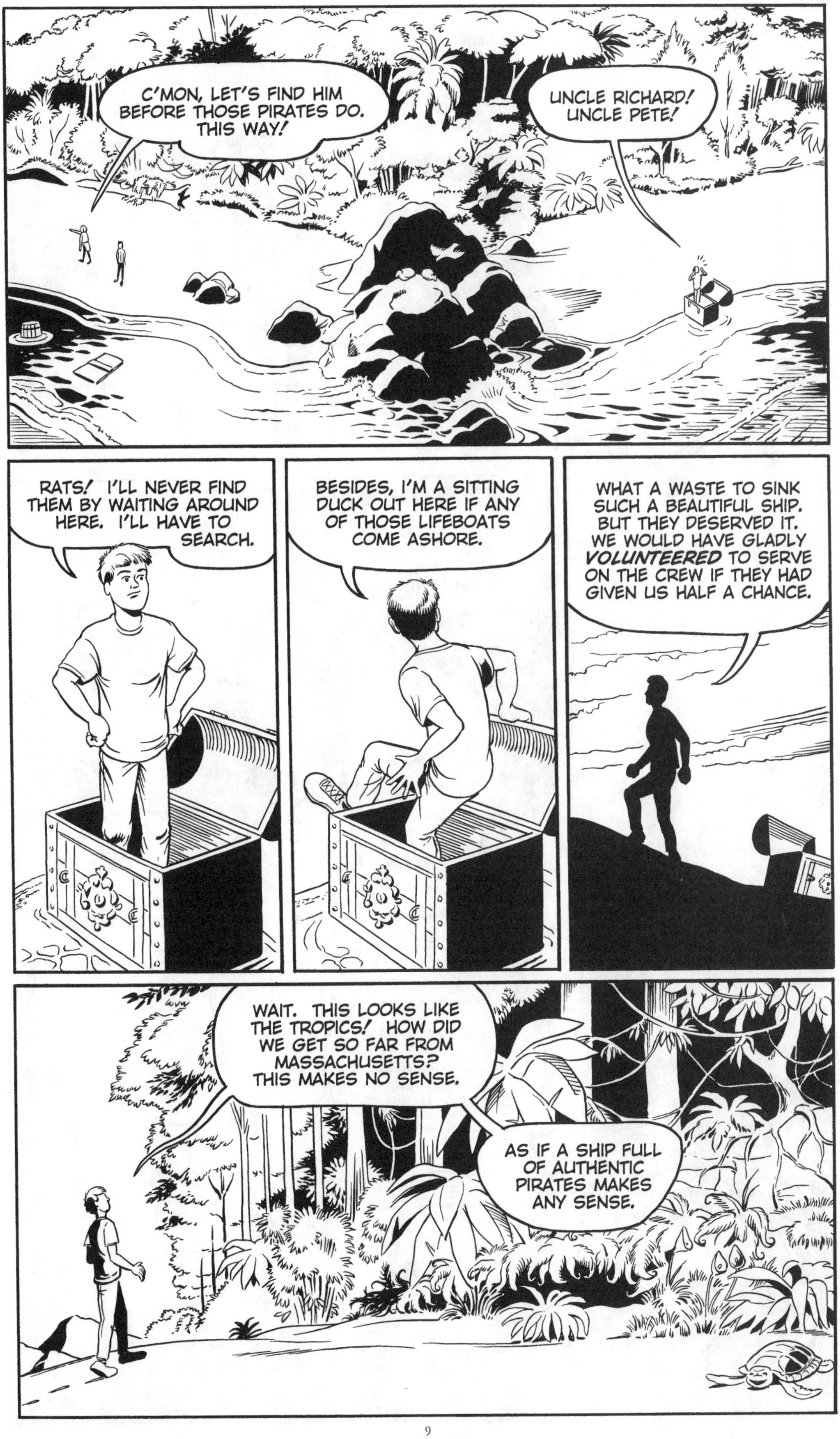
C'MON, LET'S FIND HIM BEFORE THOSE PIRATES DO. THIS WAY!
UNCLE RICHARD! UNCLE PETE!
RATS! I'LL NEVER FIND THEM BY WAITING AROUND HERE. I'LL HAVE TO SEARCH.
BESIDES, I'M A SITTING DUCK OUT HERE IF ANY OF THOSE LIFEBOATS COME ASHORE.
WHAT A WASTE TO SINK SUCH A BEAUTIFUL SHIP. BUT THEY DESERVED IT. WE WOULD HAVE GLADLY VOLUNTEERED TO SERVE ON THE CREW IF THEY HAD GIVEN US HALF A CHANCE.
WAIT. THIS LOOKS LIKE THE TROPICS! HOW DID WE GET SO FAR FROM MASSACHUSETTS? THIS MAKES NO SENSE.
AS IF A SHIP FULL OF AUTHENTIC PIRATES MAKES ANY SENSE.

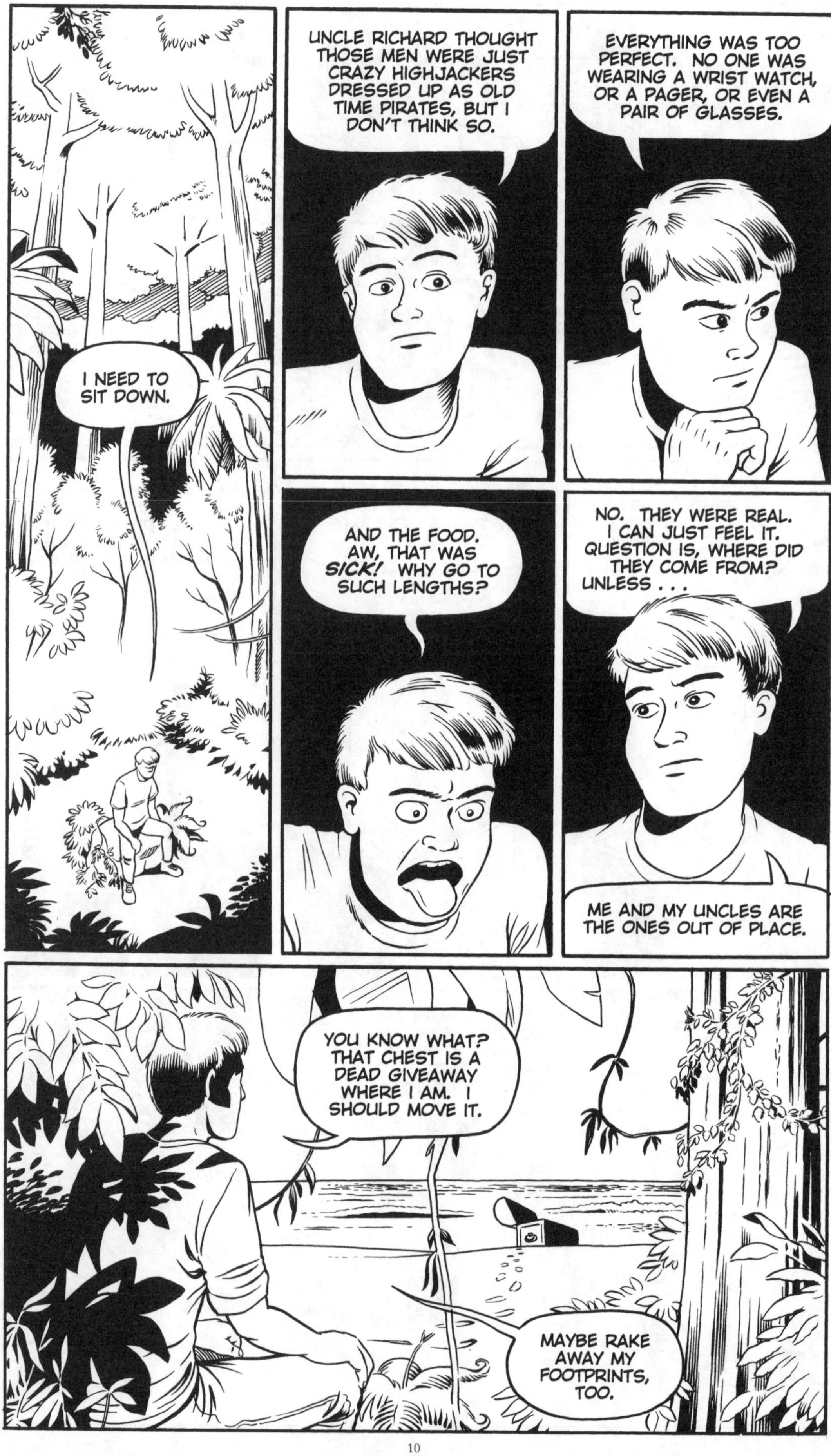
I NEED TO SIT DOWN.
UNCLE RICHARD THOUGHT THOSE MEN WERE JUST CRAZY HIGHJACKERS DRESSED UP AS OLD TIME PIRATES, BUT I DON'T THINK SO.
EVERYTHING WAS TOO PERFECT. NO ONE WAS WEARING A WRIST WATCH, OR A PAGER, OR EVEN A PAIR OF GLASSES.
AND THE FOOD. AW, THAT WAS SICK! WHY GO TO SUCH LENGTHS?
NO. THEY WERE REAL. I CAN JUST FEEL IT. QUESTION IS, WHERE DID THEY COME FROM? UNLESS . . .
ME AND MY UNCLES ARE THE ONES OUT OF PLACE.
YOU KNOW WHAT? THAT CHEST IS A DEAD GIVEAWAY WHERE I AM. I SHOULD MOVE IT.
MAYBE RAKE AWAY MY FOOTPRINTS, TOO.

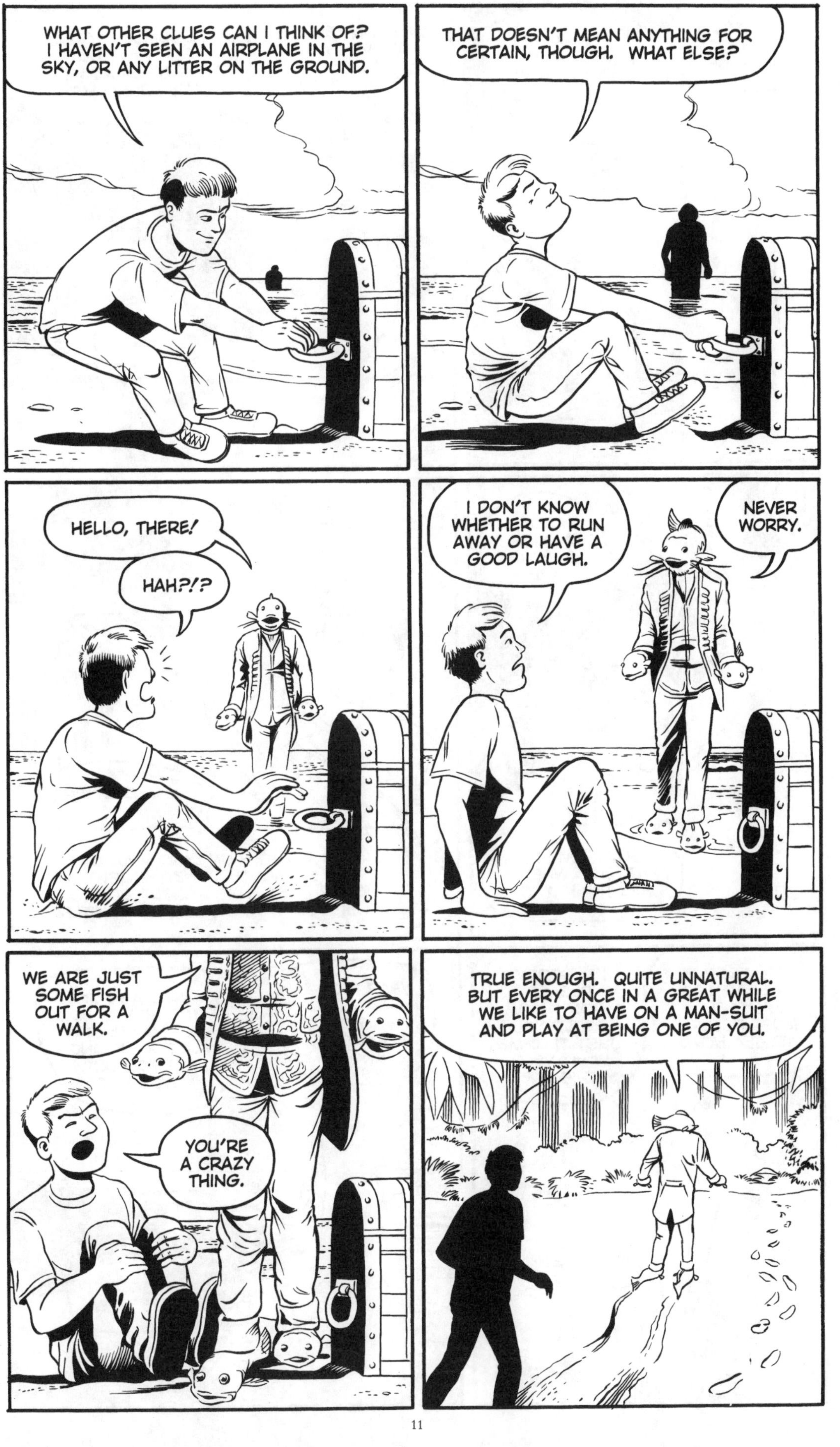
WHAT OTHER CLUES CAN I THINK OF? I HAVEN'T SEEN AN AIRPLANE IN THE SKY, OR ANY LITTER ON THE GROUND.
THAT DOESN'T MEAN ANYTHING FOR CERTAIN, THOUGH. WHAT ELSE?
HELLO, THERE!
HAH?!?
I DON'T KNOW WHETHER TO RUN AWAY OR HAVE A GOOD LAUGH.
NEVER WORRY.
WE ARE JUST SOME FISH OUT FOR A WALK.
YOU'RE A CRAZY THING.
TRUE ENOUGH. QUITE UNNATURAL. BUT EVERY ONCE IN A GREAT WHILE WE LIKE TO HAVE ON A MAN-SUIT AND PLAY AT BEING ONE OF YOU.

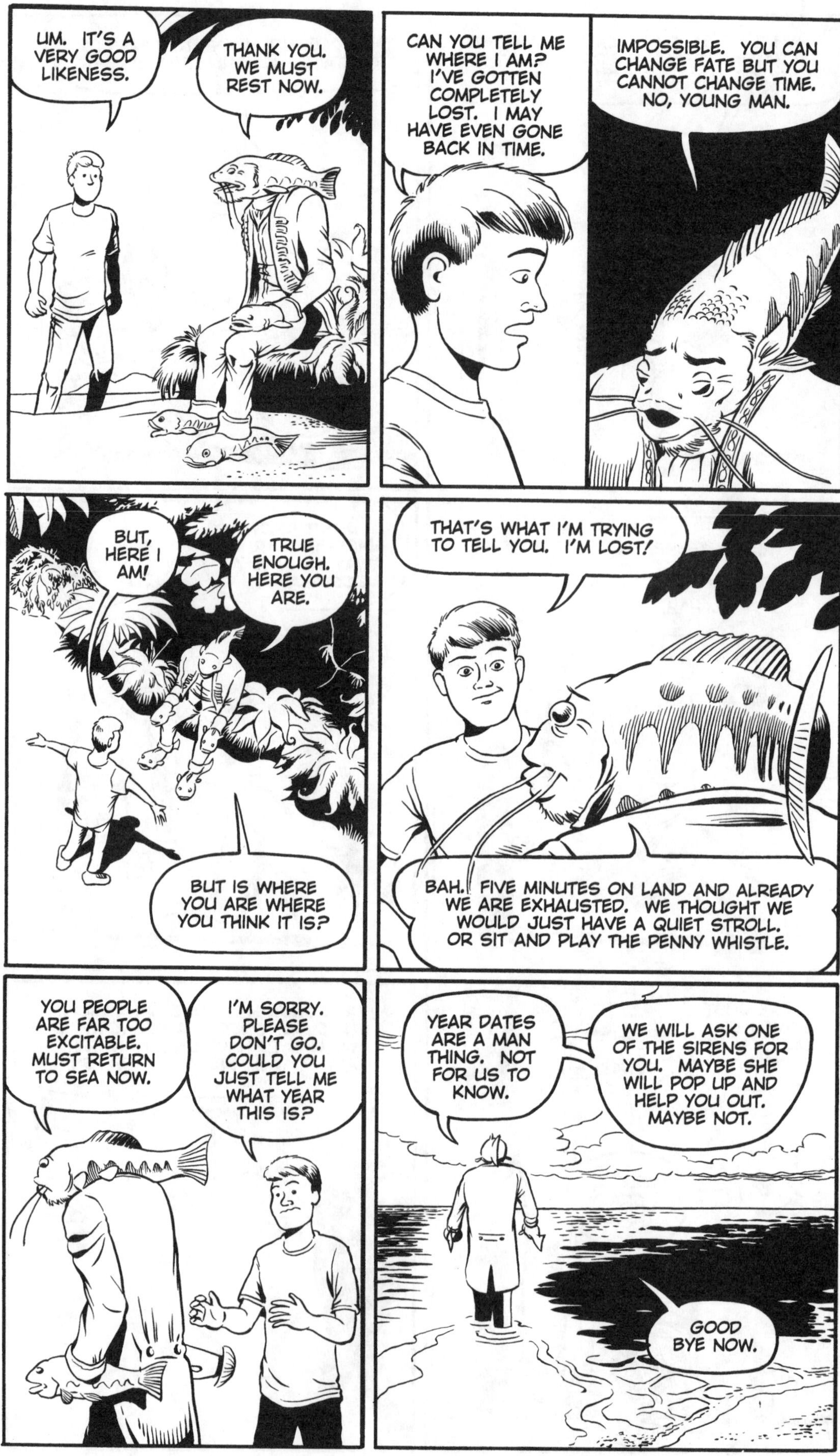
UM. IT'S A VERY GOOD LIKENESS.
THANK YOU. WE MUST REST NOW.
CAN YOU TELL ME WHERE I AM? I'VE GOTTEN COMPLETELY LOST. I MAY HAVE EVEN GONE BACK IN TIME.
IMPOSSIBLE. YOU CAN CHANGE FATE BUT YOU CANNOT CHANGE TIME. NO, YOUNG MAN.
BUT, HERE I AM!
TRUE ENOUGH. HERE YOU ARE.
BUT IS WHERE YOU ARE WHERE YOU THINK IT IS?
THAT'S WHAT I'M TRYING TO TELL YOU. I'M LOST!
BAH. FIVE MINUTES ON LAND AND ALREADY WE ARE EXHAUSTED. WE THOUGHT WE WOULD JUST HAVE A QUIET STROLL. OR SIT AND PLAY THE PENNY WHISTLE.
YOU PEOPLE ARE FAR TOO EXCITABLE. MUST RETURN TO SEA NOW.
I'M SORRY. PLEASE DON'T GO. COULD YOU JUST TELL ME WHAT YEAR THIS IS?
YEAR DATES ARE A MAN THING. NOT FOR US TO KNOW.
WE WILL ASK ONE OF THE SIRENS FOR YOU. MAYBE SHE WILL POP UP AND HELP YOU OUT. MAYBE NOT.
GOOD BYE NOW.

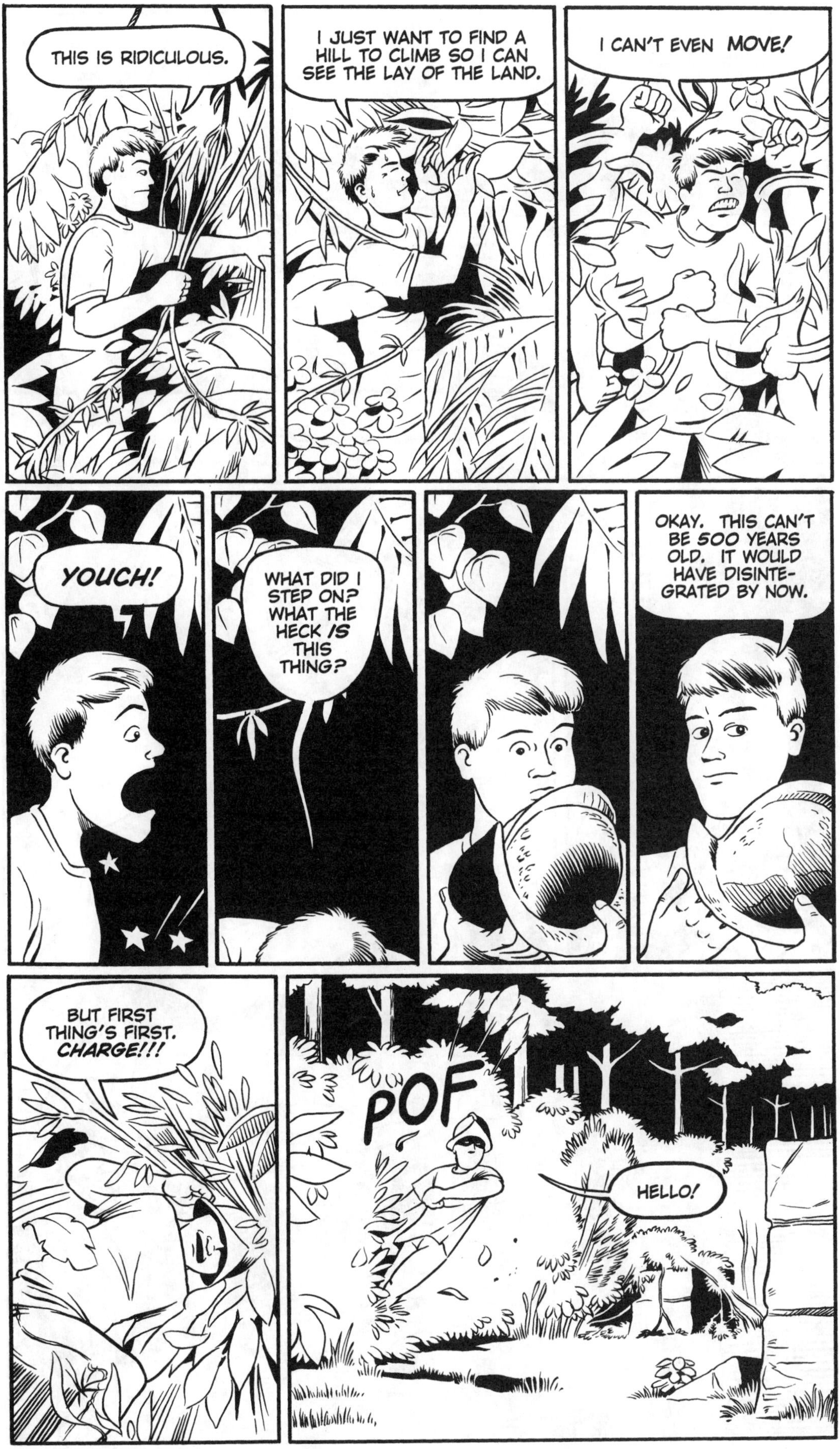
THIS IS RIDICULOUS.
I JUST WANT TO FIND A HILL TO CLIMB SO I CAN SEE THE LAY OF THE LAND.
I CAN'T EVEN MOVE!
YOUCH!
WHAT DID I STEP ON? WHAT THE HECK IS THIS THING?
OKAY. THIS CAN'T BE 500 YEARS OLD. IT WOULD HAVE DISINTE-GRATED BY NOW.
BUT FIRST THING'S FIRST. CHARGE!!!
POF
HELLO!

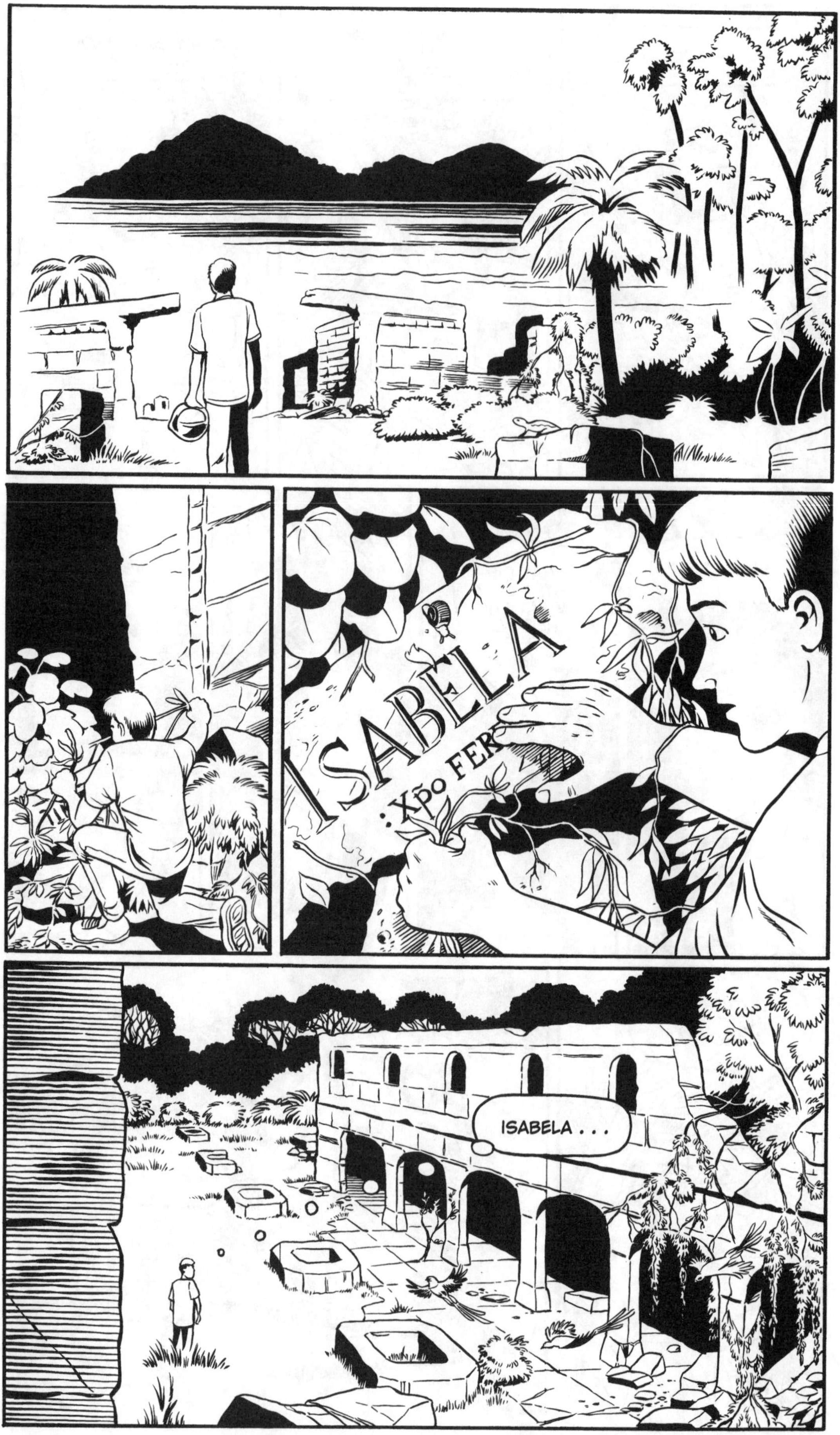
ISABELA
:Xpo FER
ISABELA . . .

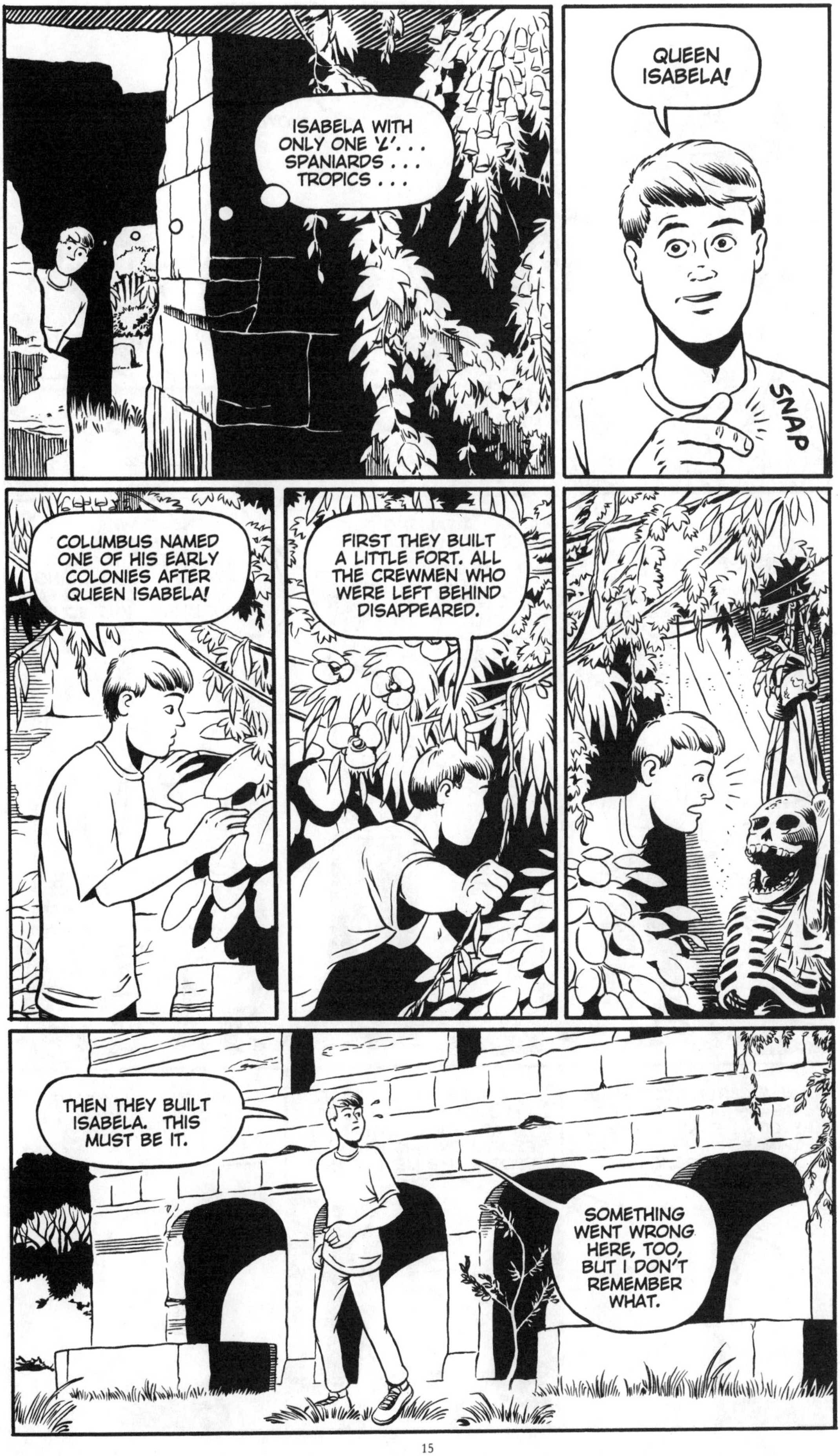
ISABELA WITH ONLY ONE 'L'... SPANIARDS... TROPICS...
QUEEN ISABELA!
SNAP
COLUMBUS NAMED ONE OF HIS EARLY COLONIES AFTER QUEEN ISABELA!
FIRST THEY BUILT A LITTLE FORT. ALL THE CREWMEN WHO WERE LEFT BEHIND DISAPPEARED.
THEN THEY BUILT ISABELA. THIS MUST BE IT.
SOMETHING WENT WRONG HERE, TOO, BUT I DON'T REMEMBER WHAT.

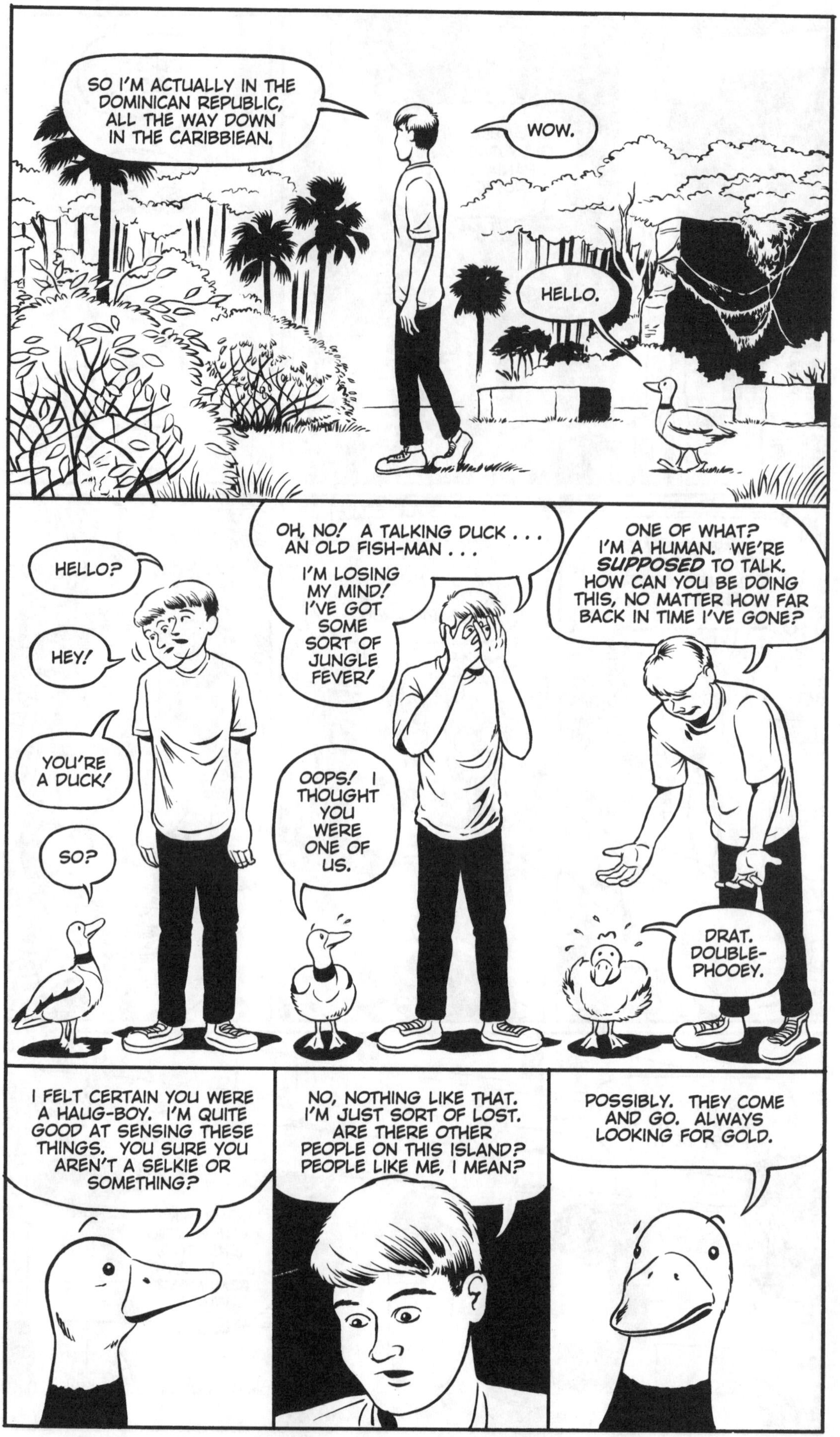
SO I'M ACTUALLY IN THE DOMINICAN REPUBLIC, ALL THE WAY DOWN IN THE CARIBBIEAN.
WOW.
HELLO.
HELLO?
HEY!
YOU'RE A DUCK!
SO?
OH, NO! A TALKING DUCK . . . AN OLD FISH-MAN . . .
I'M LOSING MY MIND! I'VE GOT SOME SORT OF JUNGLE FEVER!
OOPS! I THOUGHT YOU WERE ONE OF US.
ONE OF WHAT? I'M A HUMAN. WE'RE *SUPPOSED* TO TALK. HOW CAN YOU BE DOING THIS, NO MATTER HOW FAR BACK IN TIME I'VE GONE?
DRAT. DOUBLE-PHOOEY.
I FELT CERTAIN YOU WERE A HAUG-BOY. I'M QUITE GOOD AT SENSING THESE THINGS. YOU SURE YOU AREN'T A SELKIE OR SOMETHING?
NO, NOTHING LIKE THAT. I'M JUST SORT OF LOST. ARE THERE OTHER PEOPLE ON THIS ISLAND? PEOPLE LIKE ME, I MEAN?
POSSIBLY. THEY COME AND GO. ALWAYS LOOKING FOR GOLD.

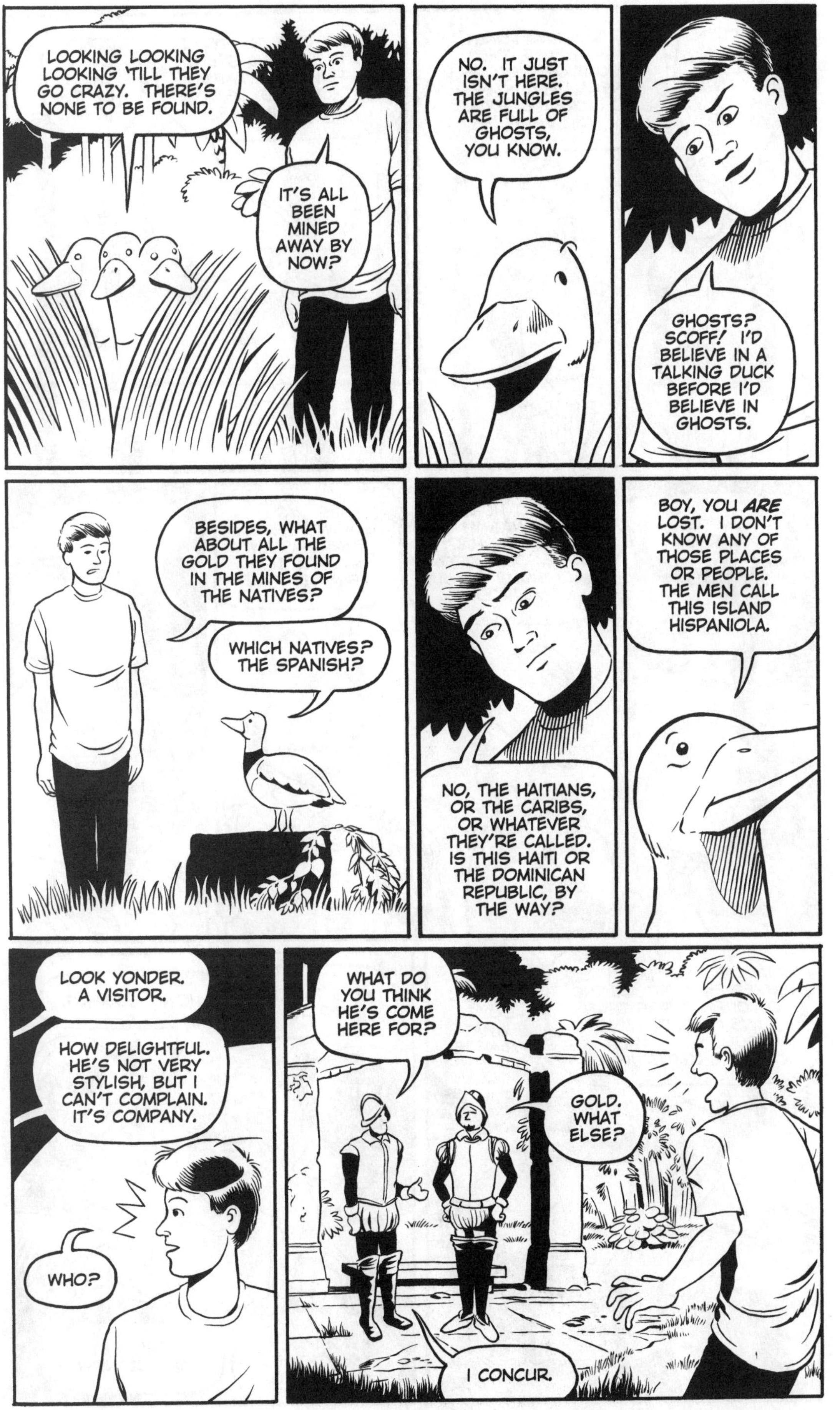
LOOKING LOOKING LOOKING 'TILL THEY GO CRAZY. THERE'S NONE TO BE FOUND.
IT'S ALL BEEN MINED AWAY BY NOW?
NO. IT JUST ISN'T HERE. THE JUNGLES ARE FULL OF GHOSTS, YOU KNOW.
GHOSTS? SCOFF! I'D BELIEVE IN A TALKING DUCK BEFORE I'D BELIEVE IN GHOSTS.
BESIDES, WHAT ABOUT ALL THE GOLD THEY FOUND IN THE MINES OF THE NATIVES?
WHICH NATIVES? THE SPANISH?
NO, THE HAITIANS, OR THE CARIBS, OR WHATEVER THEY'RE CALLED. IS THIS HAITI OR THE DOMINICAN REPUBLIC, BY THE WAY?
BOY, YOU ARE LOST. I DON'T KNOW ANY OF THOSE PLACES OR PEOPLE. THE MEN CALL THIS ISLAND HISPANIOLA.
LOOK YONDER. A VISITOR.
HOW DELIGHTFUL. HE'S NOT VERY STYLISH, BUT I CAN'T COMPLAIN. IT'S COMPANY.
WHO?
WHAT DO YOU THINK HE'S COME HERE FOR?
GOLD. WHAT ELSE?
I CONCUR.

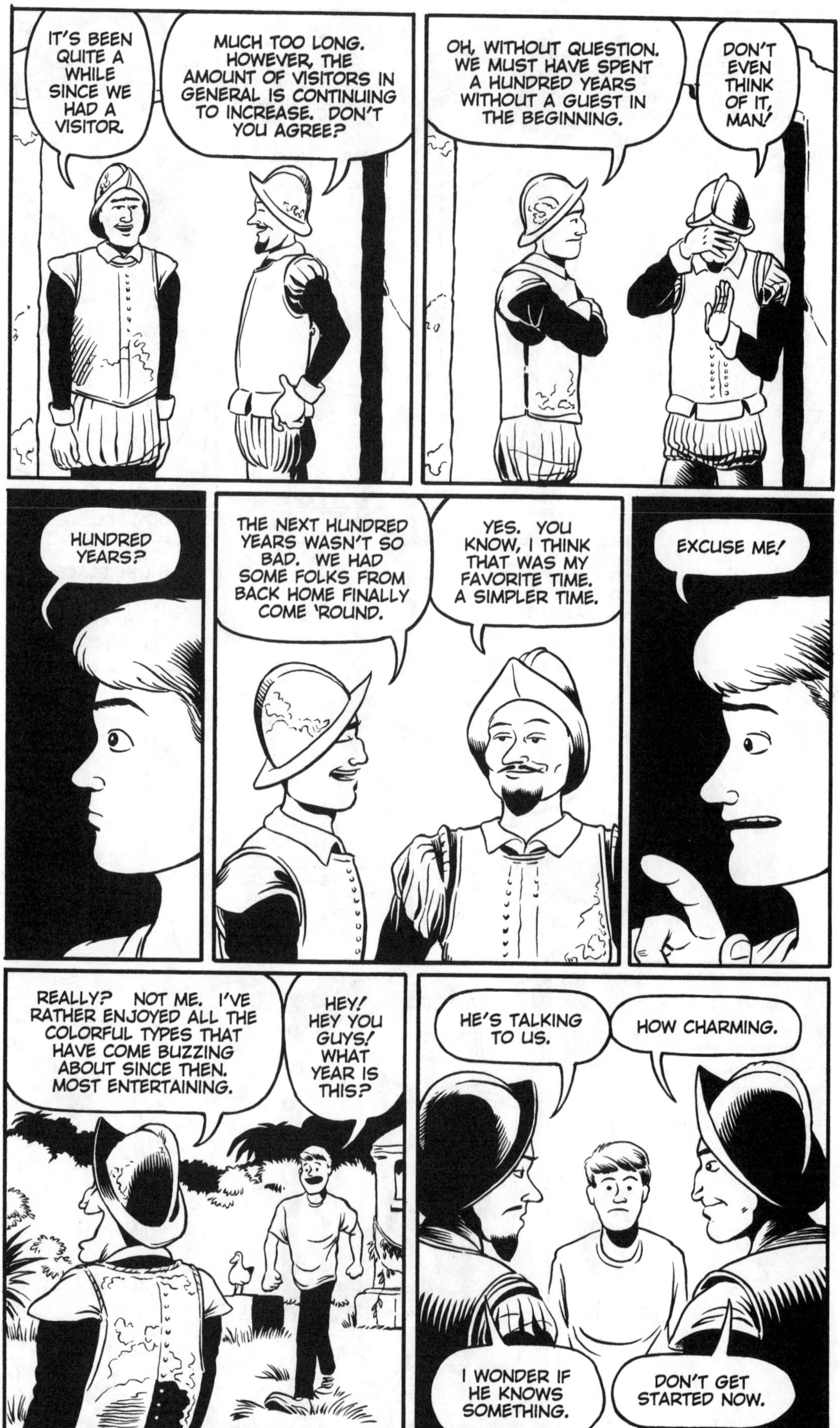

IT'S BEEN QUITE A WHILE SINCE WE HAD A VISITOR.
MUCH TOO LONG. HOWEVER, THE AMOUNT OF VISITORS IN GENERAL IS CONTINUING TO INCREASE. DON'T YOU AGREE?
OH, WITHOUT QUESTION. WE MUST HAVE SPENT A HUNDRED YEARS WITHOUT A GUEST IN THE BEGINNING.
DON'T EVEN THINK OF IT, MAN!
HUNDRED YEARS?
THE NEXT HUNDRED YEARS WASN'T SO BAD. WE HAD SOME FOLKS FROM BACK HOME FINALLY COME 'ROUND.
YES. YOU KNOW, I THINK THAT WAS MY FAVORITE TIME. A SIMPLER TIME.
EXCUSE ME!
REALLY? NOT ME. I'VE RATHER ENJOYED ALL THE COLORFUL TYPES THAT HAVE COME BUZZING ABOUT SINCE THEN. MOST ENTERTAINING.
HEY! HEY YOU GUYS! WHAT YEAR IS THIS?
HE'S TALKING TO US.
HOW CHARMING.
I WONDER IF HE KNOWS SOMETHING.
DON'T GET STARTED NOW.

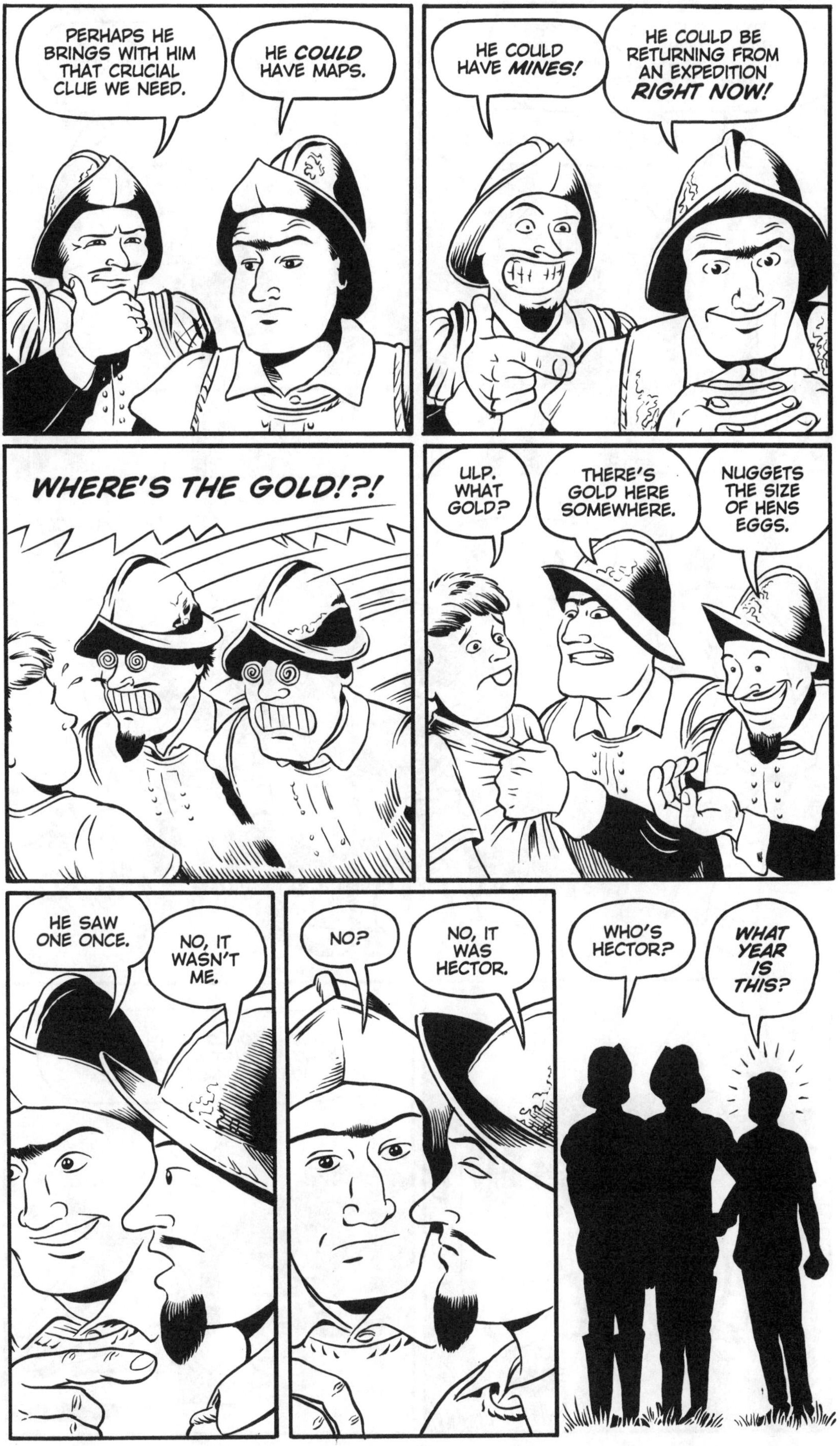
PERHAPS HE BRINGS WITH HIM THAT CRUCIAL CLUE WE NEED.
HE COULD HAVE MAPS.
HE COULD HAVE MINES!
HE COULD BE RETURNING FROM AN EXPEDITION RIGHT NOW!
WHERE'S THE GOLD!?!
ULP. WHAT GOLD?
THERE'S GOLD HERE SOMEWHERE.
NUGGETS THE SIZE OF HENS EGGS.
HE SAW ONE ONCE.
NO, IT WASN'T ME.
NO?
NO, IT WAS HECTOR.
WHO'S HECTOR?
WHAT YEAR IS THIS?

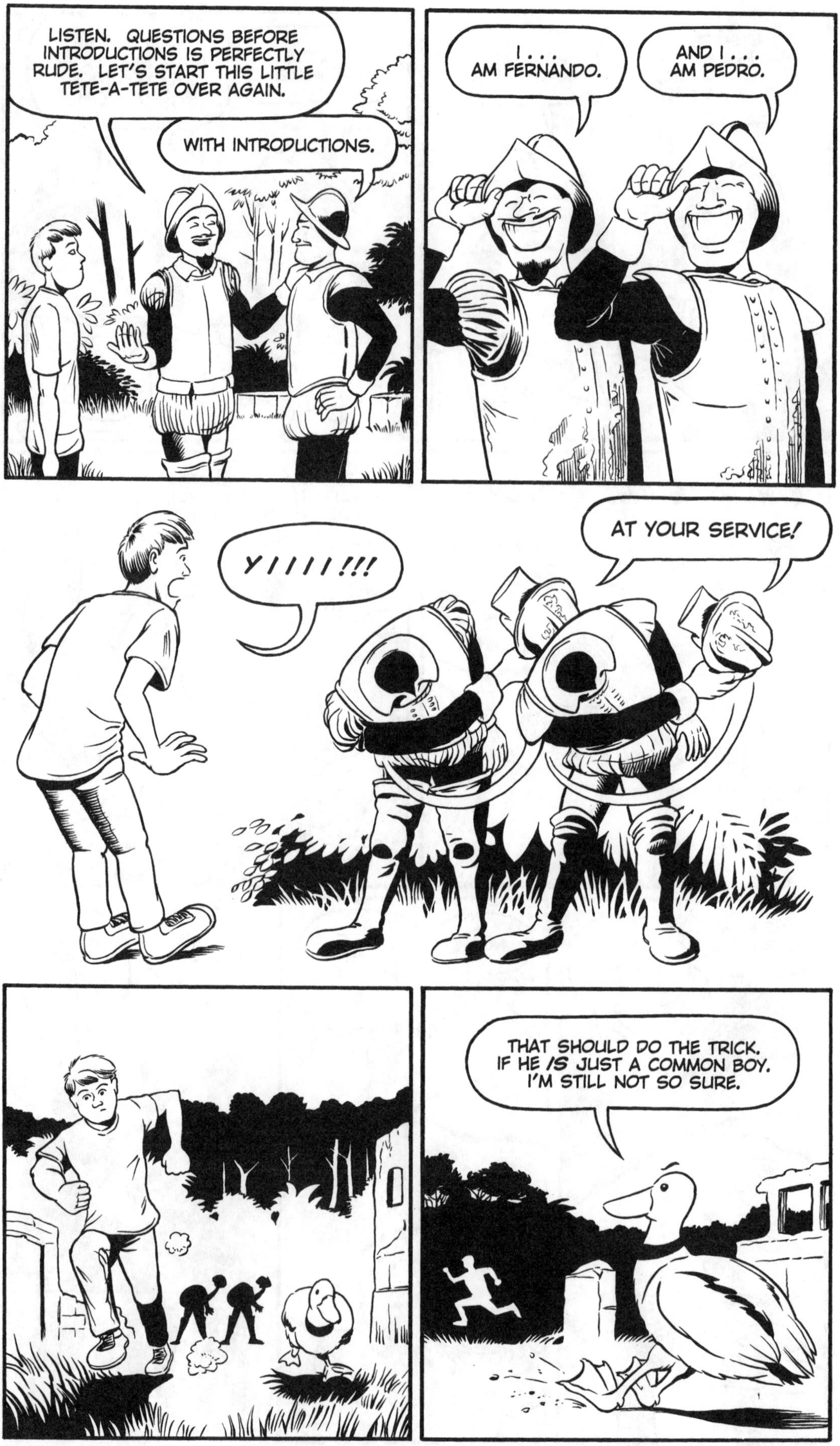
LISTEN. QUESTIONS BEFORE INTRODUCTIONS IS PERFECTLY RUDE. LET'S START THIS LITTLE TETE-A-TETE OVER AGAIN.
WITH INTRODUCTIONS.
I . . . AM FERNANDO.
AND I . . . AM PEDRO.
YIIIII!!!
AT YOUR SERVICE!
THAT SHOULD DO THE TRICK. IF HE *IS* JUST A COMMON BOY. I'M STILL NOT SO SURE.

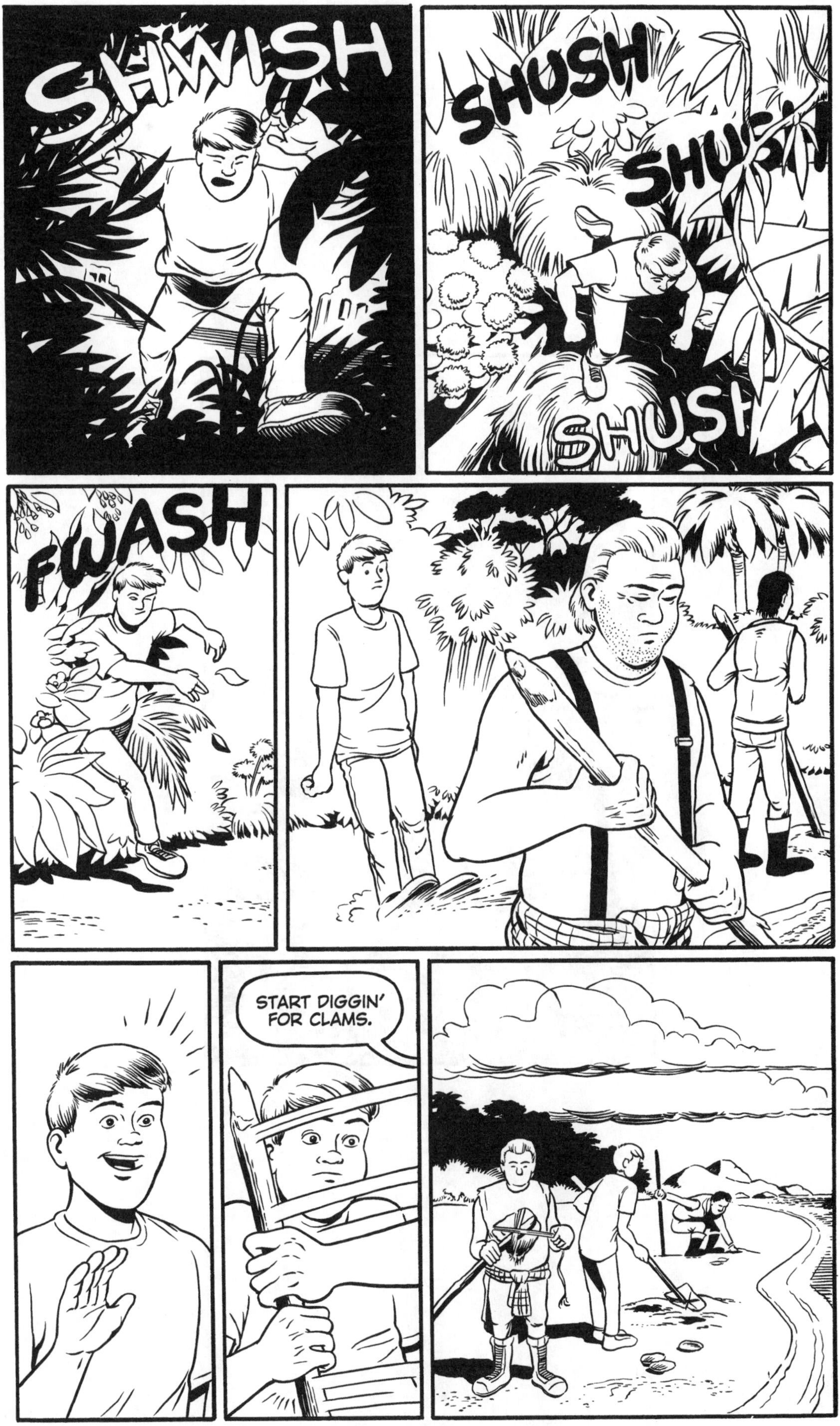
SHWISH
SHUSH
SHUSH
SHUSH
FWASH
START DIGGIN' FOR CLAMS.

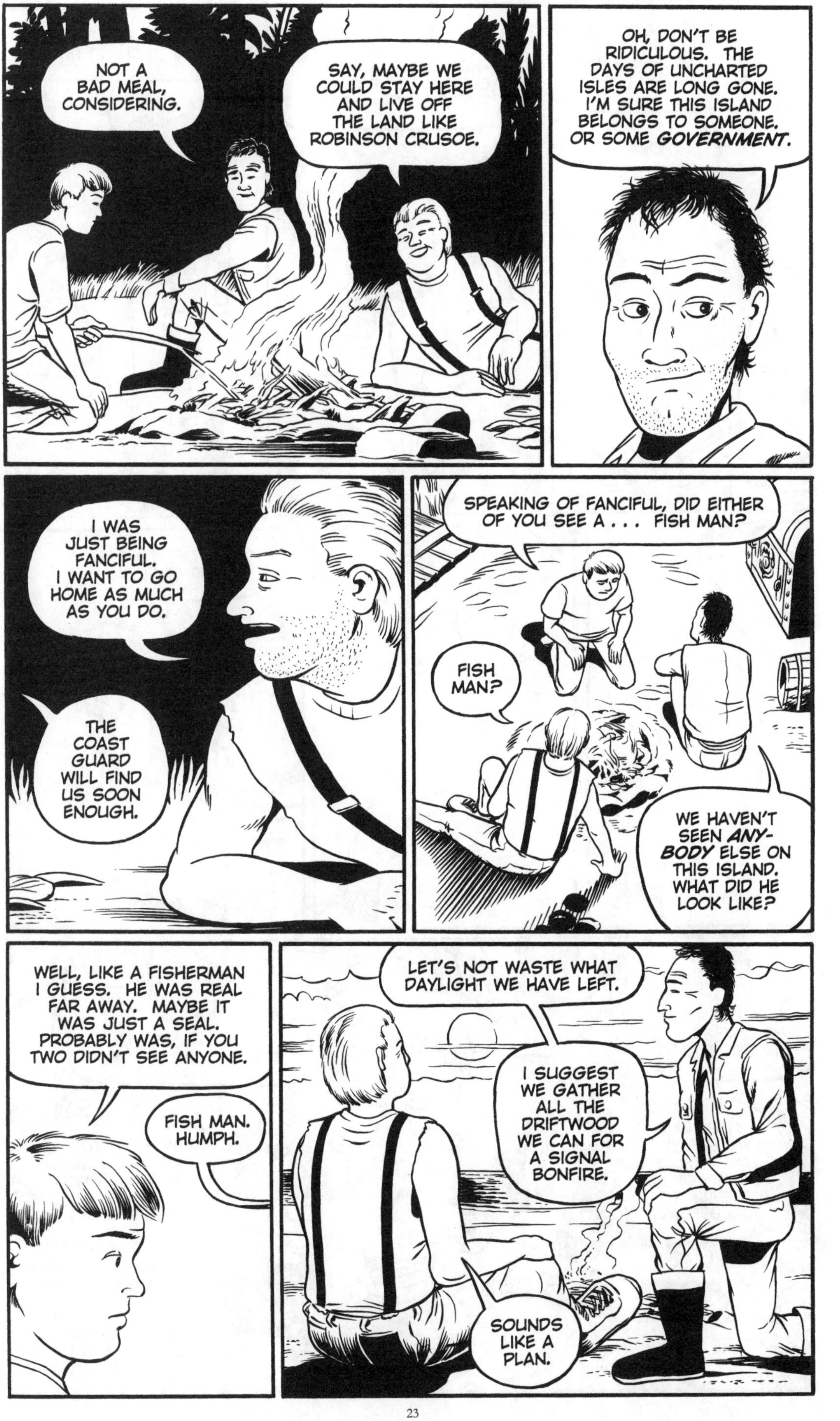
NOT A BAD MEAL, CONSIDERING.
SAY, MAYBE WE COULD STAY HERE AND LIVE OFF THE LAND LIKE ROBINSON CRUSOE.
OH, DON'T BE RIDICULOUS. THE DAYS OF UNCHARTED ISLES ARE LONG GONE. I'M SURE THIS ISLAND BELONGS TO SOMEONE. OR SOME *GOVERNMENT*.
I WAS JUST BEING FANCIFUL. I WANT TO GO HOME AS MUCH AS YOU DO.
THE COAST GUARD WILL FIND US SOON ENOUGH.
SPEAKING OF FANCIFUL, DID EITHER OF YOU SEE A . . . FISH MAN?
FISH MAN?
WE HAVEN'T SEEN *ANY-BODY* ELSE ON THIS ISLAND. WHAT DID HE LOOK LIKE?
WELL, LIKE A FISHERMAN I GUESS. HE WAS REAL FAR AWAY. MAYBE IT WAS JUST A SEAL. PROBABLY WAS, IF YOU TWO DIDN'T SEE ANYONE.
FISH MAN. HUMPH.
LET'S NOT WASTE WHAT DAYLIGHT WE HAVE LEFT.
I SUGGEST WE GATHER ALL THE DRIFTWOOD WE CAN FOR A SIGNAL BONFIRE.
SOUNDS LIKE A PLAN.

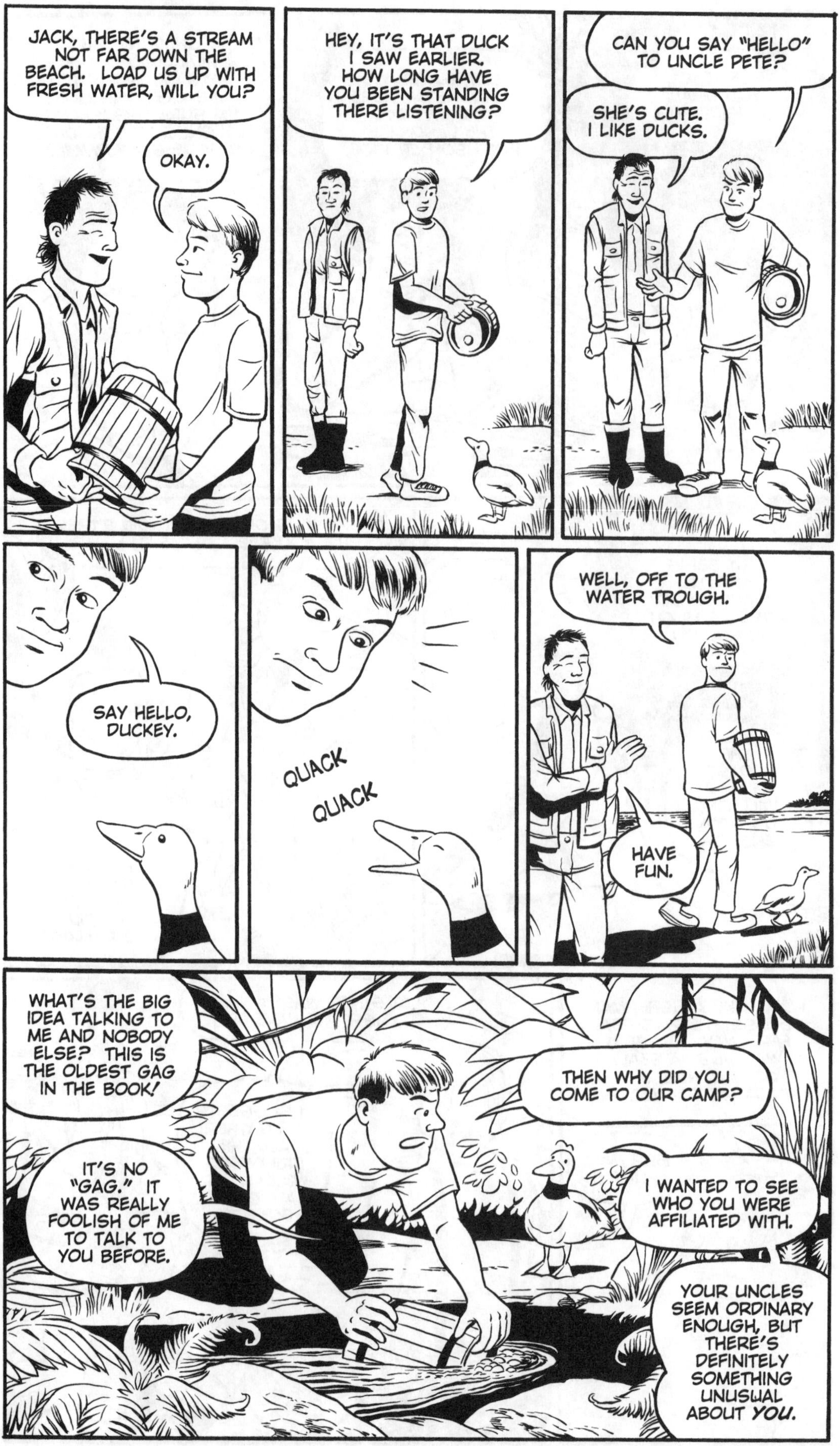
JACK, THERE'S A STREAM NOT FAR DOWN THE BEACH. LOAD US UP WITH FRESH WATER, WILL YOU?
OKAY.
HEY, IT'S THAT DUCK I SAW EARLIER. HOW LONG HAVE YOU BEEN STANDING THERE LISTENING?
CAN YOU SAY "HELLO" TO UNCLE PETE?
SHE'S CUTE. I LIKE DUCKS.
SAY HELLO, DUCKEY.
QUACK
QUACK
WELL, OFF TO THE WATER TROUGH.
HAVE FUN.
WHAT'S THE BIG IDEA TALKING TO ME AND NOBODY ELSE? THIS IS THE OLDEST GAG IN THE BOOK!
IT'S NO "GAG." IT WAS REALLY FOOLISH OF ME TO TALK TO YOU BEFORE.
THEN WHY DID YOU COME TO OUR CAMP?
I WANTED TO SEE WHO YOU WERE AFFILIATED WITH.
YOUR UNCLES SEEM ORDINARY ENOUGH, BUT THERE'S DEFINITELY SOMETHING UNUSUAL ABOUT *YOU*.

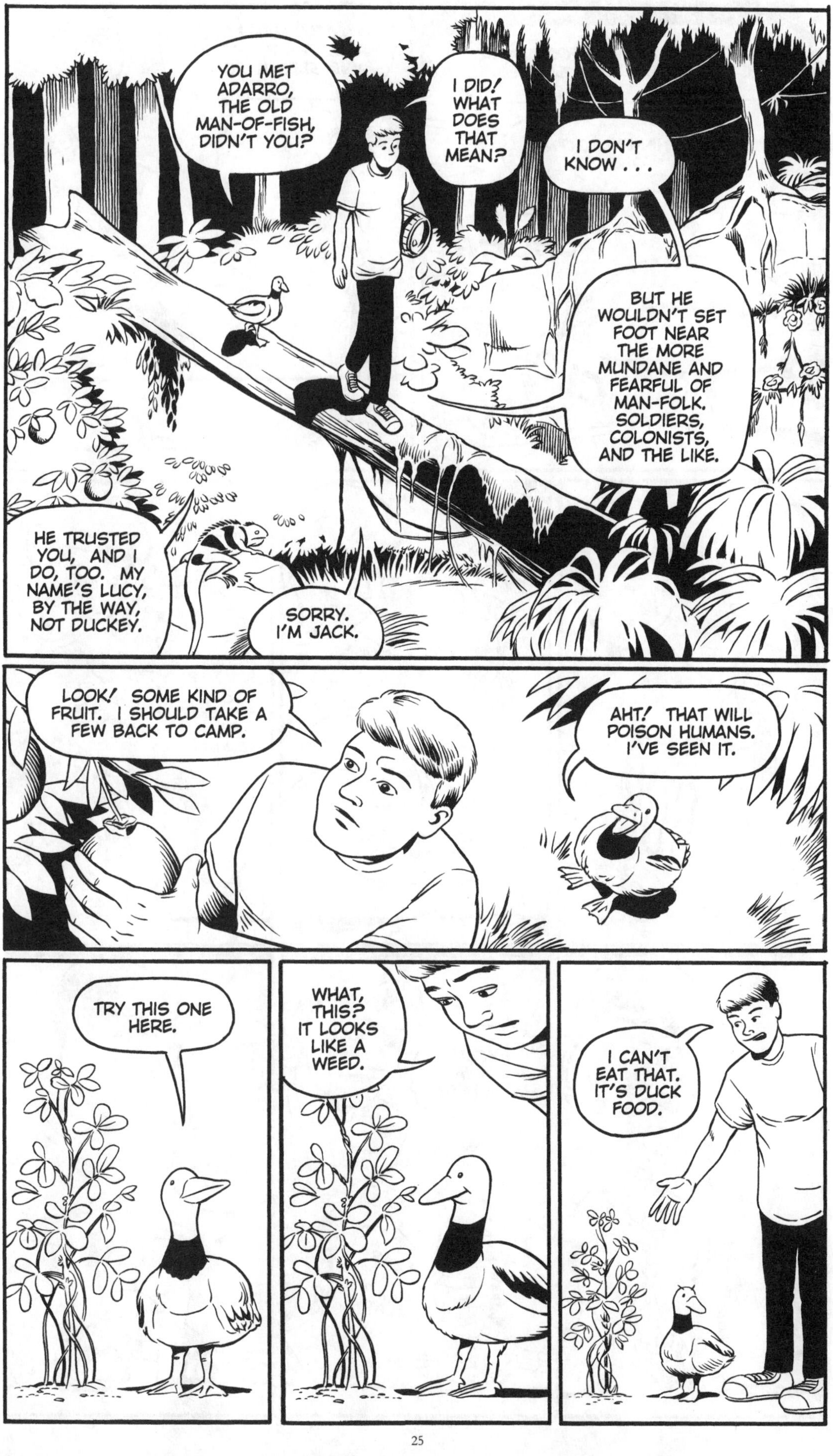
YOU MET ADARRO, THE OLD MAN-OF-FISH, DIDN'T YOU?
I DID! WHAT DOES THAT MEAN?
I DON'T KNOW . . .
BUT HE WOULDN'T SET FOOT NEAR THE MORE MUNDANE AND FEARFUL OF MAN-FOLK. SOLDIERS, COLONISTS, AND THE LIKE.
HE TRUSTED YOU, AND I DO, TOO. MY NAME'S LUCY, BY THE WAY, NOT DUCKEY.
SORRY. I'M JACK.
LOOK! SOME KIND OF FRUIT. I SHOULD TAKE A FEW BACK TO CAMP.
AHT! THAT WILL POISON HUMANS. I'VE SEEN IT.
TRY THIS ONE HERE.
WHAT, THIS? IT LOOKS LIKE A WEED.
I CAN'T EAT THAT. IT'S DUCK FOOD.

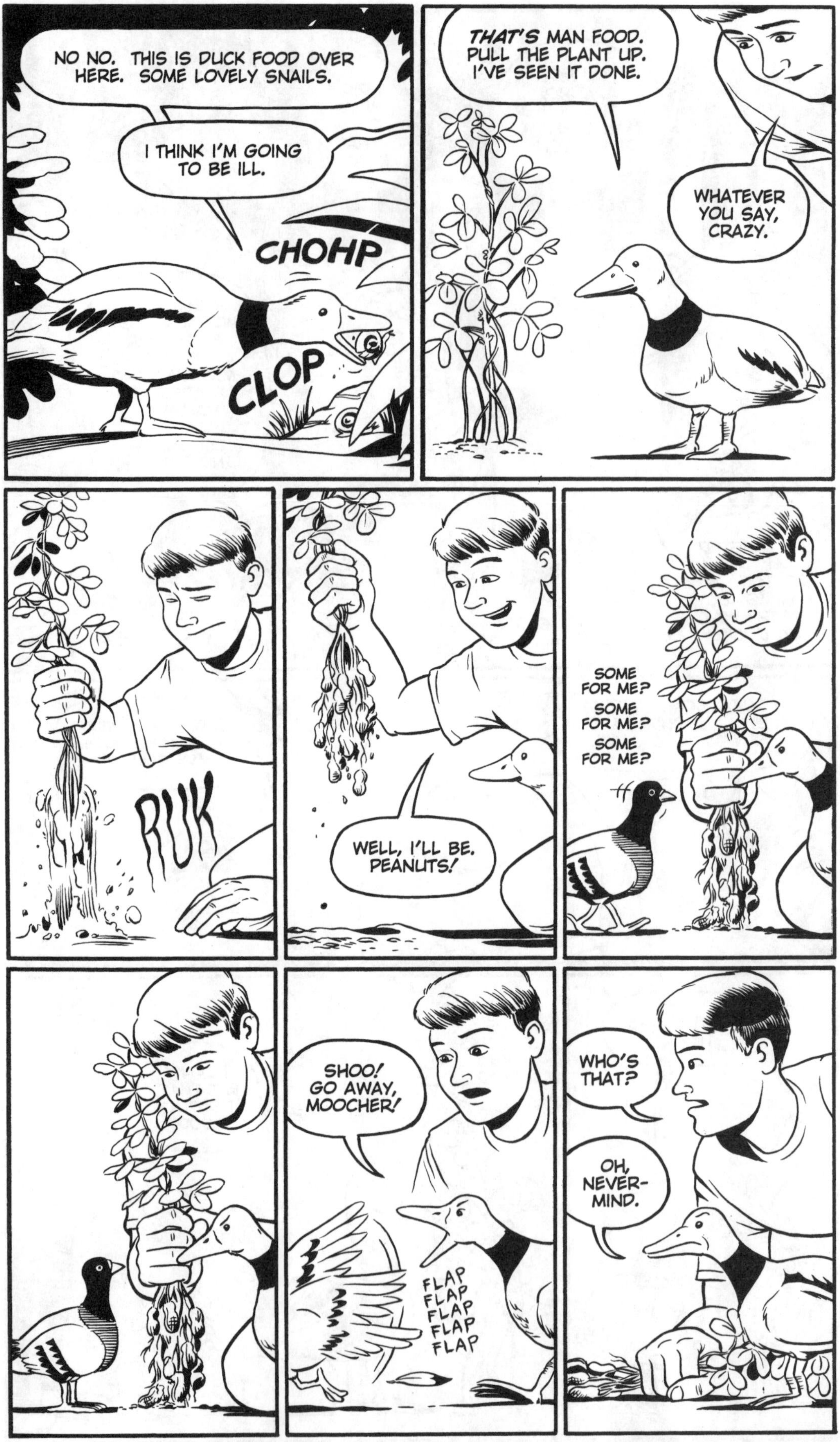
NO NO. THIS IS DUCK FOOD OVER HERE. SOME LOVELY SNAILS.
I THINK I'M GOING TO BE ILL.
CHOHP
CLOP
THAT'S MAN FOOD. PULL THE PLANT UP. I'VE SEEN IT DONE.
WHATEVER YOU SAY, CRAZY.
RUK
WELL, I'LL BE. PEANUTS!
SOME FOR ME? SOME FOR ME? SOME FOR ME?
SHOO! GO AWAY, MOOCHER!
FLAP FLAP FLAP FLAP FLAP FLAP
WHO'S THAT?
OH, NEVER-MIND.

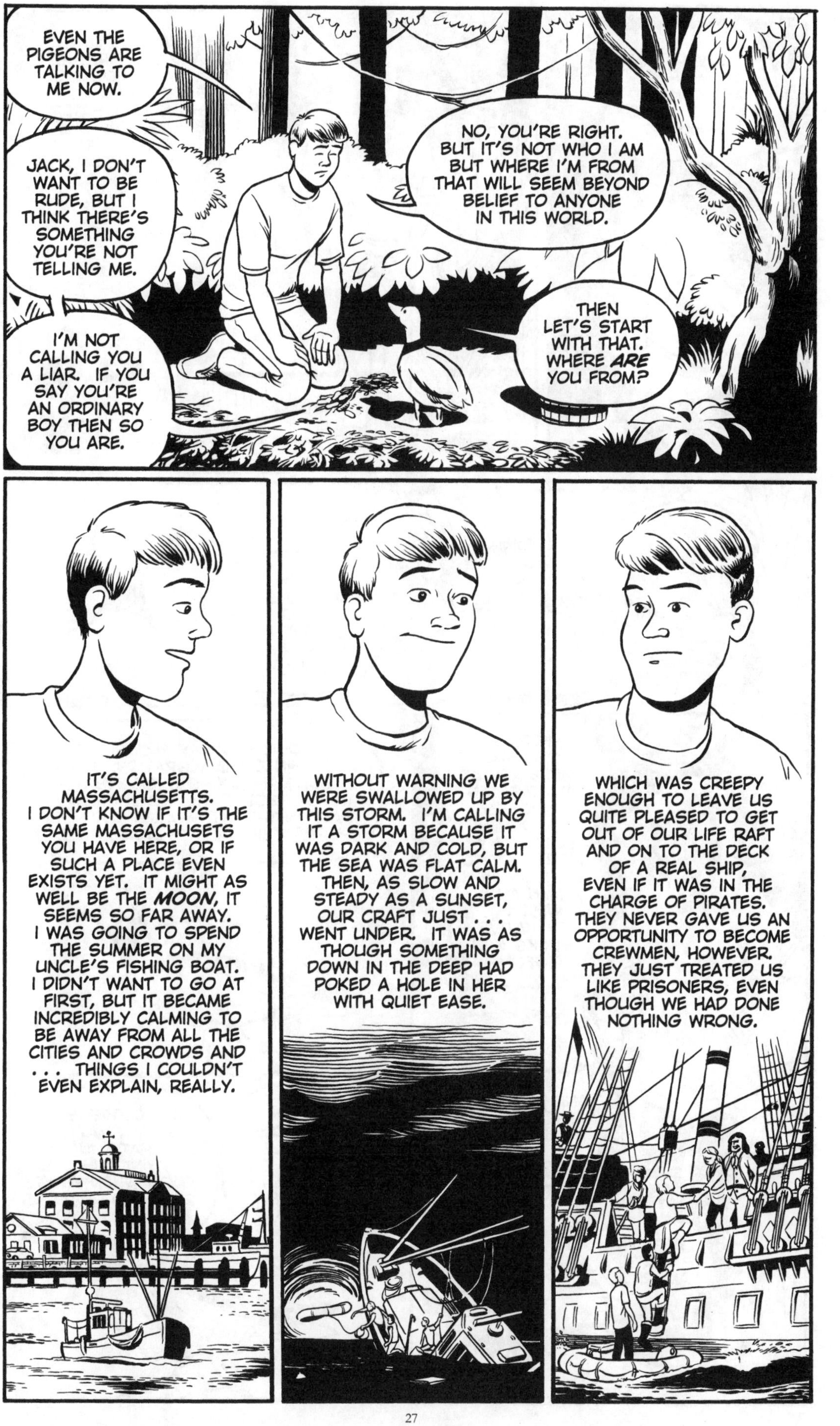
EVEN THE PIGEONS ARE TALKING TO ME NOW.
JACK, I DON'T WANT TO BE RUDE, BUT I THINK THERE'S SOMETHING YOU'RE NOT TELLING ME.
I'M NOT CALLING YOU A LIAR. IF YOU SAY YOU'RE AN ORDINARY BOY THEN SO YOU ARE.
NO, YOU'RE RIGHT. BUT IT'S NOT WHO I AM BUT WHERE I'M FROM THAT WILL SEEM BEYOND BELIEF TO ANYONE IN THIS WORLD.
THEN LET'S START WITH THAT. WHERE *ARE* YOU FROM?
IT'S CALLED MASSACHUSETTS. I DON'T KNOW IF IT'S THE SAME MASSACHUSETS YOU HAVE HERE, OR IF SUCH A PLACE EVEN EXISTS YET. IT MIGHT AS WELL BE THE *MOON*, IT SEEMS SO FAR AWAY. I WAS GOING TO SPEND THE SUMMER ON MY UNCLE'S FISHING BOAT. I DIDN'T WANT TO GO AT FIRST, BUT IT BECAME INCREDIBLY CALMING TO BE AWAY FROM ALL THE CITIES AND CROWDS AND . . . THINGS I COULDN'T EVEN EXPLAIN, REALLY.
WITHOUT WARNING WE WERE SWALLOWED UP BY THIS STORM. I'M CALLING IT A STORM BECAUSE IT WAS DARK AND COLD, BUT THE SEA WAS FLAT CALM. THEN, AS SLOW AND STEADY AS A SUNSET, OUR CRAFT JUST . . . WENT UNDER. IT WAS AS THOUGH SOMETHING DOWN IN THE DEEP HAD POKED A HOLE IN HER WITH QUIET EASE.
WHICH WAS CREEPY ENOUGH TO LEAVE US QUITE PLEASED TO GET OUT OF OUR LIFE RAFT AND ON TO THE DECK OF A REAL SHIP, EVEN IF IT WAS IN THE CHARGE OF PIRATES. THEY NEVER GAVE US AN OPPORTUNITY TO BECOME CREWMEN, HOWEVER. THEY JUST TREATED US LIKE PRISONERS, EVEN THOUGH WE HAD DONE NOTHING WRONG.

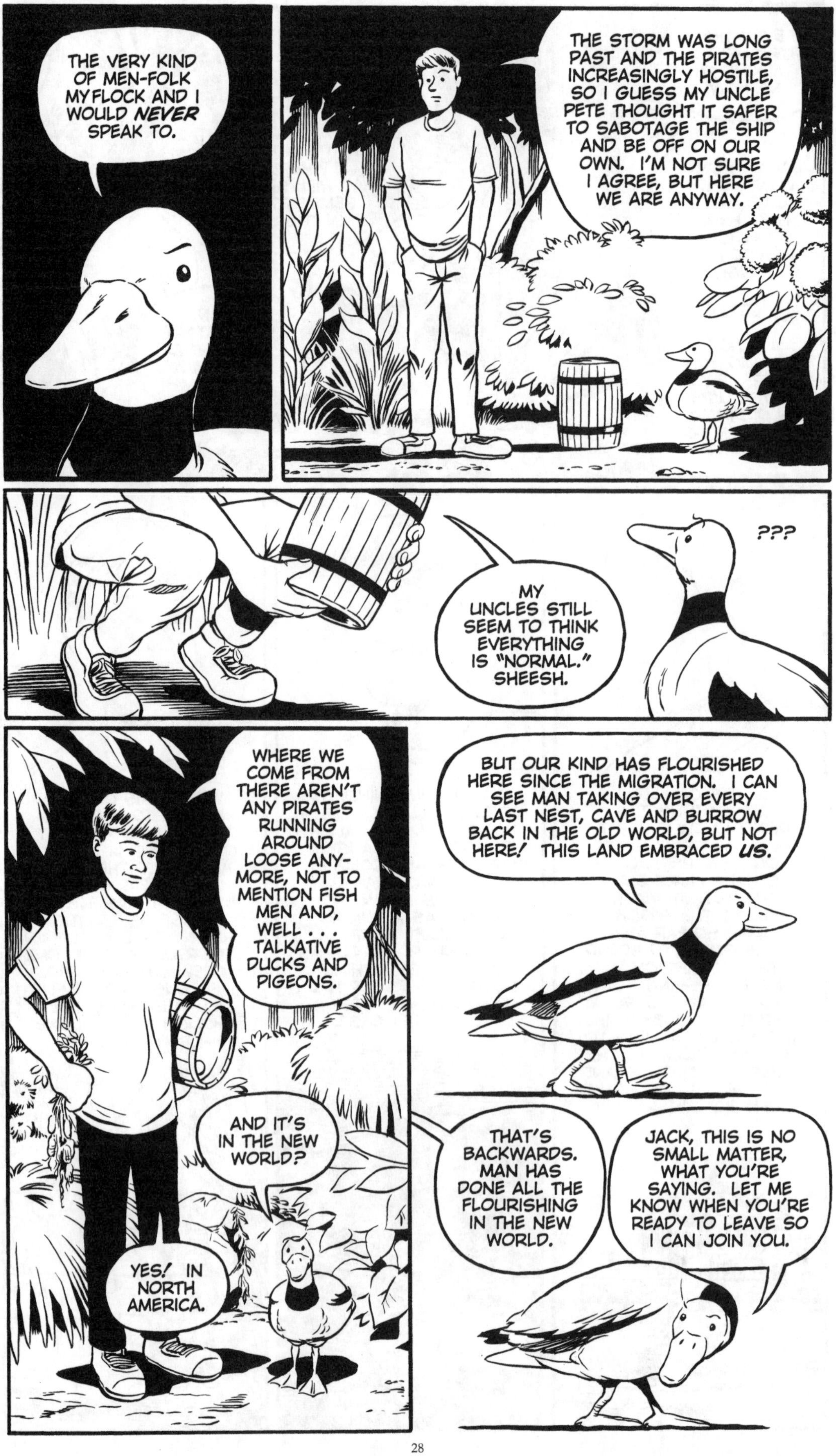
THE VERY KIND OF MEN-FOLK MY FLOCK AND I WOULD NEVER SPEAK TO.
THE STORM WAS LONG PAST AND THE PIRATES INCREASINGLY HOSTILE, SO I GUESS MY UNCLE PETE THOUGHT IT SAFER TO SABOTAGE THE SHIP AND BE OFF ON OUR OWN. I'M NOT SURE I AGREE, BUT HERE WE ARE ANYWAY.
MY UNCLES STILL SEEM TO THINK EVERYTHING IS "NORMAL." SHEESH.
???
WHERE WE COME FROM THERE AREN'T ANY PIRATES RUNNING AROUND LOOSE ANY-MORE, NOT TO MENTION FISH MEN AND, WELL . . . TALKATIVE DUCKS AND PIGEONS.
AND IT'S IN THE NEW WORLD?
YES! IN NORTH AMERICA.
BUT OUR KIND HAS FLOURISHED HERE SINCE THE MIGRATION. I CAN SEE MAN TAKING OVER EVERY LAST NEST, CAVE AND BURROW BACK IN THE OLD WORLD, BUT NOT HERE! THIS LAND EMBRACED US.
THAT'S BACKWARDS. MAN HAS DONE ALL THE FLOURISHING IN THE NEW WORLD.
JACK, THIS IS NO SMALL MATTER, WHAT YOU'RE SAYING. LET ME KNOW WHEN YOU'RE READY TO LEAVE SO I CAN JOIN YOU.

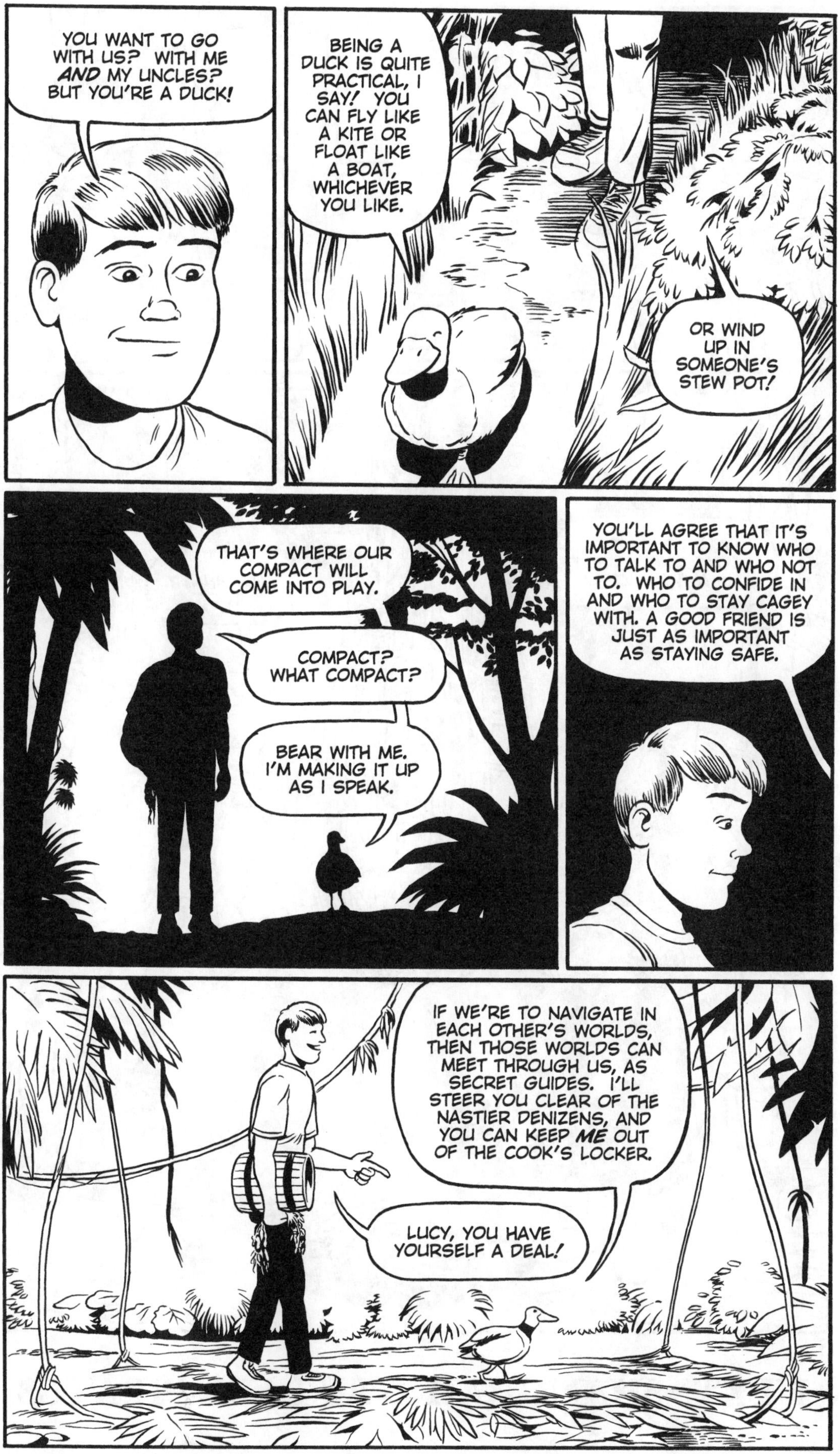
YOU WANT TO GO WITH US? WITH ME *AND* MY UNCLES? BUT YOU'RE A DUCK!
BEING A DUCK IS QUITE PRACTICAL, I SAY! YOU CAN FLY LIKE A KITE OR FLOAT LIKE A BOAT, WHICHEVER YOU LIKE.
OR WIND UP IN SOMEONE'S STEW POT!
THAT'S WHERE OUR COMPACT WILL COME INTO PLAY.
COMPACT? WHAT COMPACT?
BEAR WITH ME. I'M MAKING IT UP AS I SPEAK.
YOU'LL AGREE THAT IT'S IMPORTANT TO KNOW WHO TO TALK TO AND WHO NOT TO. WHO TO CONFIDE IN AND WHO TO STAY CAGEY WITH. A GOOD FRIEND IS JUST AS IMPORTANT AS STAYING SAFE.
IF WE'RE TO NAVIGATE IN EACH OTHER'S WORLDS, THEN THOSE WORLDS CAN MEET THROUGH US, AS SECRET GUIDES. I'LL STEER YOU CLEAR OF THE NASTIER DENIZENS, AND YOU CAN KEEP *ME* OUT OF THE COOK'S LOCKER.
LUCY, YOU HAVE YOURSELF A DEAL!

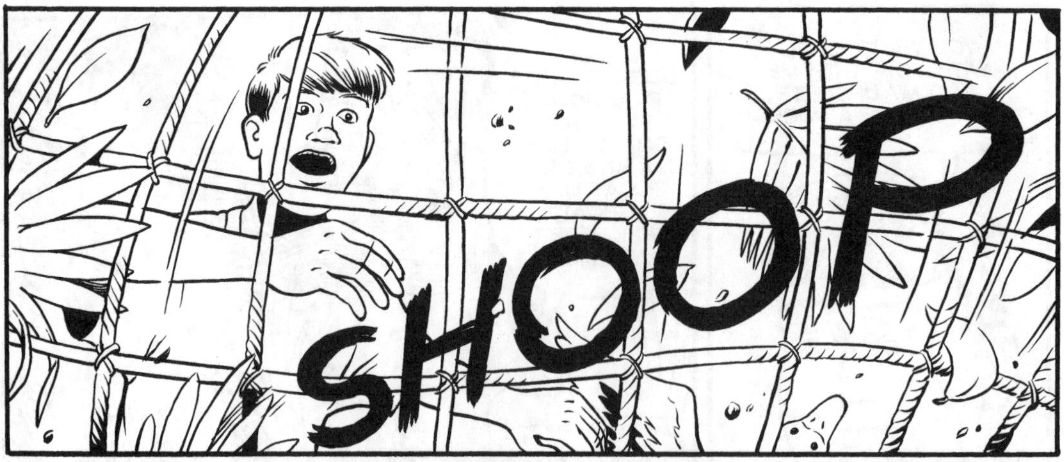
SHOOP

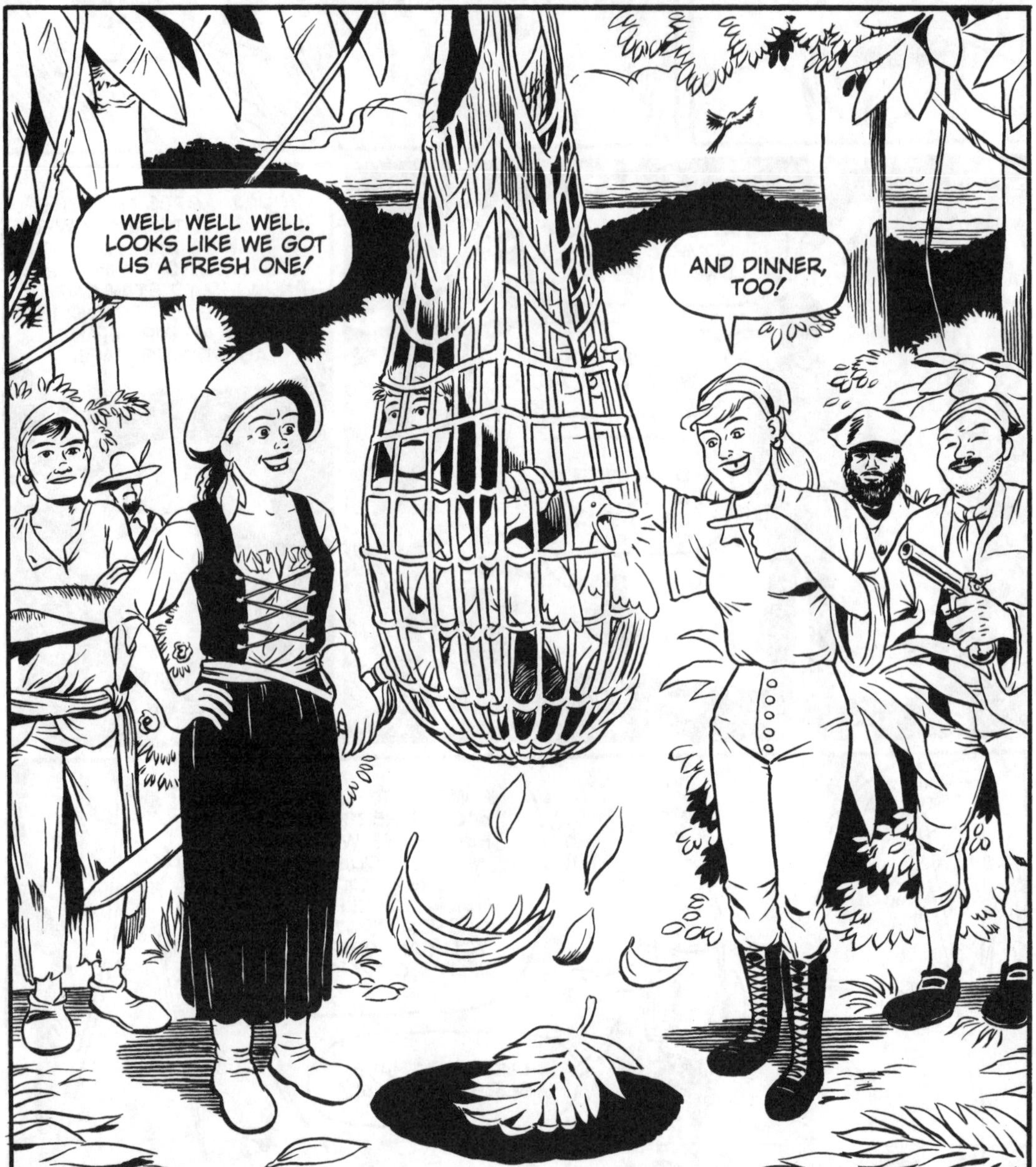
WELL WELL WELL. LOOKS LIKE WE GOT US A FRESH ONE!
AND DINNER, TOO!

NEXT: SHANGHAIED BY LADY PIRATES

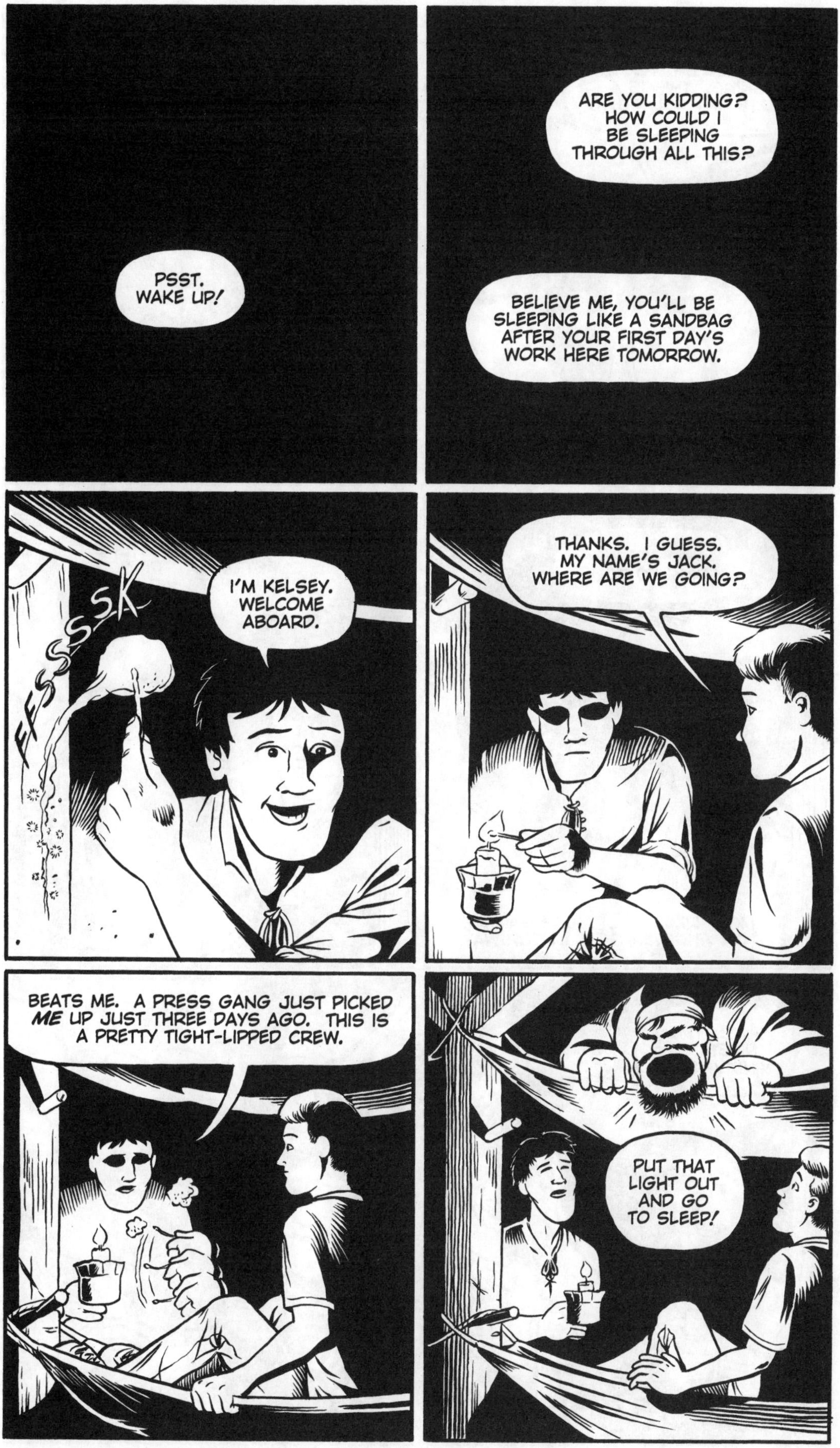
PSST. WAKE UP!
ARE YOU KIDDING? HOW COULD I BE SLEEPING THROUGH ALL THIS?
BELIEVE ME, YOU'LL BE SLEEPING LIKE A SANDBAG AFTER YOUR FIRST DAY'S WORK HERE TOMORROW.
FFSSSSK
I'M KELSEY. WELCOME ABOARD.
THANKS. I GUESS. MY NAME'S JACK. WHERE ARE WE GOING?
BEATS ME. A PRESS GANG JUST PICKED ME UP JUST THREE DAYS AGO. THIS IS A PRETTY TIGHT-LIPPED CREW.
PUT THAT LIGHT OUT AND GO TO SLEEP!

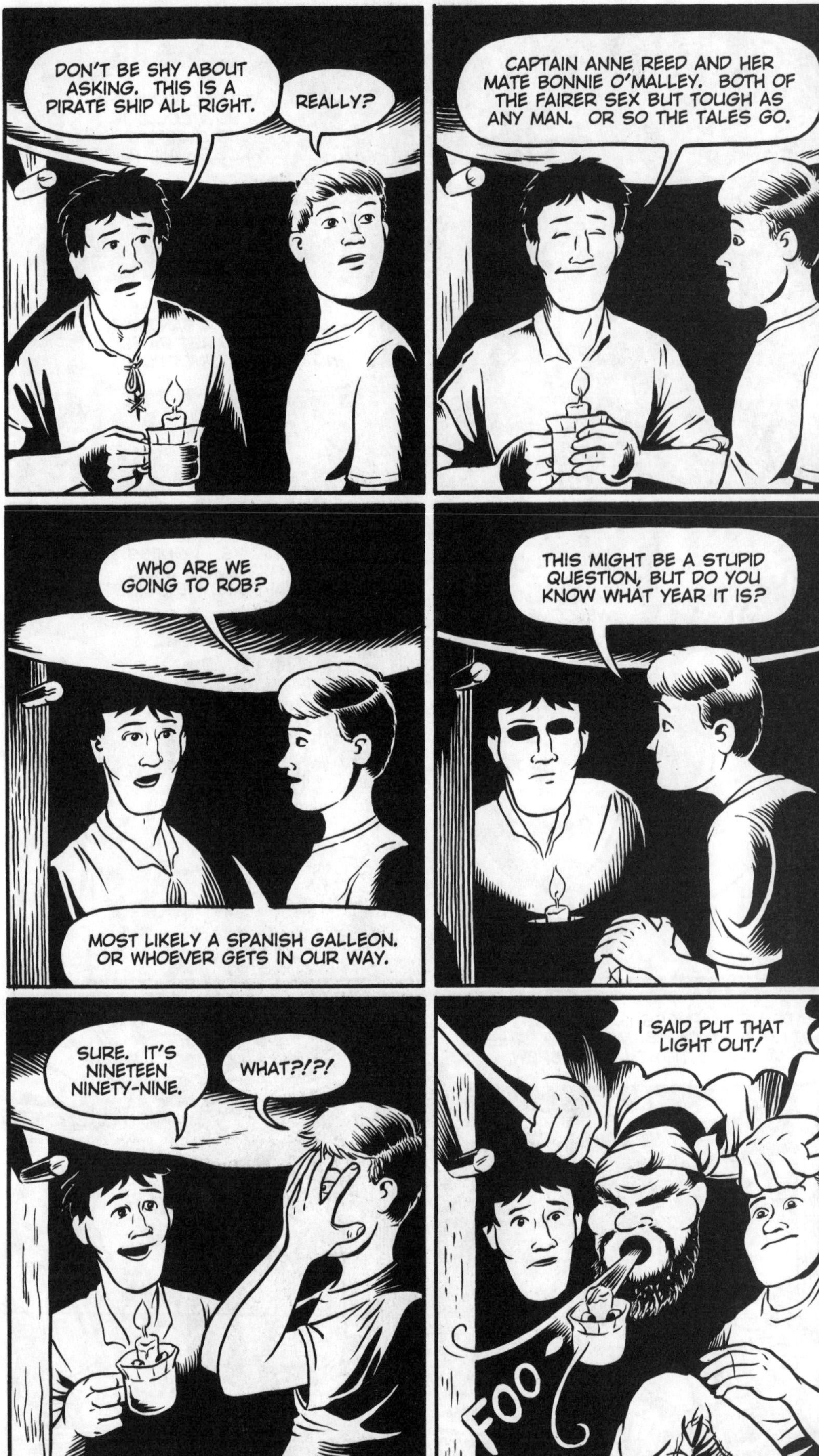
DON'T BE SHY ABOUT ASKING. THIS IS A PIRATE SHIP ALL RIGHT.
REALLY?
CAPTAIN ANNE REED AND HER MATE BONNIE O'MALLEY. BOTH OF THE FAIRER SEX BUT TOUGH AS ANY MAN. OR SO THE TALES GO.
WHO ARE WE GOING TO ROB?
MOST LIKELY A SPANISH GALLEON. OR WHOEVER GETS IN OUR WAY.
THIS MIGHT BE A STUPID QUESTION, BUT DO YOU KNOW WHAT YEAR IT IS?
SURE. IT'S NINETEEN NINETY-NINE.
WHAT?!?!
I SAID PUT THAT LIGHT OUT!
FOO

SHANGHAIED

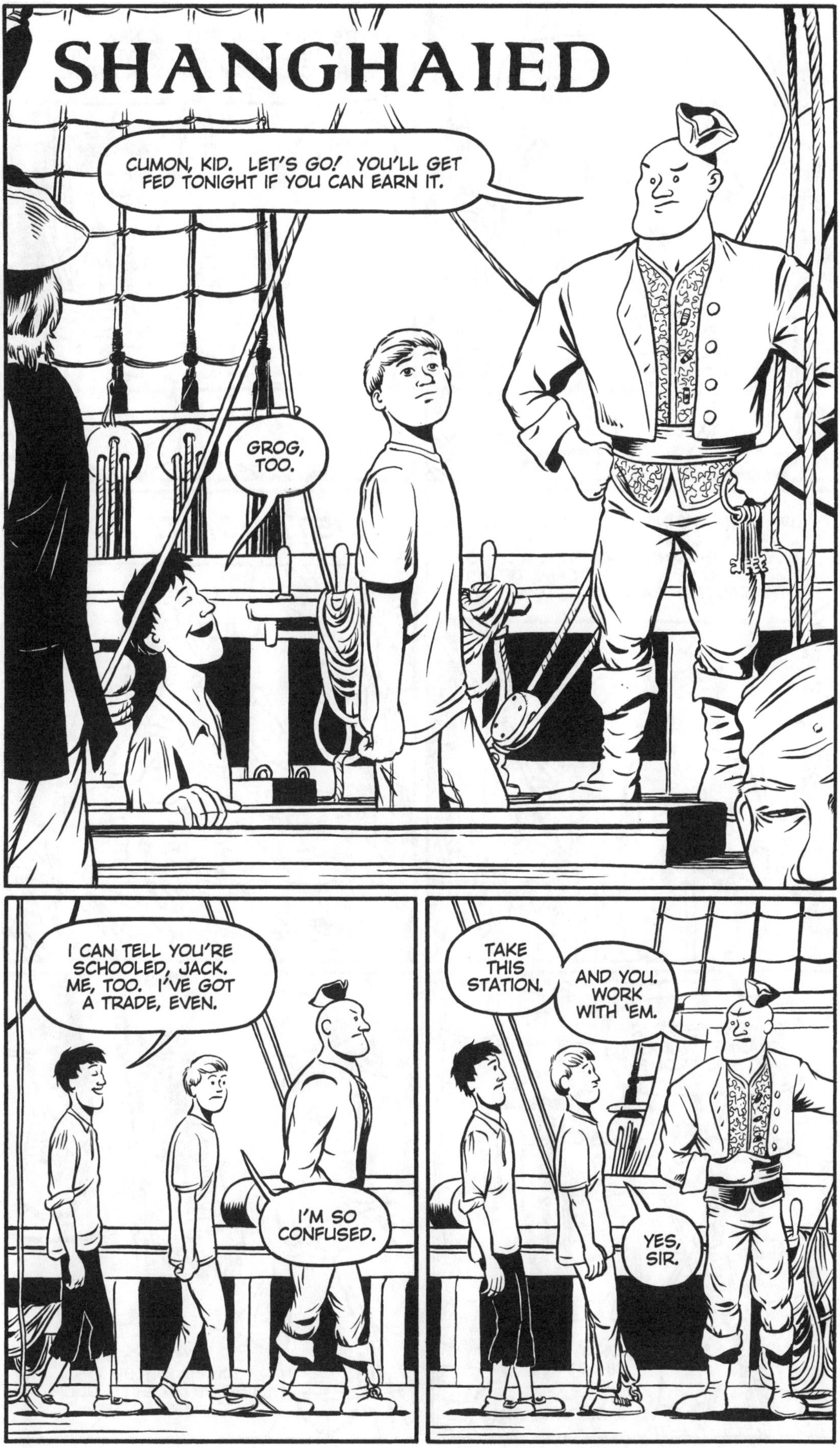
CUMON, KID. LET'S GO! YOU'LL GET FED TONIGHT IF YOU CAN EARN IT.
GROG, TOO.
I CAN TELL YOU'RE SCHOOLED, JACK. ME, TOO. I'VE GOT A TRADE, EVEN.
I'M SO CONFUSED.
TAKE THIS STATION.
AND YOU. WORK WITH 'EM.
YES, SIR.

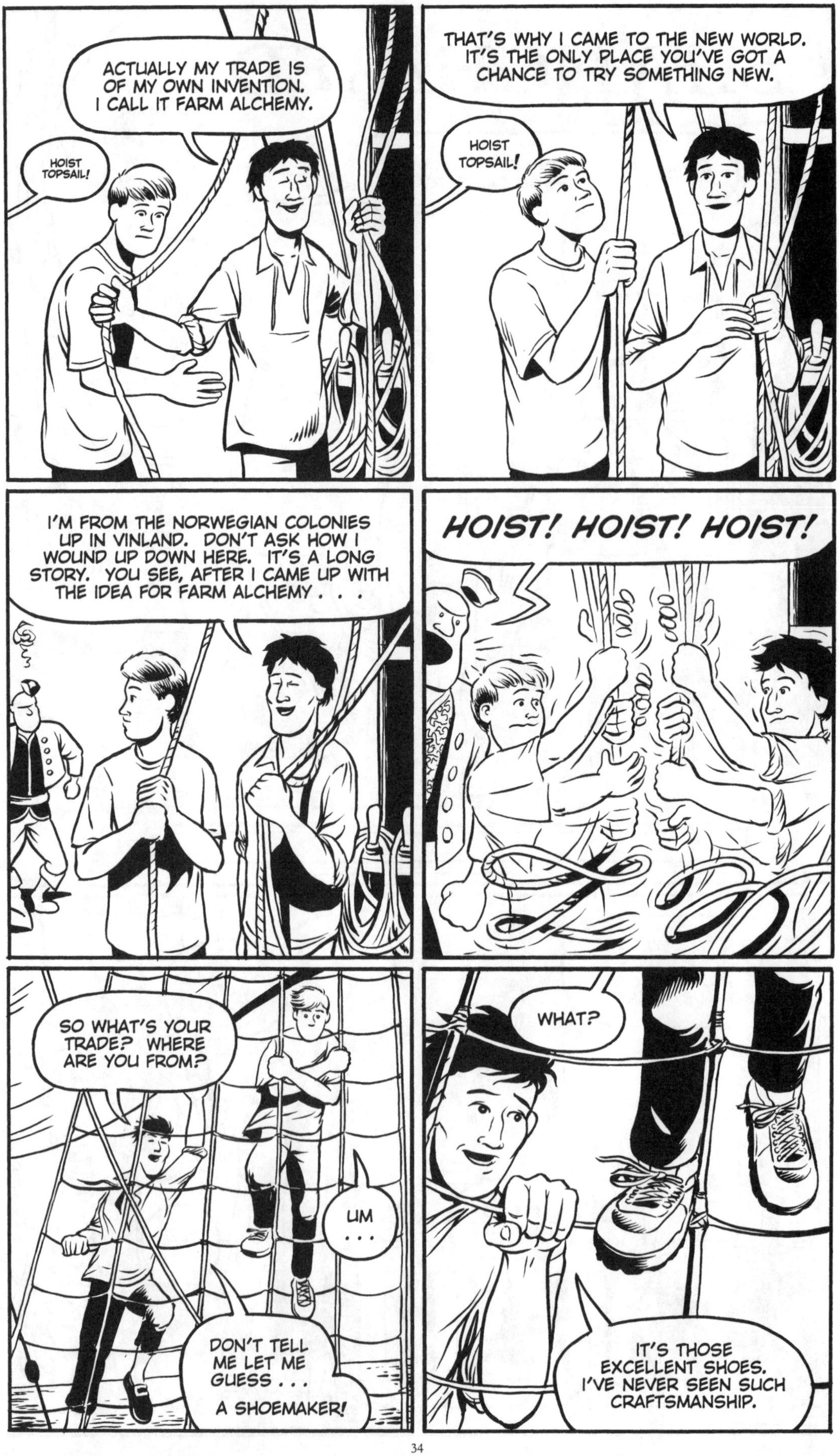
ACTUALLY MY TRADE IS OF MY OWN INVENTION. I CALL IT FARM ALCHEMY.
HOIST TOPSAIL!
THAT'S WHY I CAME TO THE NEW WORLD. IT'S THE ONLY PLACE YOU'VE GOT A CHANCE TO TRY SOMETHING NEW.
HOIST TOPSAIL!
I'M FROM THE NORWEGIAN COLONIES UP IN VINLAND. DON'T ASK HOW I WOUND UP DOWN HERE. IT'S A LONG STORY. YOU SEE, AFTER I CAME UP WITH THE IDEA FOR FARM ALCHEMY . . .
HOIST! HOIST! HOIST!
SO WHAT'S YOUR TRADE? WHERE ARE YOU FROM?
UM . . .
DON'T TELL ME LET ME GUESS . . . A SHOEMAKER!
WHAT?
IT'S THOSE EXCELLENT SHOES. I'VE NEVER SEEN SUCH CRAFTSMANSHIP.

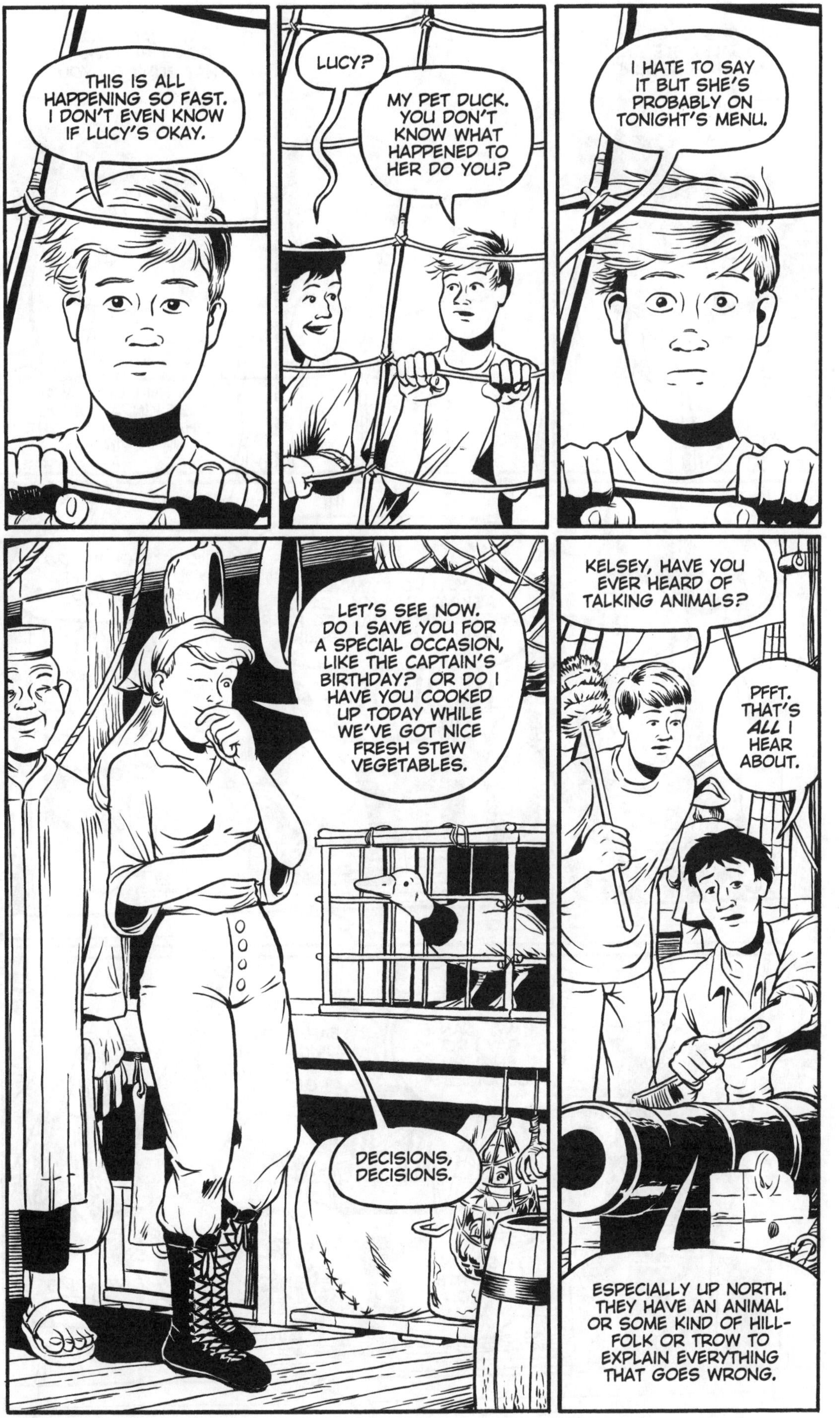
THIS IS ALL HAPPENING SO FAST. I DON'T EVEN KNOW IF LUCY'S OKAY.
LUCY?
MY PET DUCK. YOU DON'T KNOW WHAT HAPPENED TO HER DO YOU?
I HATE TO SAY IT BUT SHE'S PROBABLY ON TONIGHT'S MENU.
LET'S SEE NOW. DO I SAVE YOU FOR A SPECIAL OCCASION, LIKE THE CAPTAIN'S BIRTHDAY? OR DO I HAVE YOU COOKED UP TODAY WHILE WE'VE GOT NICE FRESH STEW VEGETABLES.
DECISIONS, DECISIONS.
KELSEY, HAVE YOU EVER HEARD OF TALKING ANIMALS?
PFFT. THAT'S *ALL* I HEAR ABOUT.
ESPECIALLY UP NORTH. THEY HAVE AN ANIMAL OR SOME KIND OF HILL-FOLK OR TROW TO EXPLAIN EVERYTHING THAT GOES WRONG.

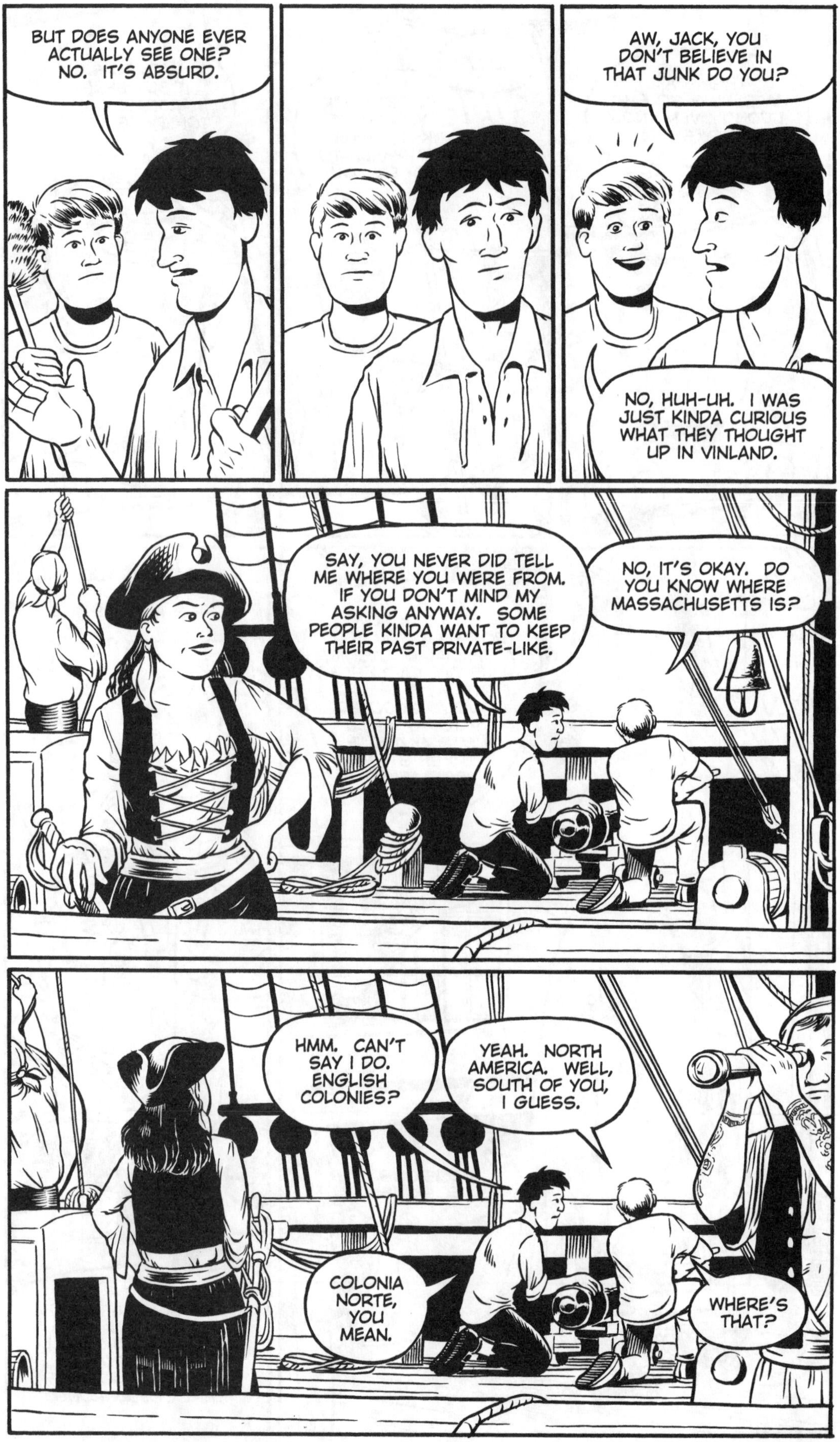
BUT DOES ANYONE EVER ACTUALLY SEE ONE? NO. IT'S ABSURD.
AW, JACK, YOU DON'T BELIEVE IN THAT JUNK DO YOU?
NO, HUH-UH. I WAS JUST KINDA CURIOUS WHAT THEY THOUGHT UP IN VINLAND.
SAY, YOU NEVER DID TELL ME WHERE YOU WERE FROM. IF YOU DON'T MIND MY ASKING ANYWAY. SOME PEOPLE KINDA WANT TO KEEP THEIR PAST PRIVATE-LIKE.
NO, IT'S OKAY. DO YOU KNOW WHERE MASSACHUSETTS IS?
HMM. CAN'T SAY I DO. ENGLISH COLONIES?
YEAH. NORTH AMERICA. WELL, SOUTH OF YOU, I GUESS.
COLONIA NORTE, YOU MEAN.
WHERE'S THAT?

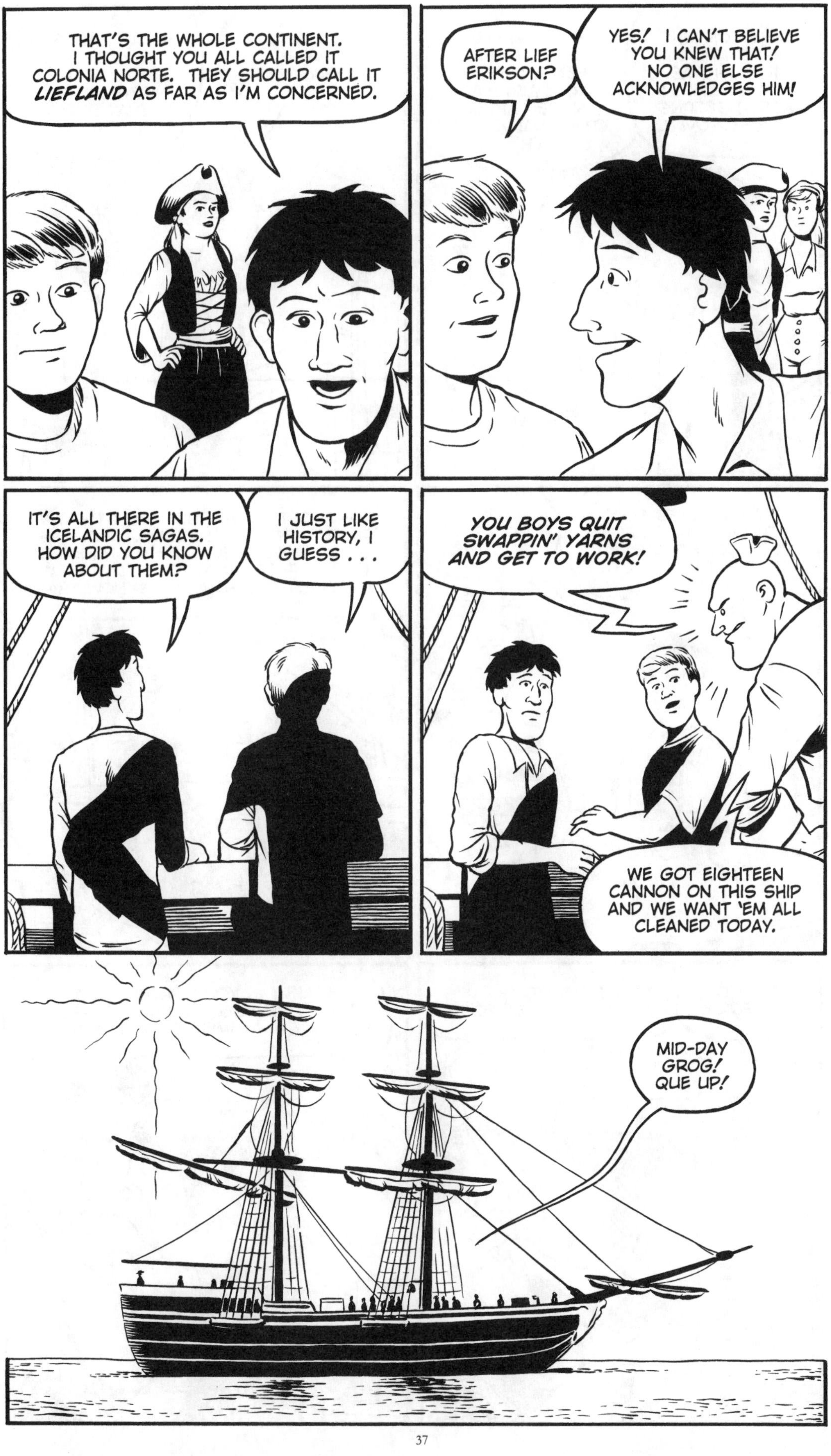
THAT'S THE WHOLE CONTINENT. I THOUGHT YOU ALL CALLED IT COLONIA NORTE. THEY SHOULD CALL IT *LIEFLAND* AS FAR AS I'M CONCERNED.
AFTER LIEF ERIKSON?
YES! I CAN'T BELIEVE YOU KNEW THAT! NO ONE ELSE ACKNOWLEDGES HIM!
IT'S ALL THERE IN THE ICELANDIC SAGAS. HOW DID YOU KNOW ABOUT THEM?
I JUST LIKE HISTORY, I GUESS . . .
YOU BOYS QUIT SWAPPIN' YARNS AND GET TO WORK!
WE GOT EIGHTEEN CANNON ON THIS SHIP AND WE WANT 'EM ALL CLEANED TODAY.
MID-DAY GROG! QUE UP!

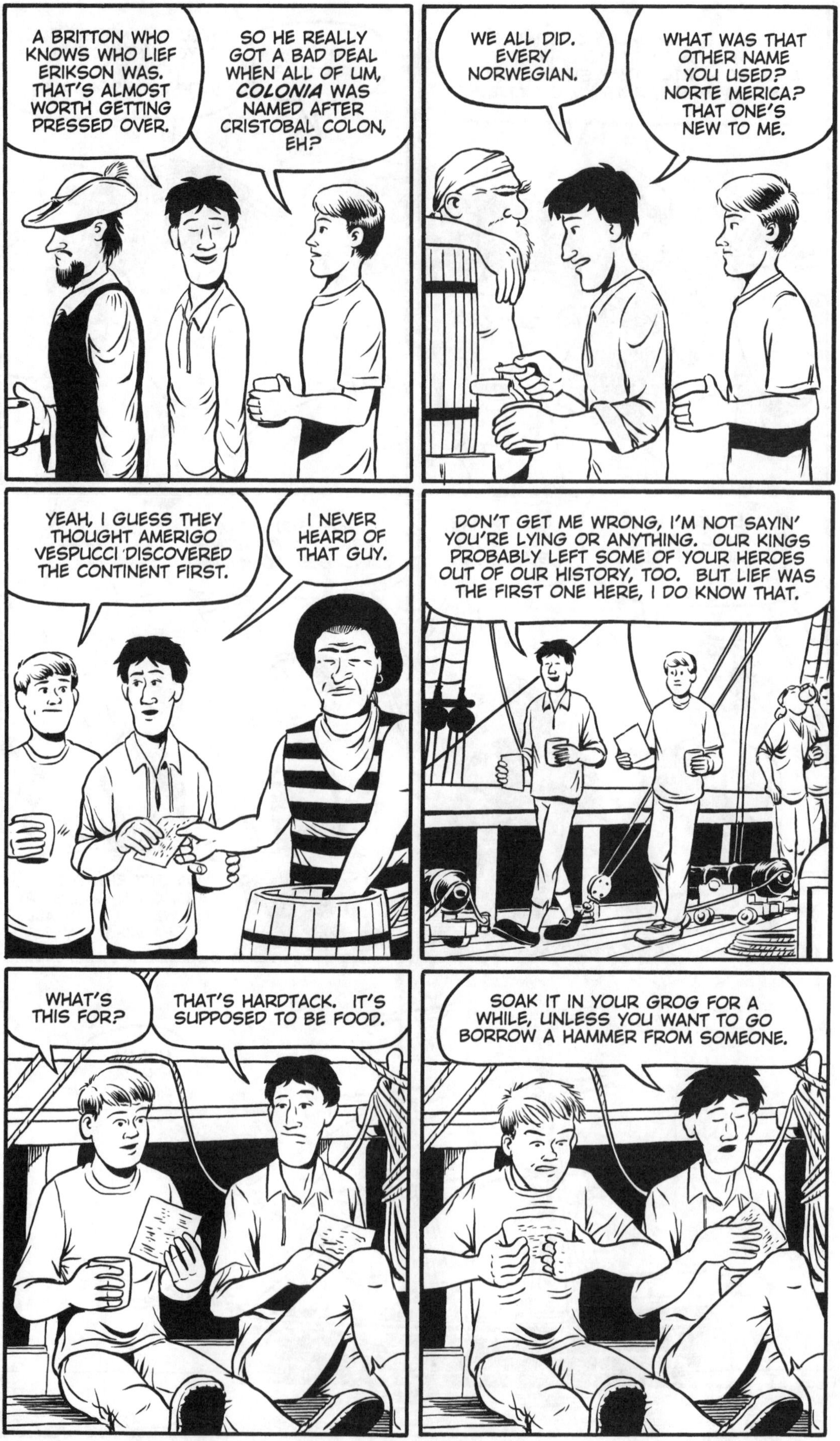
A BRITTON WHO KNOWS WHO LIEF ERIKSON WAS. THAT'S ALMOST WORTH GETTING PRESSED OVER.
SO HE REALLY GOT A BAD DEAL WHEN ALL OF UM, *COLONIA* WAS NAMED AFTER CRISTOBAL COLON, EH?
WE ALL DID. EVERY NORWEGIAN.
WHAT WAS THAT OTHER NAME YOU USED? NORTE MERICA? THAT ONE'S NEW TO ME.
YEAH, I GUESS THEY THOUGHT AMERIGO VESPUCCI DISCOVERED THE CONTINENT FIRST.
I NEVER HEARD OF THAT GUY.
DON'T GET ME WRONG, I'M NOT SAYIN' YOU'RE LYING OR ANYTHING. OUR KINGS PROBABLY LEFT SOME OF YOUR HEROES OUT OF OUR HISTORY, TOO. BUT LIEF WAS THE FIRST ONE HERE, I DO KNOW THAT.
WHAT'S THIS FOR?
THAT'S HARDTACK. IT'S SUPPOSED TO BE FOOD.
SOAK IT IN YOUR GROG FOR A WHILE, UNLESS YOU WANT TO GO BORROW A HAMMER FROM SOMEONE.

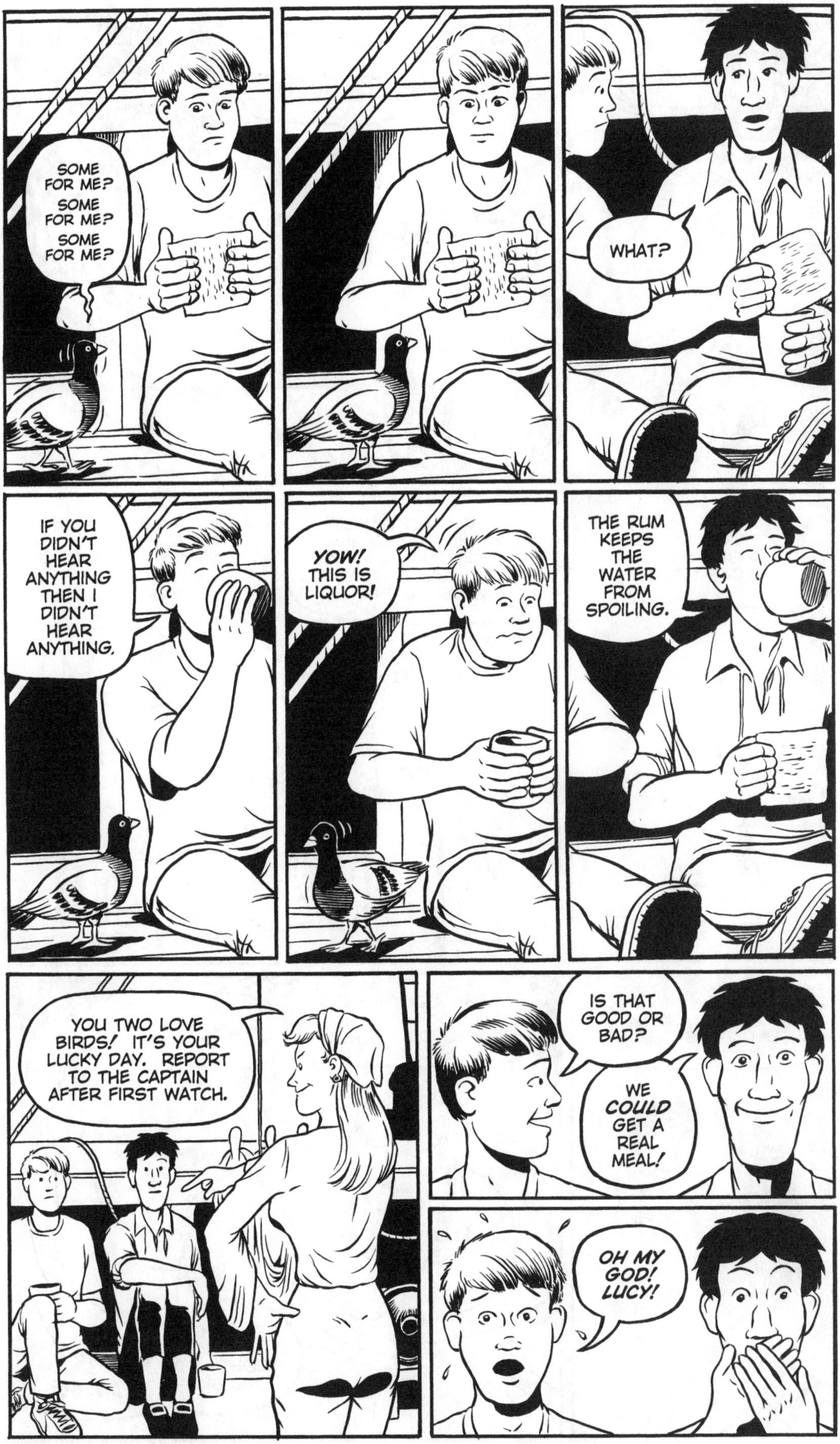
SOME FOR ME? SOME FOR ME? SOME FOR ME?
WHAT?
IF YOU DIDN'T HEAR ANYTHING THEN I DIDN'T HEAR ANYTHING.
YOW! THIS IS LIQUOR!
THE RUM KEEPS THE WATER FROM SPOILING.
YOU TWO LOVE BIRDS! IT'S YOUR LUCKY DAY. REPORT TO THE CAPTAIN AFTER FIRST WATCH.
IS THAT GOOD OR BAD?
WE COULD GET A REAL MEAL!
OH MY GOD! LUCY!

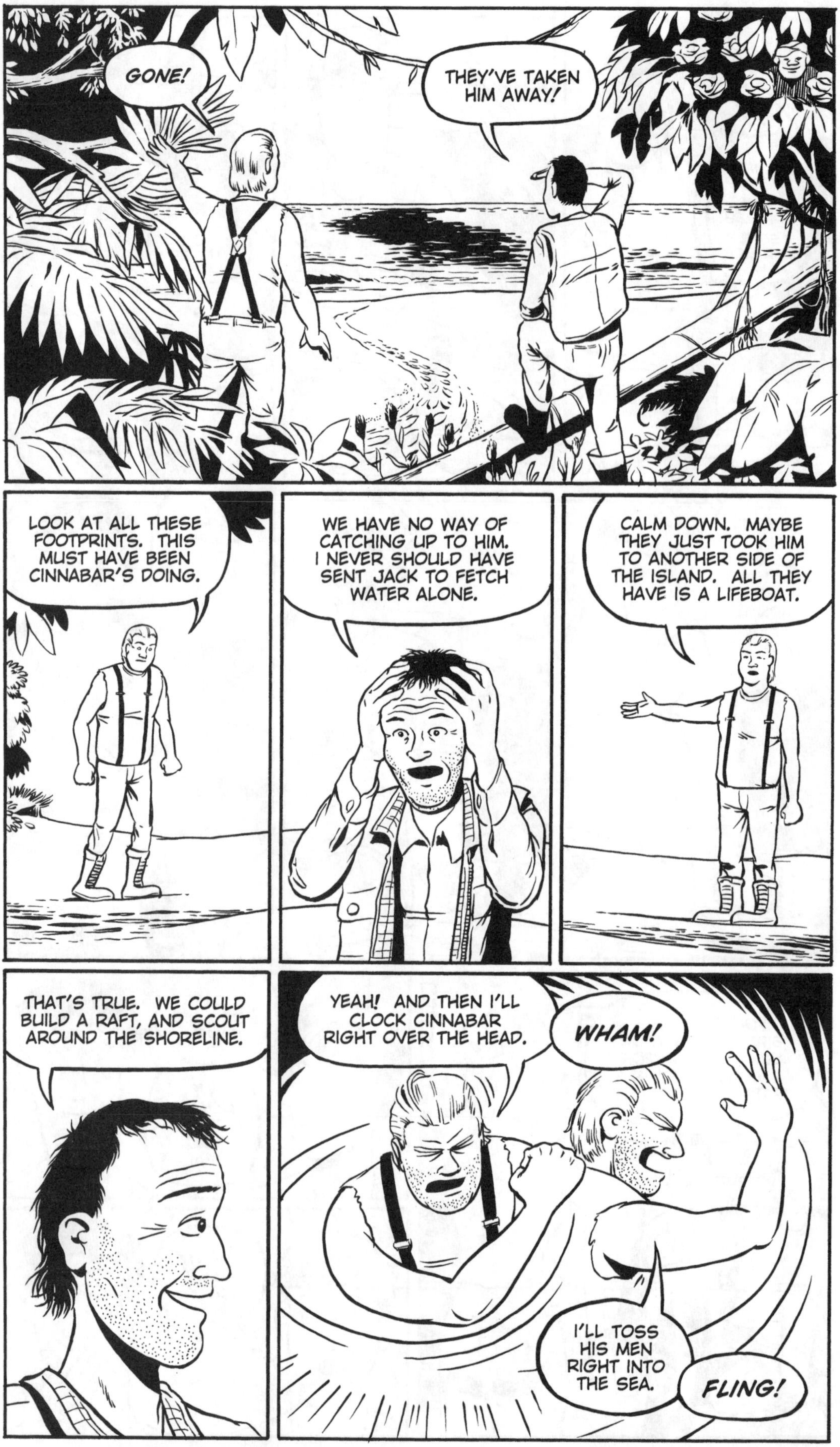
GONE!
THEY'VE TAKEN HIM AWAY!
LOOK AT ALL THESE FOOTPRINTS. THIS MUST HAVE BEEN CINNABAR'S DOING.
WE HAVE NO WAY OF CATCHING UP TO HIM. I NEVER SHOULD HAVE SENT JACK TO FETCH WATER ALONE.
CALM DOWN. MAYBE THEY JUST TOOK HIM TO ANOTHER SIDE OF THE ISLAND. ALL THEY HAVE IS A LIFEBOAT.
THAT'S TRUE. WE COULD BUILD A RAFT, AND SCOUT AROUND THE SHORELINE.
YEAH! AND THEN I'LL CLOCK CINNABAR RIGHT OVER THE HEAD.
WHAM!
I'LL TOSS HIS MEN RIGHT INTO THE SEA.
FLING!

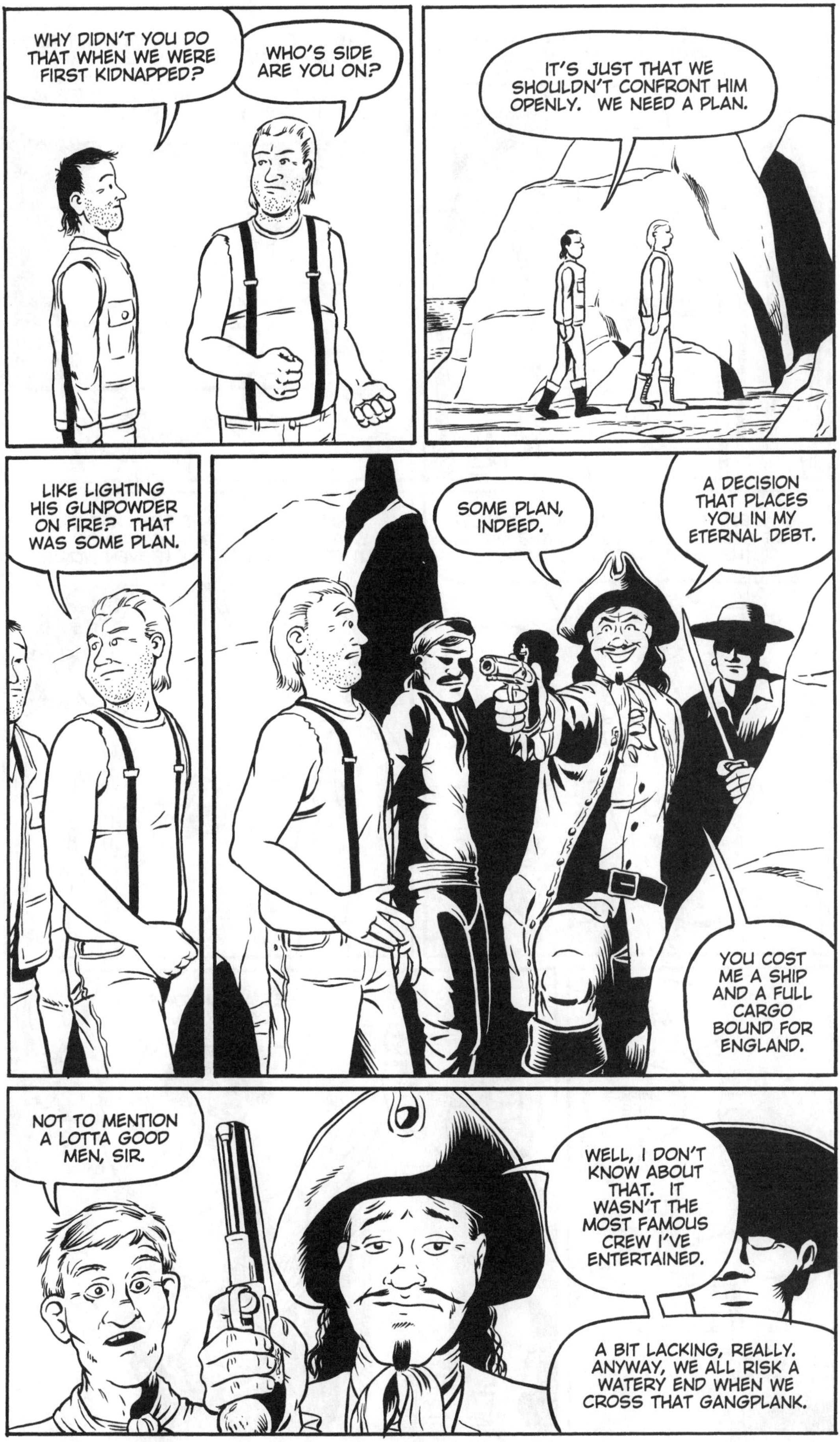

WHY DIDN'T YOU DO THAT WHEN WE WERE FIRST KIDNAPPED?
WHO'S SIDE ARE YOU ON?
IT'S JUST THAT WE SHOULDN'T CONFRONT HIM OPENLY. WE NEED A PLAN.
LIKE LIGHTING HIS GUNPOWDER ON FIRE? THAT WAS SOME PLAN.
SOME PLAN, INDEED.
A DECISION THAT PLACES YOU IN MY ETERNAL DEBT.
YOU COST ME A SHIP AND A FULL CARGO BOUND FOR ENGLAND.
NOT TO MENTION A LOTTA GOOD MEN, SIR.
WELL, I DON'T KNOW ABOUT THAT. IT WASN'T THE MOST FAMOUS CREW I'VE ENTERTAINED.
A BIT LACKING, REALLY. ANYWAY, WE ALL RISK A WATERY END WHEN WE CROSS THAT GANGPLANK.

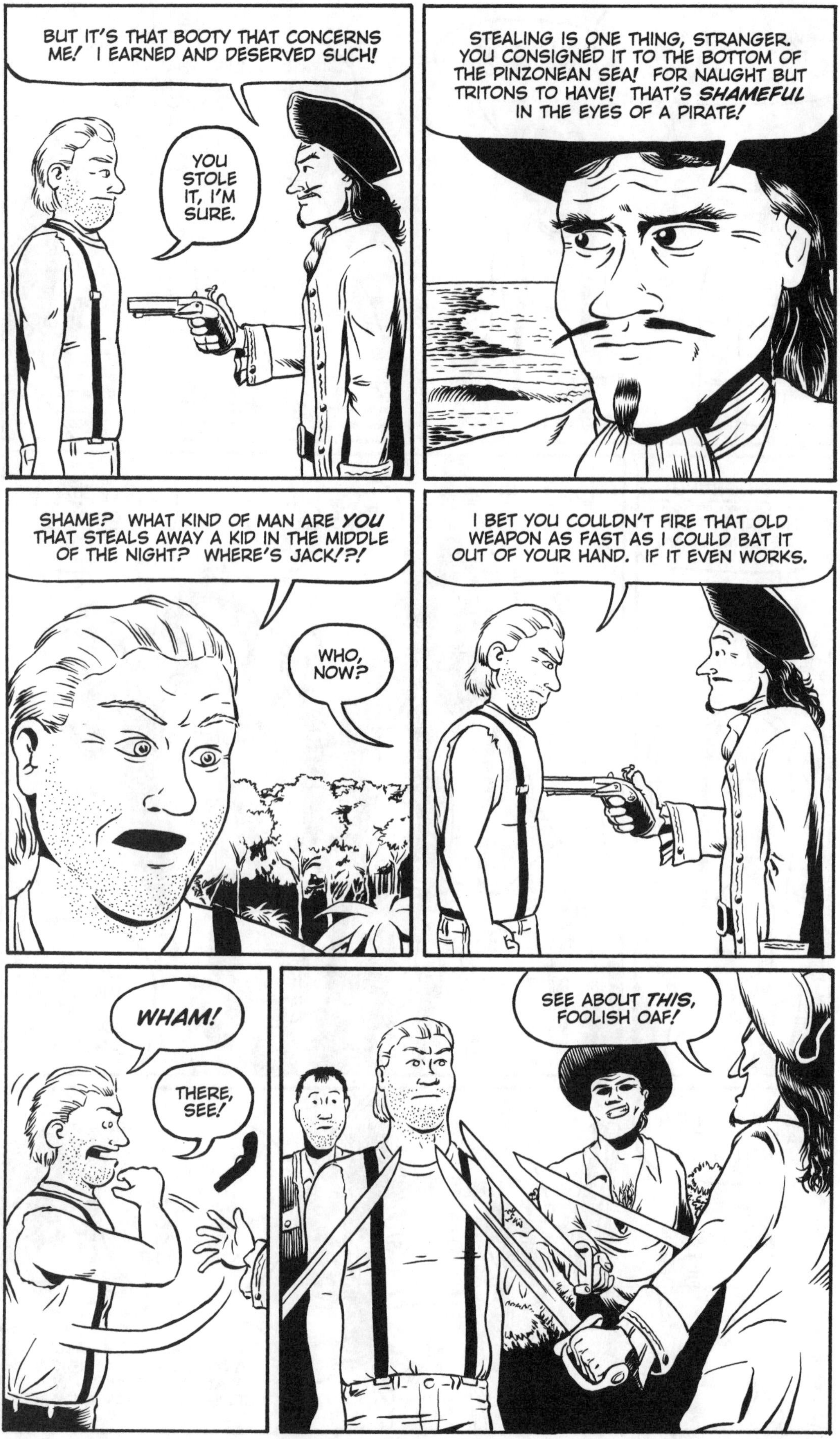
BUT IT'S THAT BOOTY THAT CONCERNS ME! I EARNED AND DESERVED SUCH!
YOU STOLE IT, I'M SURE.
STEALING IS ONE THING, STRANGER. YOU CONSIGNED IT TO THE BOTTOM OF THE PINZONEAN SEA! FOR NAUGHT BUT TRITONS TO HAVE! THAT'S SHAMEFUL IN THE EYES OF A PIRATE!
SHAME? WHAT KIND OF MAN ARE YOU THAT STEALS AWAY A KID IN THE MIDDLE OF THE NIGHT? WHERE'S JACK!?!
WHO, NOW?
I BET YOU COULDN'T FIRE THAT OLD WEAPON AS FAST AS I COULD BAT IT OUT OF YOUR HAND. IF IT EVEN WORKS.
WHAM!
THERE, SEE!
SEE ABOUT THIS, FOOLISH OAF!

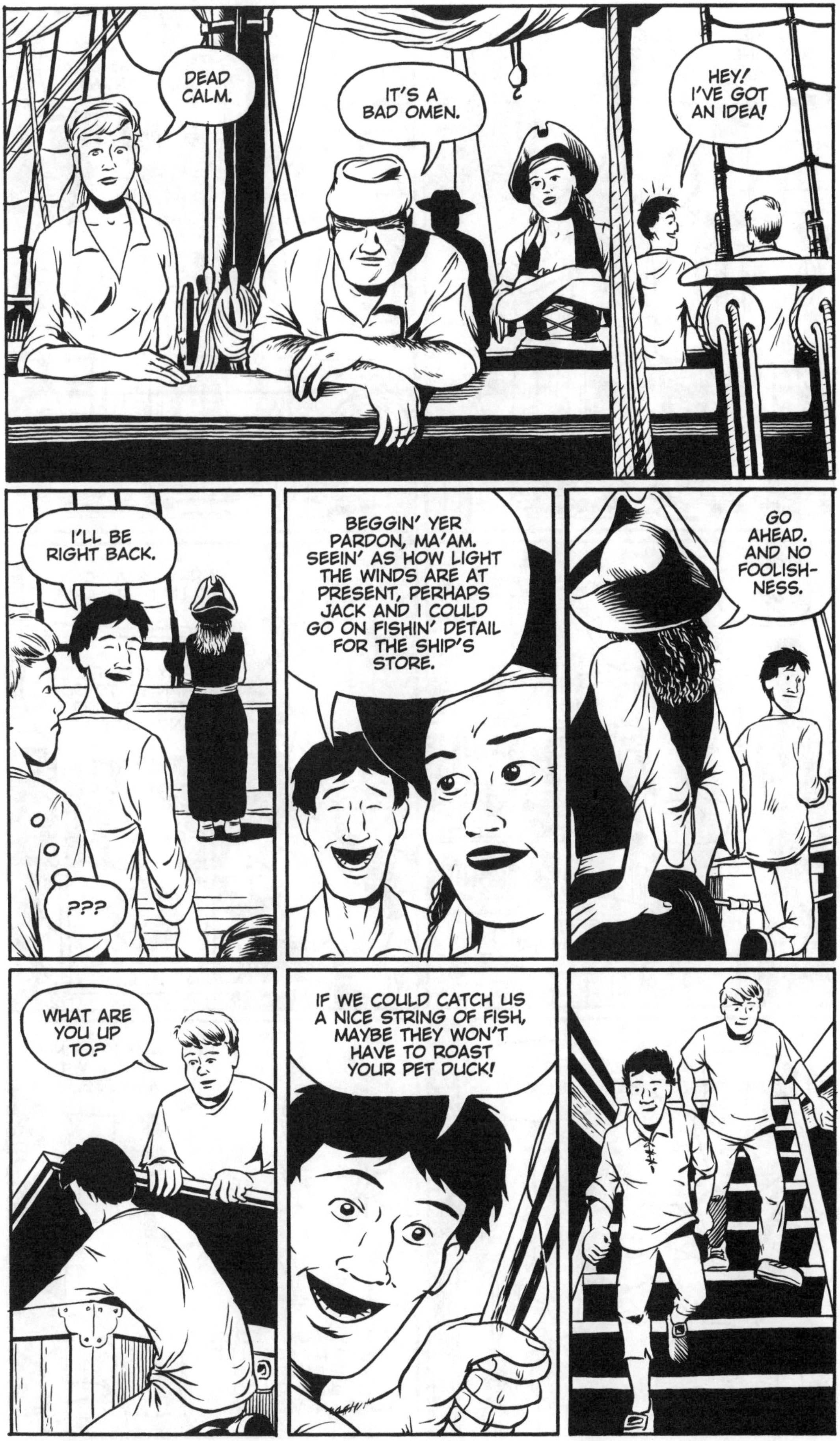
DEAD CALM.
IT'S A BAD OMEN.
HEY! I'VE GOT AN IDEA!
I'LL BE RIGHT BACK.
???
BEGGIN' YER PARDON, MA'AM. SEEIN' AS HOW LIGHT THE WINDS ARE AT PRESENT, PERHAPS JACK AND I COULD GO ON FISHIN' DETAIL FOR THE SHIP'S STORE.
GO AHEAD. AND NO FOOLISHNESS.
WHAT ARE YOU UP TO?
IF WE COULD CATCH US A NICE STRING OF FISH, MAYBE THEY WON'T HAVE TO ROAST YOUR PET DUCK!

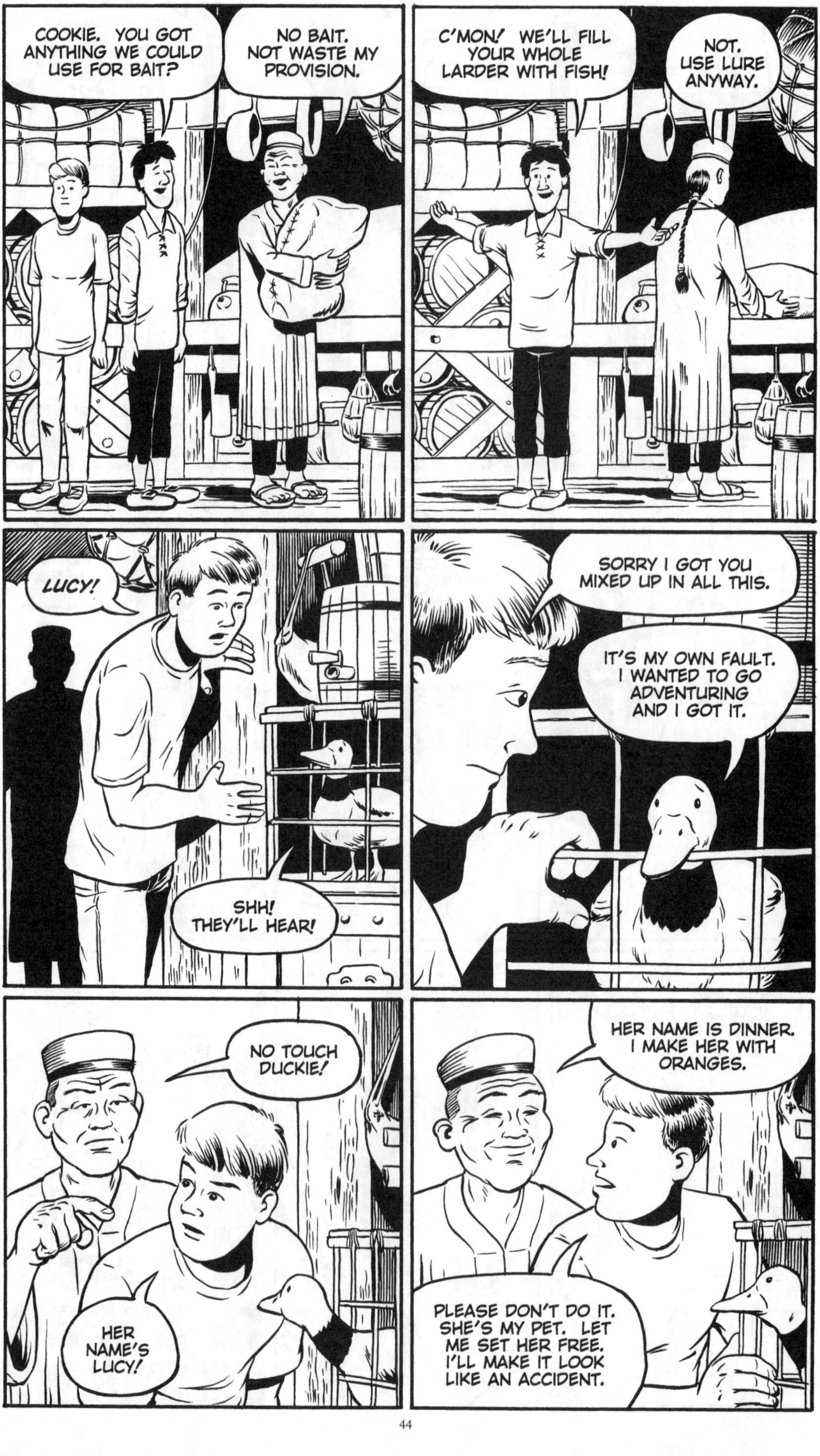
COOKIE. YOU GOT ANYTHING WE COULD USE FOR BAIT?
NO BAIT. NOT WASTE MY PROVISION.
C'MON! WE'LL FILL YOUR WHOLE LARDER WITH FISH!
NOT. USE LURE ANYWAY.
LUCY!
SHH! THEY'LL HEAR!
SORRY I GOT YOU MIXED UP IN ALL THIS.
IT'S MY OWN FAULT. I WANTED TO GO ADVENTURING AND I GOT IT.
NO TOUCH DUCKIE!
HER NAME'S LUCY!
HER NAME IS DINNER. I MAKE HER WITH ORANGES.
PLEASE DON'T DO IT. SHE'S MY PET. LET ME SET HER FREE. I'LL MAKE IT LOOK LIKE AN ACCIDENT.

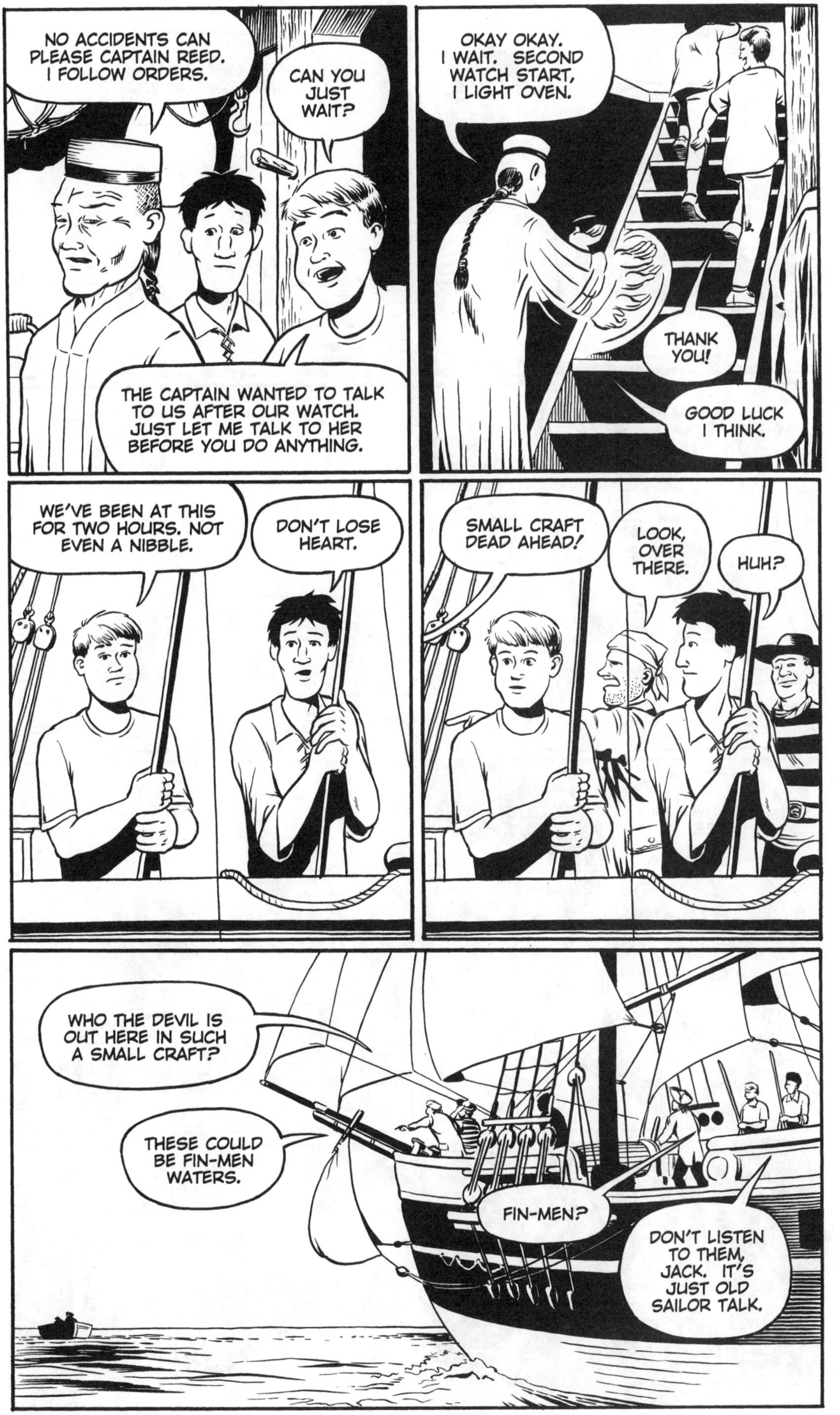

NO ACCIDENTS CAN PLEASE CAPTAIN REED. I FOLLOW ORDERS.
CAN YOU JUST WAIT?
THE CAPTAIN WANTED TO TALK TO US AFTER OUR WATCH. JUST LET ME TALK TO HER BEFORE YOU DO ANYTHING.
OKAY OKAY. I WAIT. SECOND WATCH START, I LIGHT OVEN.
THANK YOU!
GOOD LUCK I THINK.
WE'VE BEEN AT THIS FOR TWO HOURS. NOT EVEN A NIBBLE.
DON'T LOSE HEART.
SMALL CRAFT DEAD AHEAD!
LOOK, OVER THERE.
HUH?
WHO THE DEVIL IS OUT HERE IN SUCH A SMALL CRAFT?
THESE COULD BE FIN-MEN WATERS.
FIN-MEN?
DON'T LISTEN TO THEM, JACK. IT'S JUST OLD SAILOR TALK.

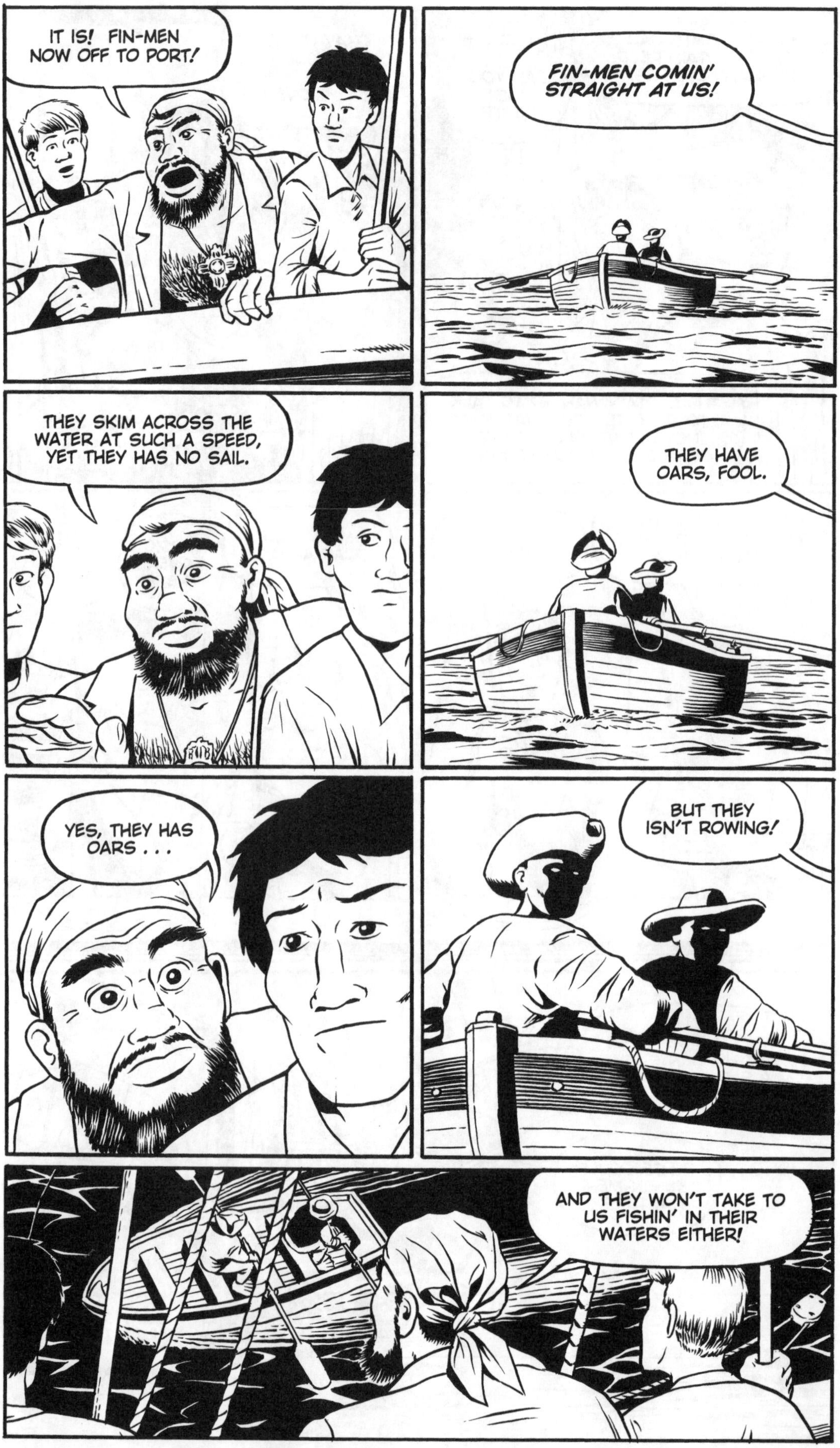
IT IS! FIN-MEN NOW OFF TO PORT!
FIN-MEN COMIN' STRAIGHT AT US!
THEY SKIM ACROSS THE WATER AT SUCH A SPEED, YET THEY HAS NO SAIL.
THEY HAVE OARS, FOOL.
YES, THEY HAS OARS . . .
BUT THEY ISN'T ROWING!
AND THEY WON'T TAKE TO US FISHIN' IN THEIR WATERS EITHER!

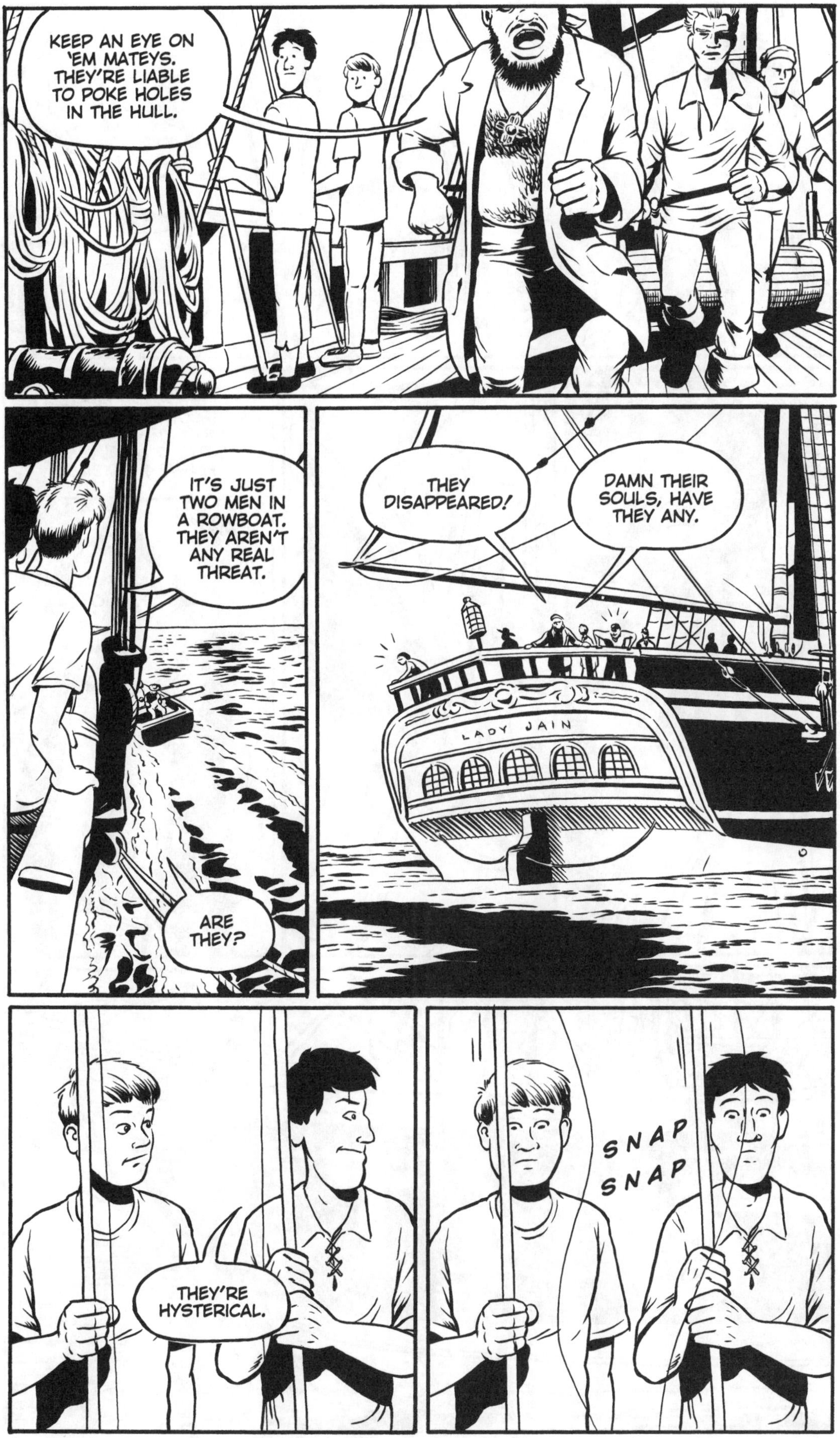
KEEP AN EYE ON 'EM MATEYS. THEY'RE LIABLE TO POKE HOLES IN THE HULL.
IT'S JUST TWO MEN IN A ROWBOAT. THEY AREN'T ANY REAL THREAT.
ARE THEY?
THEY DISAPPEARED!
DAMN THEIR SOULS, HAVE THEY ANY.
LADY JAIN
THEY'RE HYSTERICAL.
SNAP
SNAP

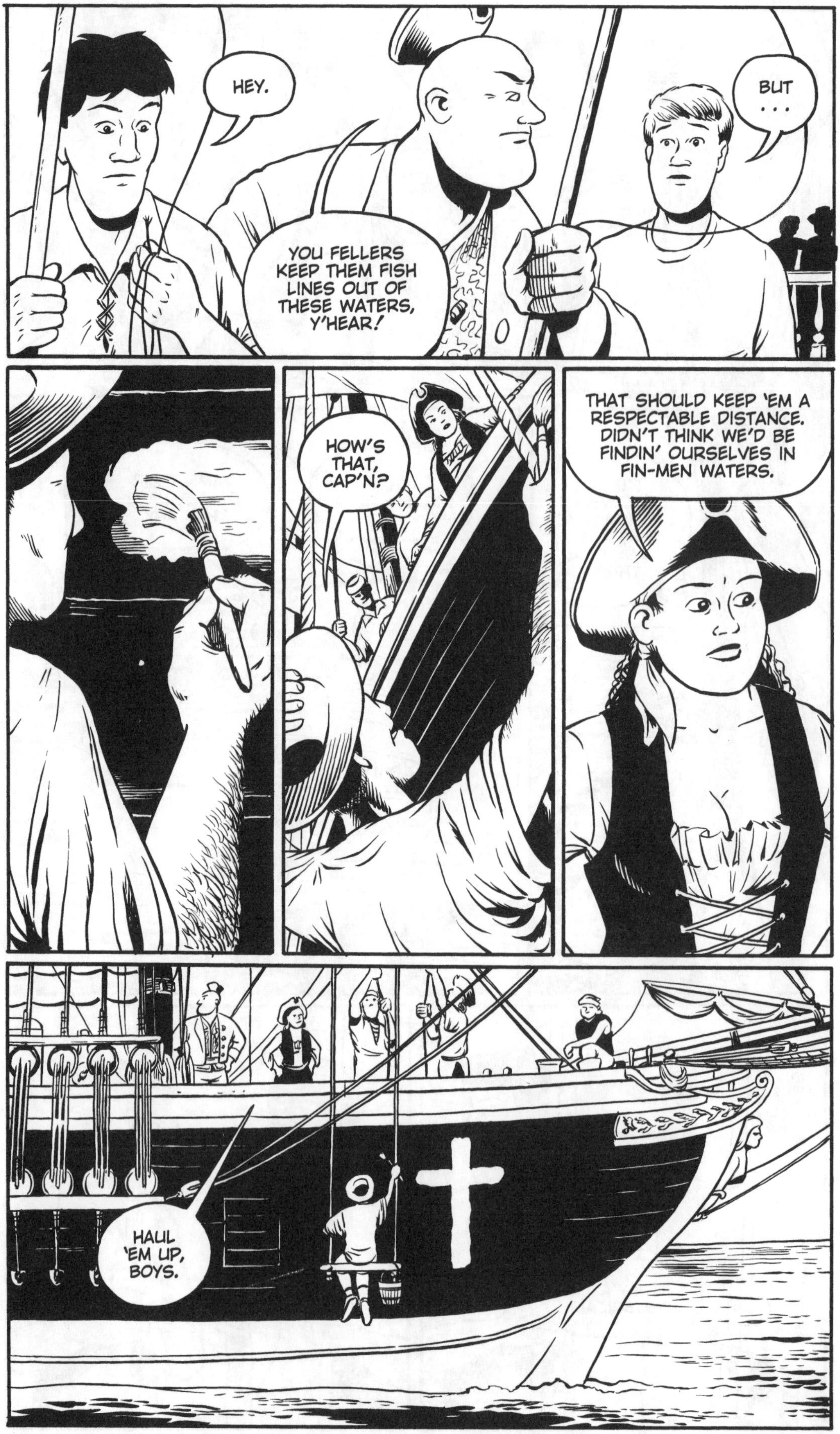
HEY.
YOU FELLERS KEEP THEM FISH LINES OUT OF THESE WATERS, Y'HEAR!
BUT . . .
HOW'S THAT, CAP'N?
THAT SHOULD KEEP 'EM A RESPECTABLE DISTANCE. DIDN'T THINK WE'D BE FINDIN' OURSELVES IN FIN-MEN WATERS.
HAUL 'EM UP, BOYS.

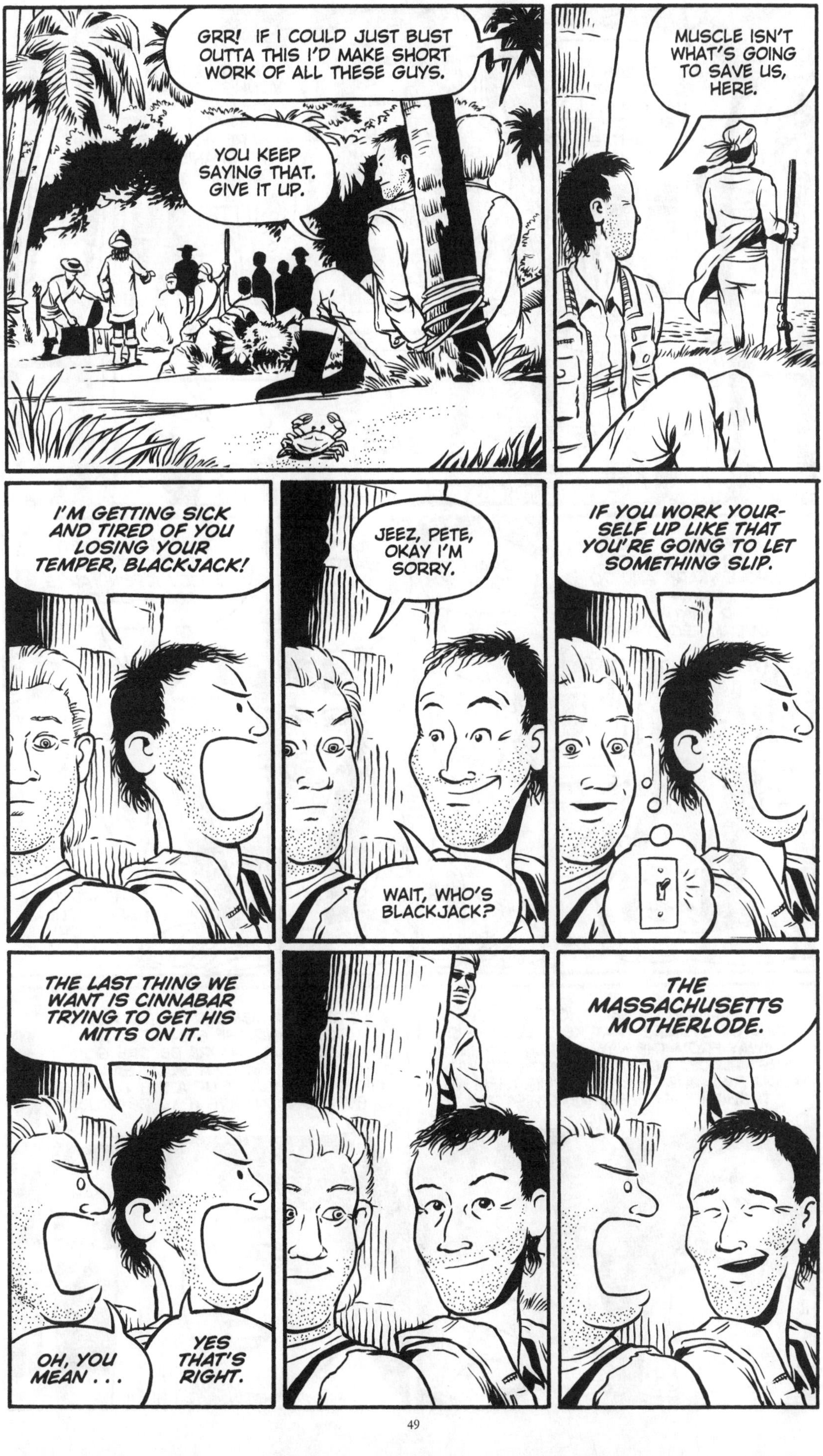
GRR! IF I COULD JUST BUST OUTTA THIS I'D MAKE SHORT WORK OF ALL THESE GUYS.
YOU KEEP SAYING THAT. GIVE IT UP.
MUSCLE ISN'T WHAT'S GOING TO SAVE US, HERE.
I'M GETTING SICK AND TIRED OF YOU LOSING YOUR TEMPER, BLACKJACK!
JEEZ, PETE, OKAY I'M SORRY.
WAIT, WHO'S BLACKJACK?
IF YOU WORK YOURSELF UP LIKE THAT YOU'RE GOING TO LET SOMETHING SLIP.
THE LAST THING WE WANT IS CINNABAR TRYING TO GET HIS MITTS ON IT.
OH, YOU MEAN . . .
YES THAT'S RIGHT.
THE MASSACHUSETTS MOTHERLODE.

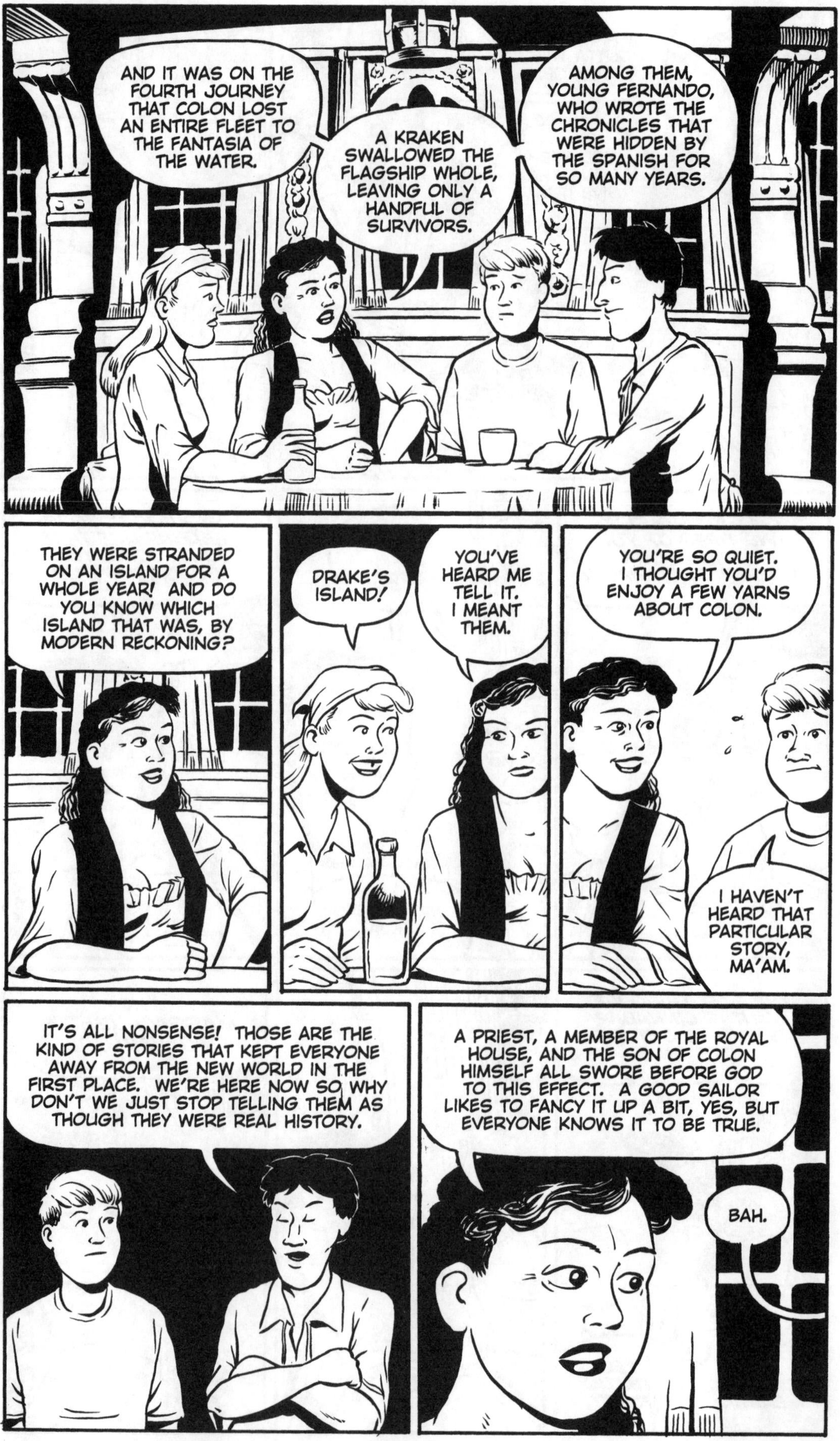
AND IT WAS ON THE FOURTH JOURNEY THAT COLON LOST AN ENTIRE FLEET TO THE FANTASIA OF THE WATER.
A KRAKEN SWALLOWED THE FLAGSHIP WHOLE, LEAVING ONLY A HANDFUL OF SURVIVORS.
AMONG THEM, YOUNG FERNANDO, WHO WROTE THE CHRONICLES THAT WERE HIDDEN BY THE SPANISH FOR SO MANY YEARS.
THEY WERE STRANDED ON AN ISLAND FOR A WHOLE YEAR! AND DO YOU KNOW WHICH ISLAND THAT WAS, BY MODERN RECKONING?
DRAKE'S ISLAND!
YOU'VE HEARD ME TELL IT. I MEANT THEM.
YOU'RE SO QUIET. I THOUGHT YOU'D ENJOY A FEW YARNS ABOUT COLON.
I HAVEN'T HEARD THAT PARTICULAR STORY, MA'AM.
IT'S ALL NONSENSE! THOSE ARE THE KIND OF STORIES THAT KEPT EVERYONE AWAY FROM THE NEW WORLD IN THE FIRST PLACE. WE'RE HERE NOW SO WHY DON'T WE JUST STOP TELLING THEM AS THOUGH THEY WERE REAL HISTORY.
A PRIEST, A MEMBER OF THE ROYAL HOUSE, AND THE SON OF COLON HIMSELF ALL SWORE BEFORE GOD TO THIS EFFECT. A GOOD SAILOR LIKES TO FANCY IT UP A BIT, YES, BUT EVERYONE KNOWS IT TO BE TRUE.
BAH.

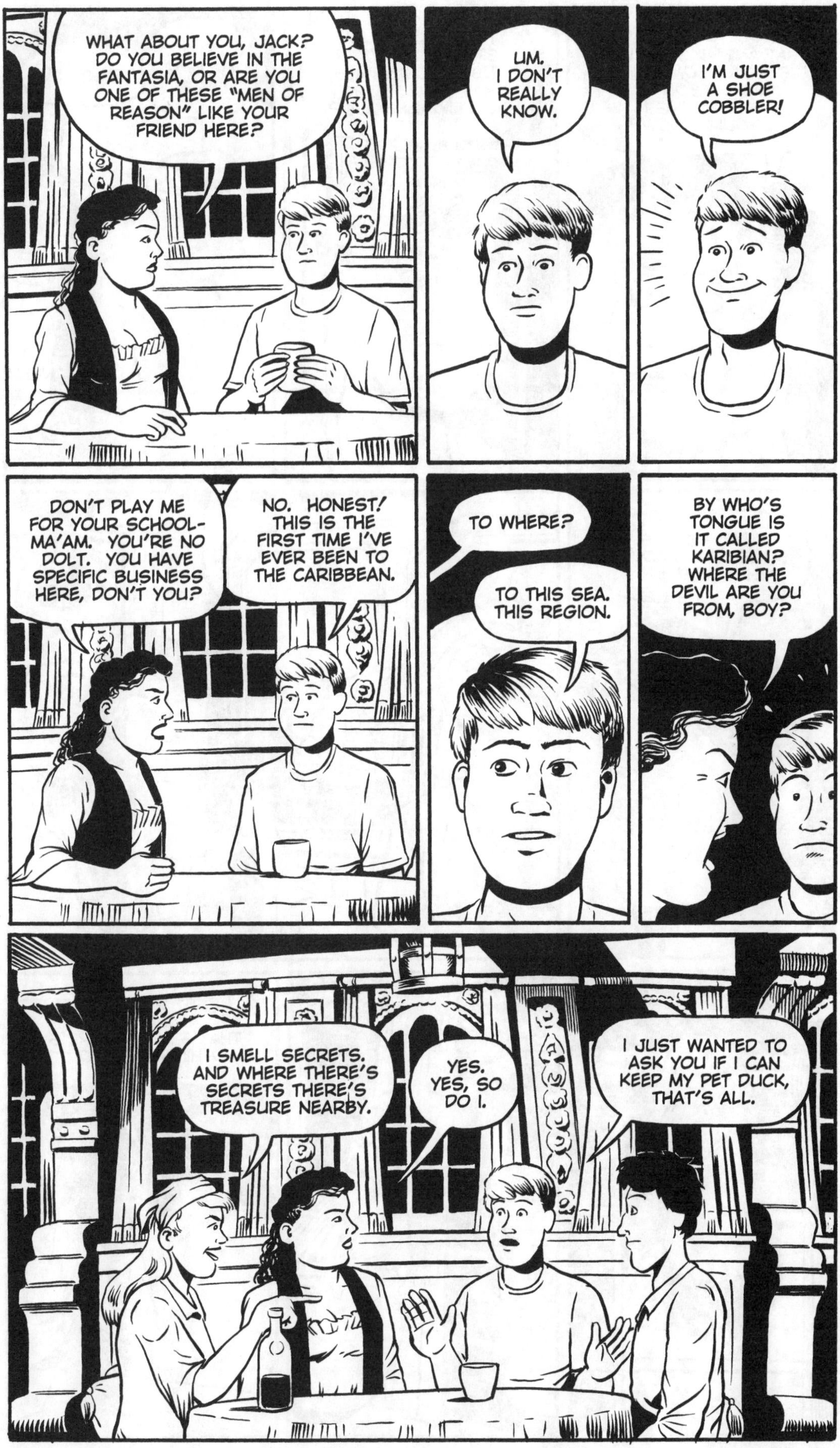
WHAT ABOUT YOU, JACK? DO YOU BELIEVE IN THE FANTASIA, OR ARE YOU ONE OF THESE "MEN OF REASON" LIKE YOUR FRIEND HERE?
UM. I DON'T REALLY KNOW.
I'M JUST A SHOE COBBLER!
DON'T PLAY ME FOR YOUR SCHOOL-MA'AM. YOU'RE NO DOLT. YOU HAVE SPECIFIC BUSINESS HERE, DON'T YOU?
NO. HONEST! THIS IS THE FIRST TIME I'VE EVER BEEN TO THE CARIBBEAN.
TO WHERE?
TO THIS SEA. THIS REGION.
BY WHO'S TONGUE IS IT CALLED KARIBIAN? WHERE THE DEVIL ARE YOU FROM, BOY?
I SMELL SECRETS. AND WHERE THERE'S SECRETS THERE'S TREASURE NEARBY.
YES. YES, SO DO I.
I JUST WANTED TO ASK YOU IF I CAN KEEP MY PET DUCK, THAT'S ALL.

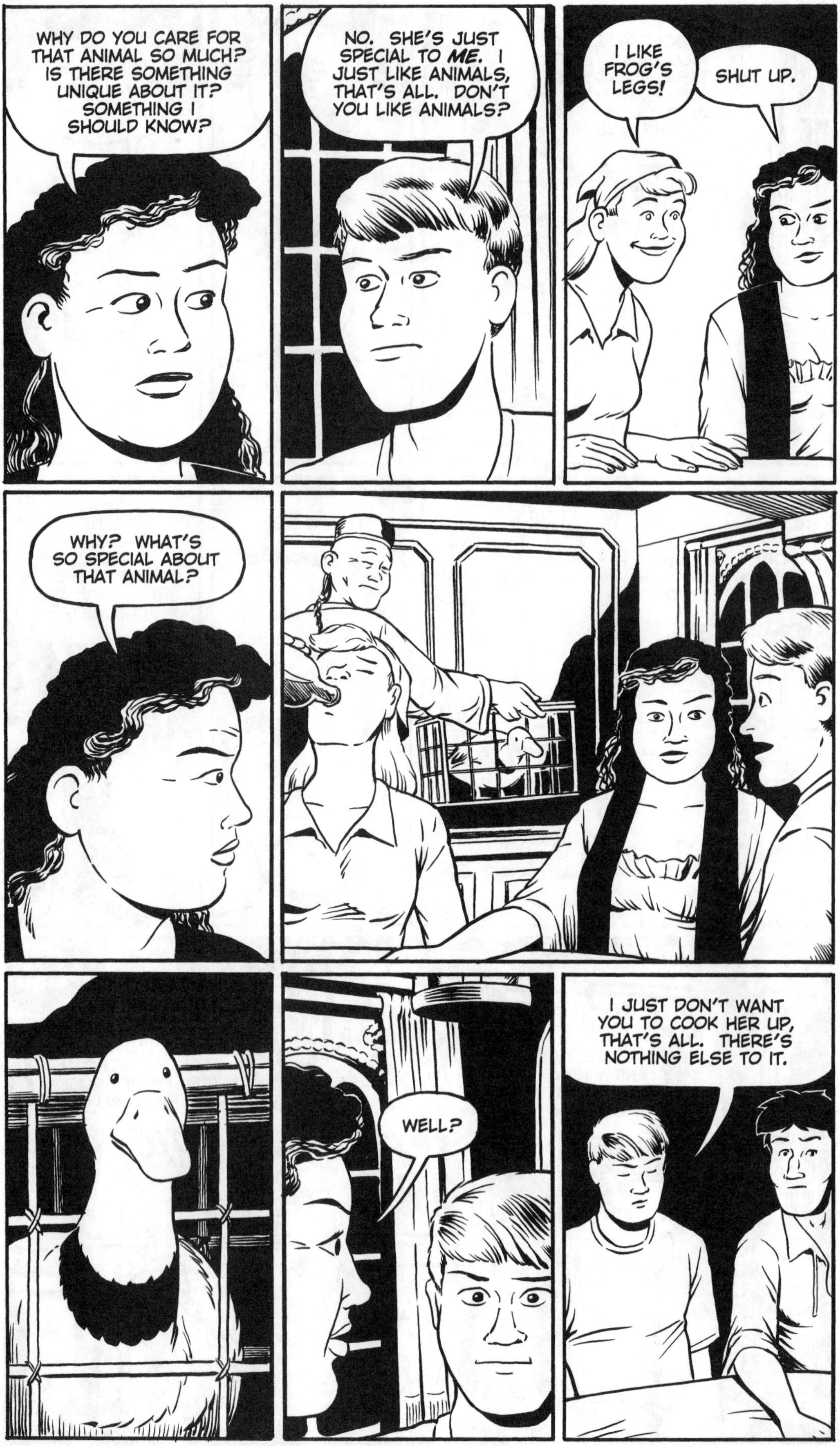
WHY DO YOU CARE FOR THAT ANIMAL SO MUCH? IS THERE SOMETHING UNIQUE ABOUT IT? SOMETHING I SHOULD KNOW?
NO. SHE'S JUST SPECIAL TO *ME.* I JUST LIKE ANIMALS, THAT'S ALL. DON'T YOU LIKE ANIMALS?
I LIKE FROG'S LEGS!
SHUT UP.
WHY? WHAT'S SO SPECIAL ABOUT THAT ANIMAL?
WELL?
I JUST DON'T WANT YOU TO COOK HER UP, THAT'S ALL. THERE'S NOTHING ELSE TO IT.

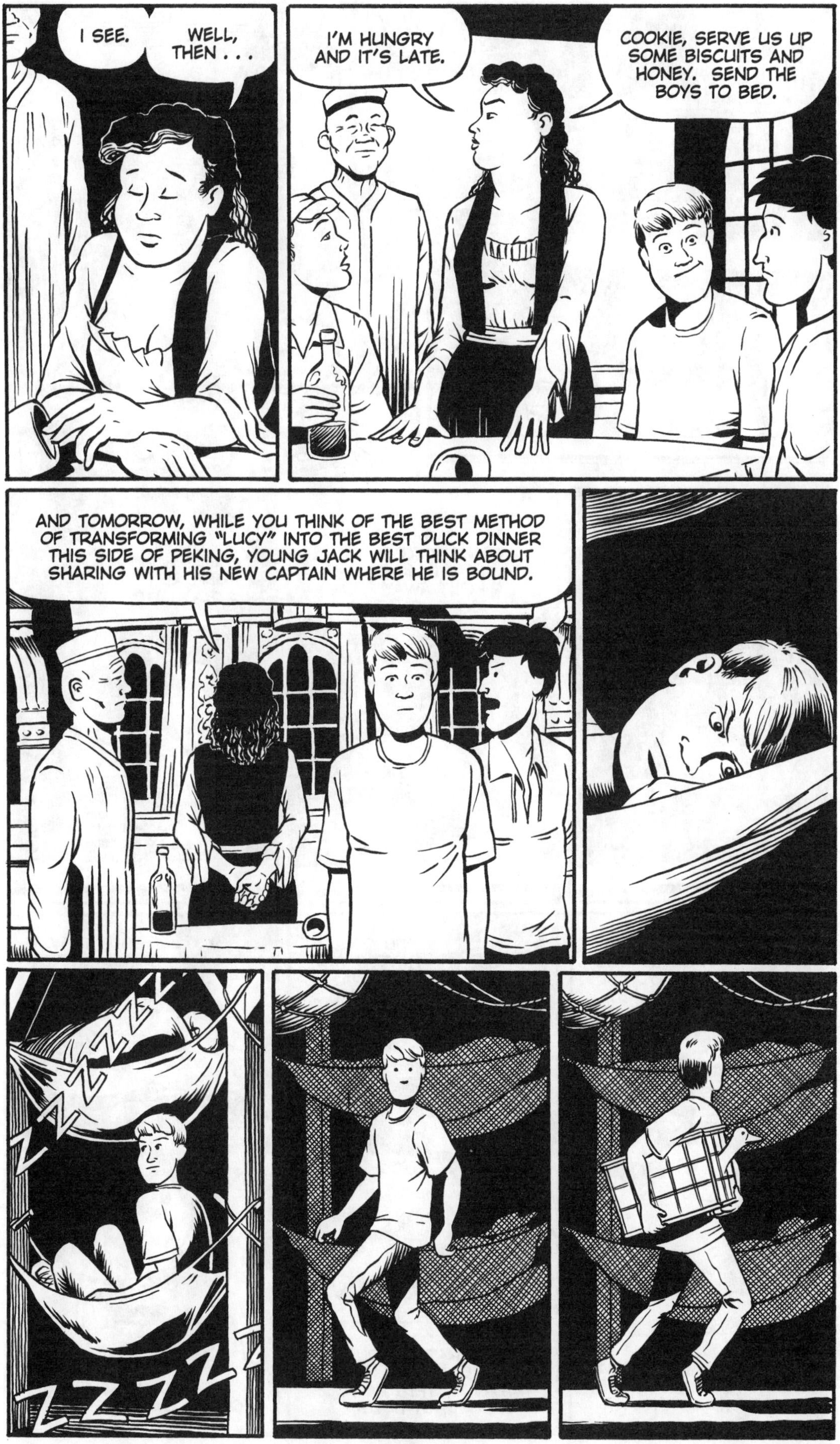

I SEE.
WELL, THEN . . .
I'M HUNGRY AND IT'S LATE.
COOKIE, SERVE US UP SOME BISCUITS AND HONEY. SEND THE BOYS TO BED.
AND TOMORROW, WHILE YOU THINK OF THE BEST METHOD OF TRANSFORMING "LUCY" INTO THE BEST DUCK DINNER THIS SIDE OF PEKING, YOUNG JACK WILL THINK ABOUT SHARING WITH HIS NEW CAPTAIN WHERE HE IS BOUND.

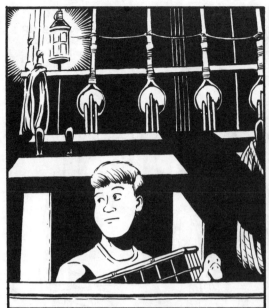

I THINK WE'RE SAFE OVER HERE.

WHAT WAS I THINKING, GOING OFF WITH HUMANS? NOW I'VE GOTTEN YOU IN HOT WATER.

IT'S NOT YOUR FAULT. GETTING SHANGHAIED WASN'T PART OF OUR PLAN. AT LEAST YOU CAN GET AWAY FROM ALL THIS NOW.

GO ON. GET HOME BEFORE IT'S TOO LATE.

BUT THEY'LL KNOW IT WAS YOU. YOU'LL SURELY BE FLOGGED, OR WORSE.

YOU COULD HAVE GIVEN ME AWAY, THAT I WAS A TALKER, BUT YOU DIDN'T.

BUT THEY SURELY WOULD HAVE GONE POKING AROUND MY ISLAND FOR GOLD AND CAUSING MAYHEM.

I'LL WORRY ABOUT THAT LATER. YOU HAVE TO GET OUT OF HERE TONIGHT.

THOSE PIRATES WOULDN'T HAVE EATEN ME IF YOU HAD . . . THEY'RE TOO SUPERSTITIOUS.

YOU SAW THE BIG PICTURE, SAME AS WE DO.

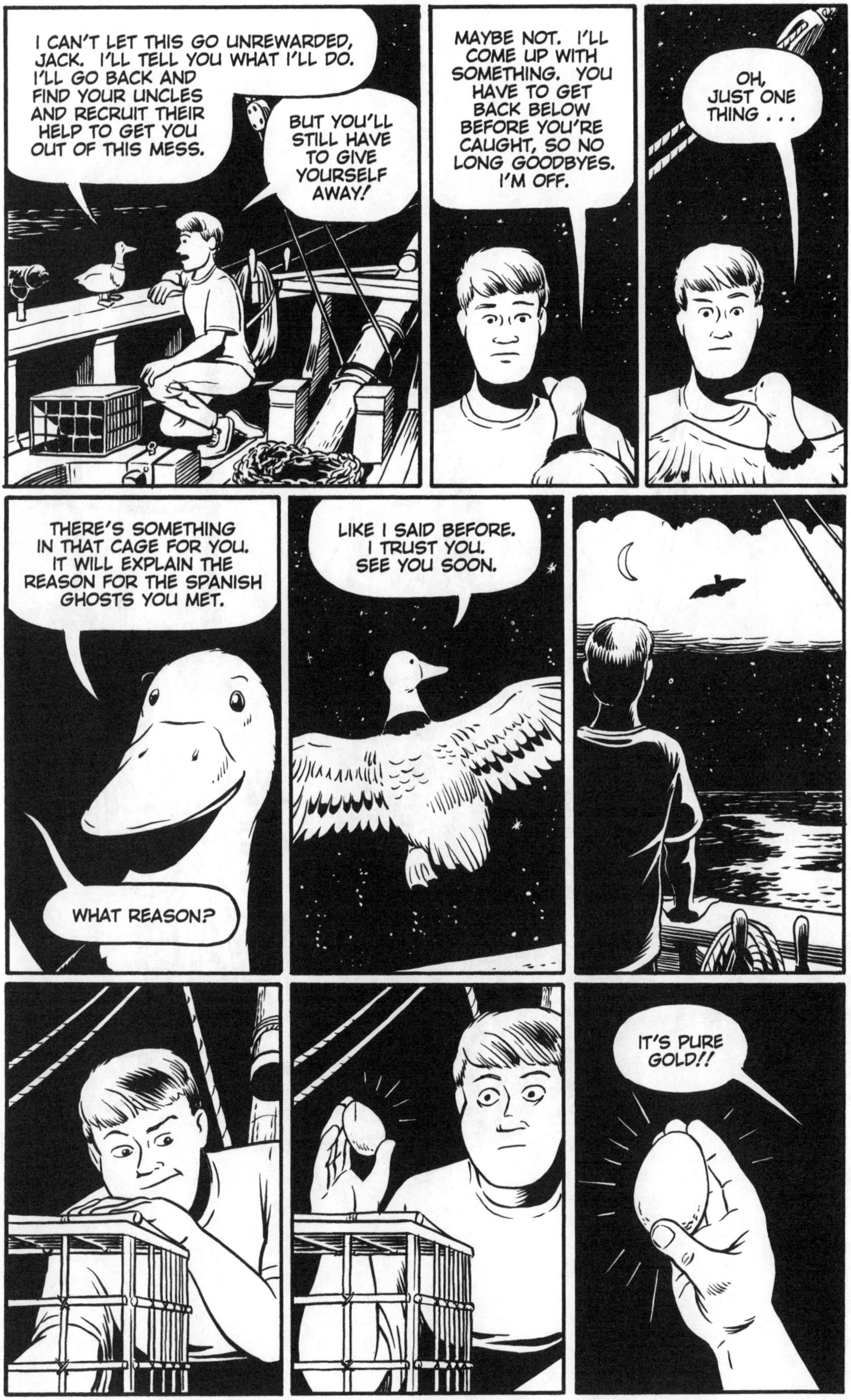
I CAN'T LET THIS GO UNREWARDED, JACK. I'LL TELL YOU WHAT I'LL DO. I'LL GO BACK AND FIND YOUR UNCLES AND RECRUIT THEIR HELP TO GET YOU OUT OF THIS MESS.
BUT YOU'LL STILL HAVE TO GIVE YOURSELF AWAY!
MAYBE NOT. I'LL COME UP WITH SOMETHING. YOU HAVE TO GET BACK BELOW BEFORE YOU'RE CAUGHT, SO NO LONG GOODBYES. I'M OFF.
OH, JUST ONE THING . . .
THERE'S SOMETHING IN THAT CAGE FOR YOU. IT WILL EXPLAIN THE REASON FOR THE SPANISH GHOSTS YOU MET.
WHAT REASON?
LIKE I SAID BEFORE. I TRUST YOU. SEE YOU SOON.
IT'S PURE GOLD!!

NEXT: BOARDING PARTY

OVER

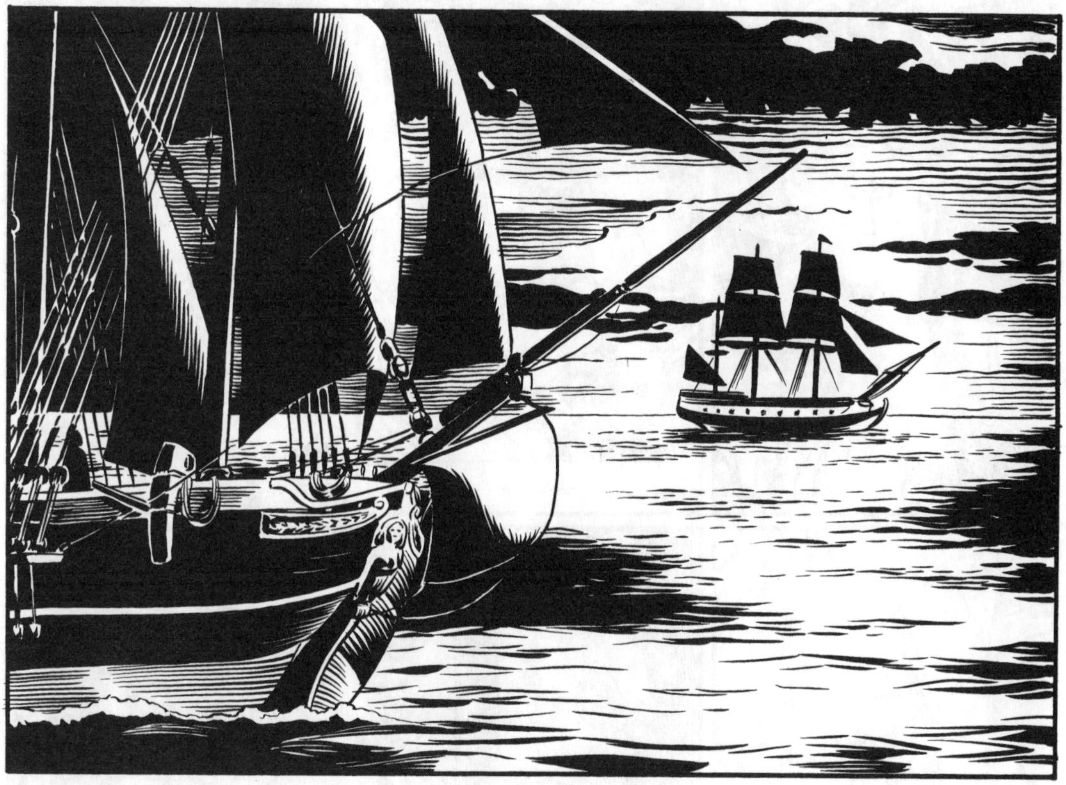

AND

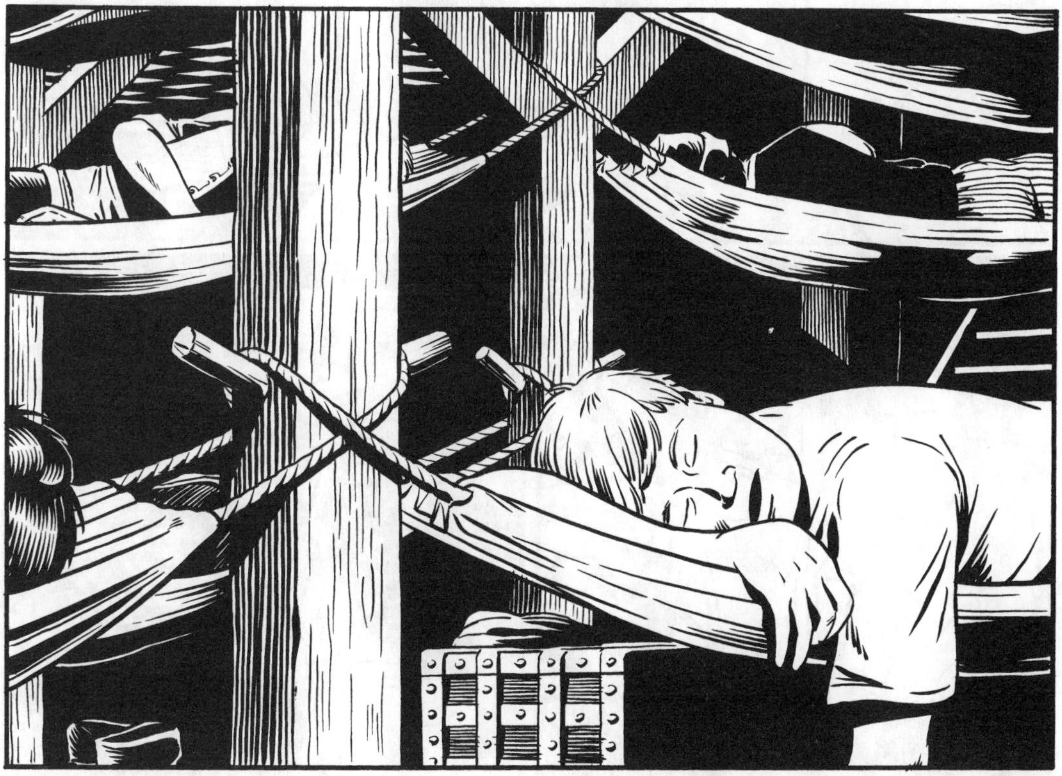

UNDER

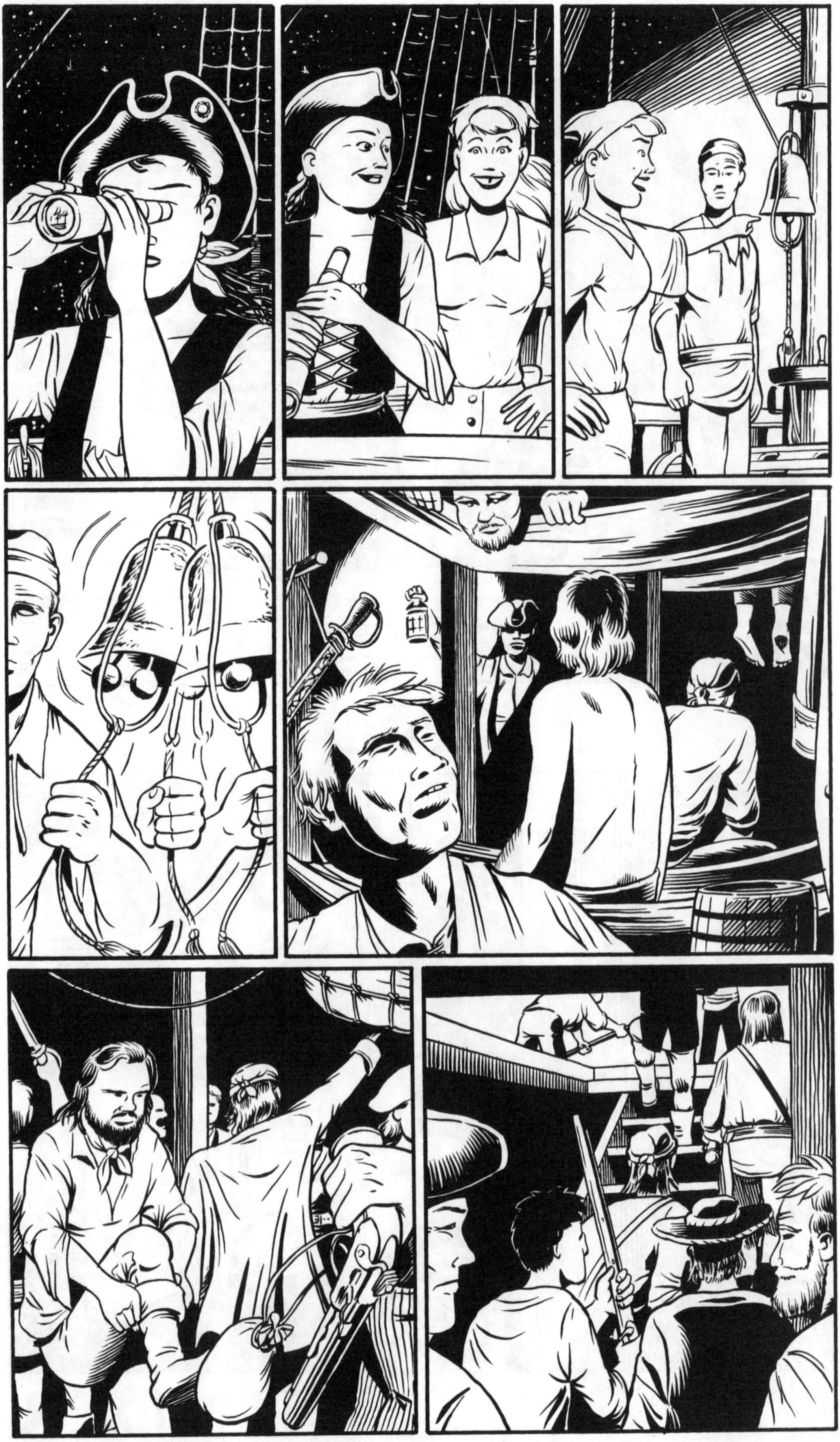

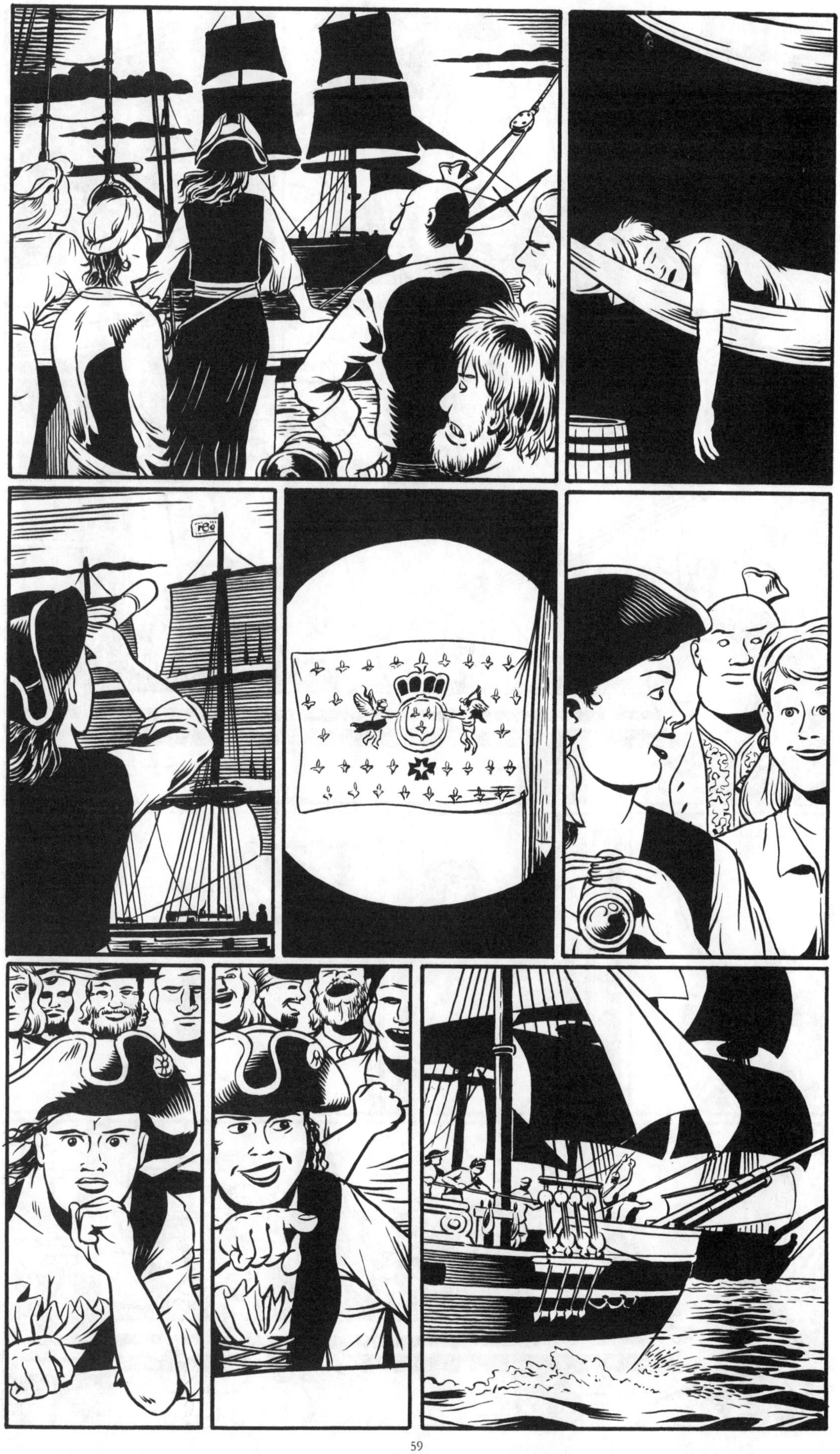

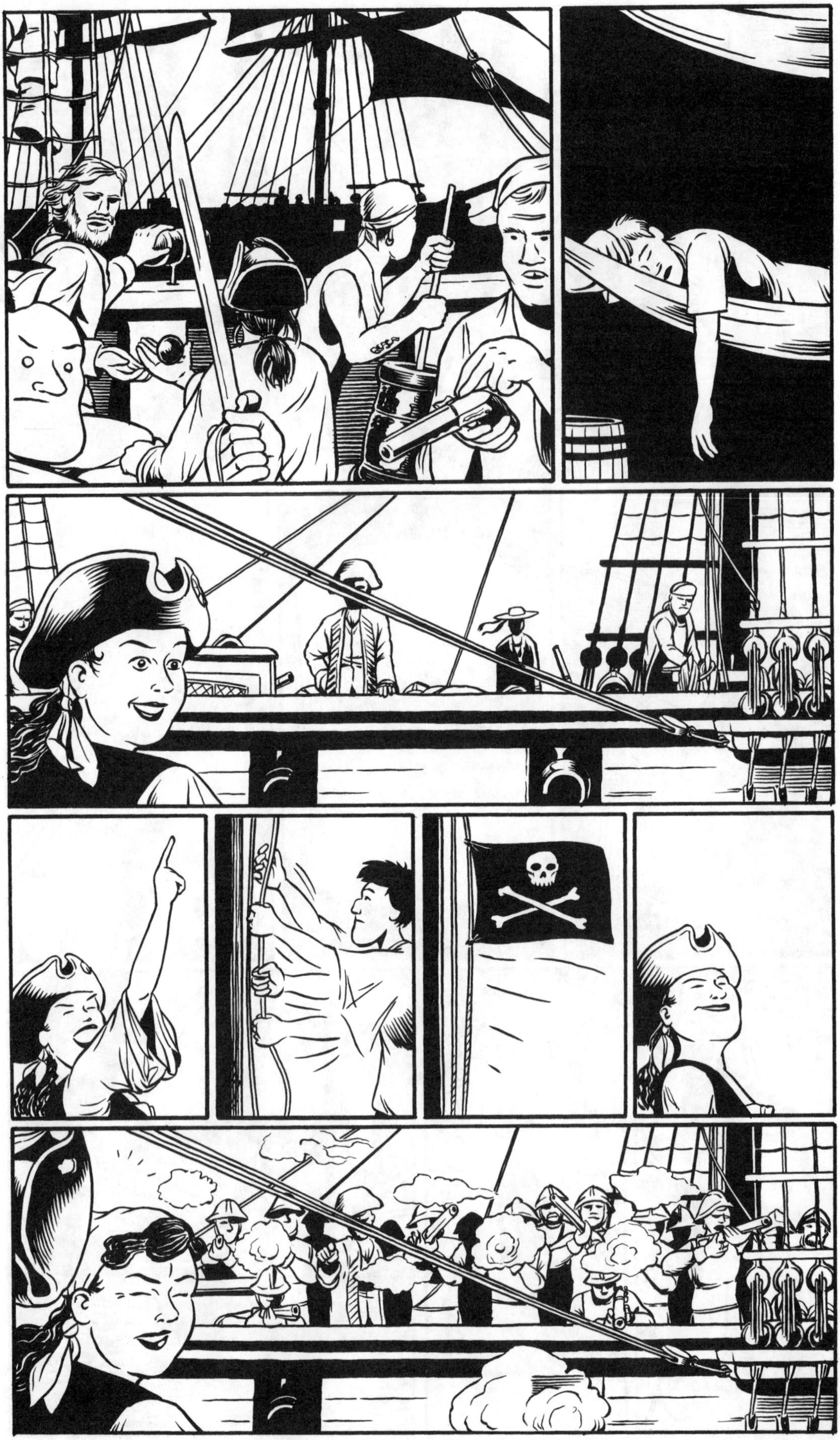

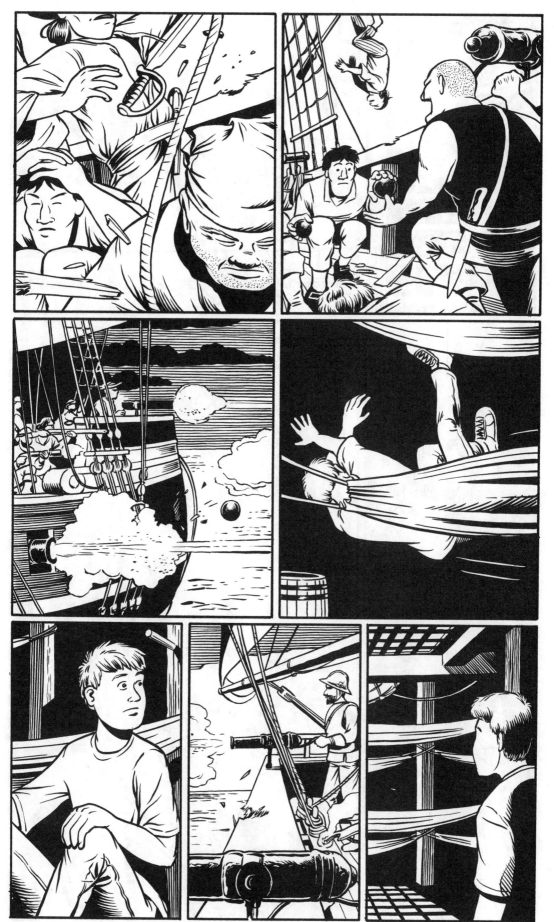

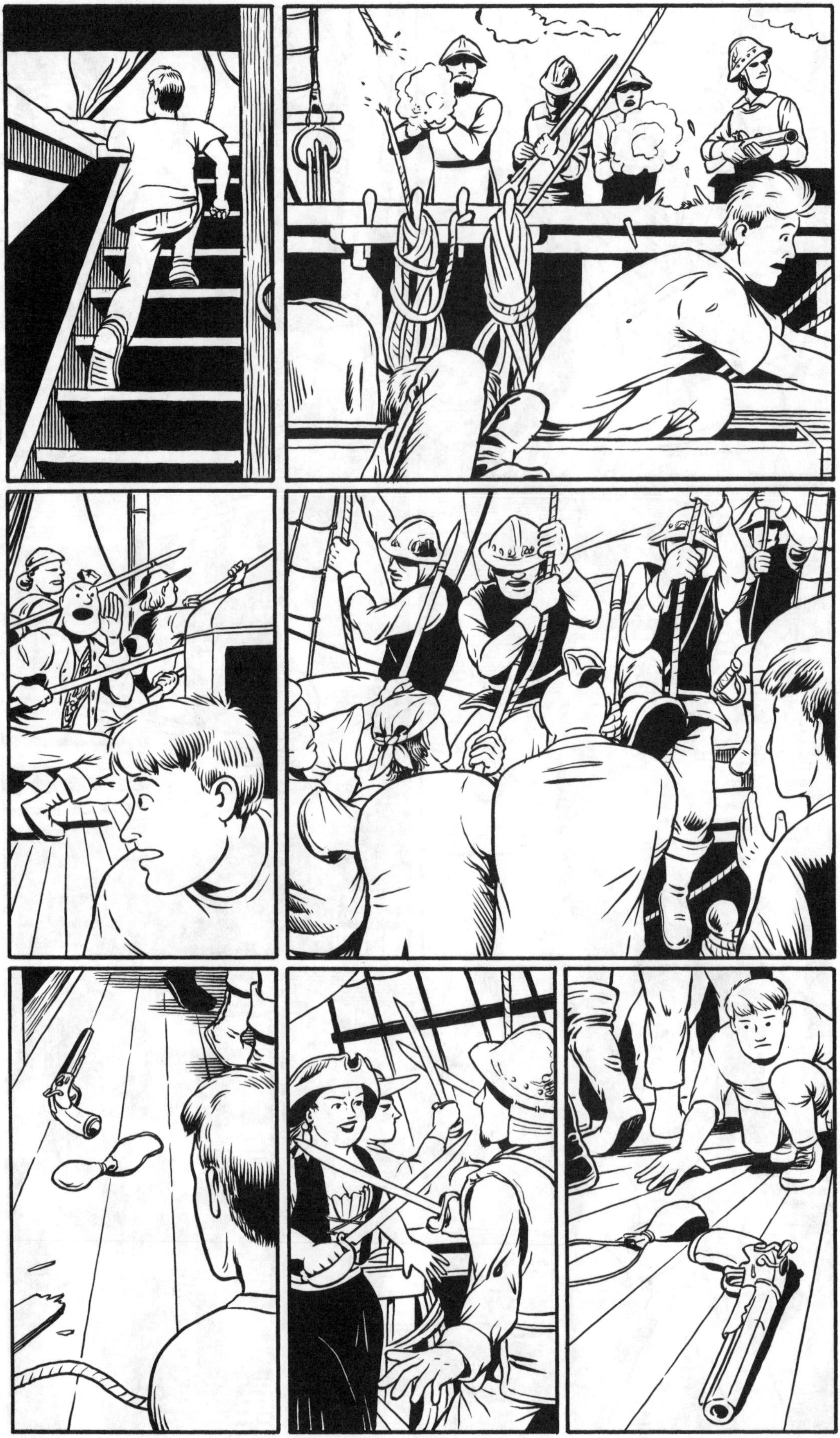

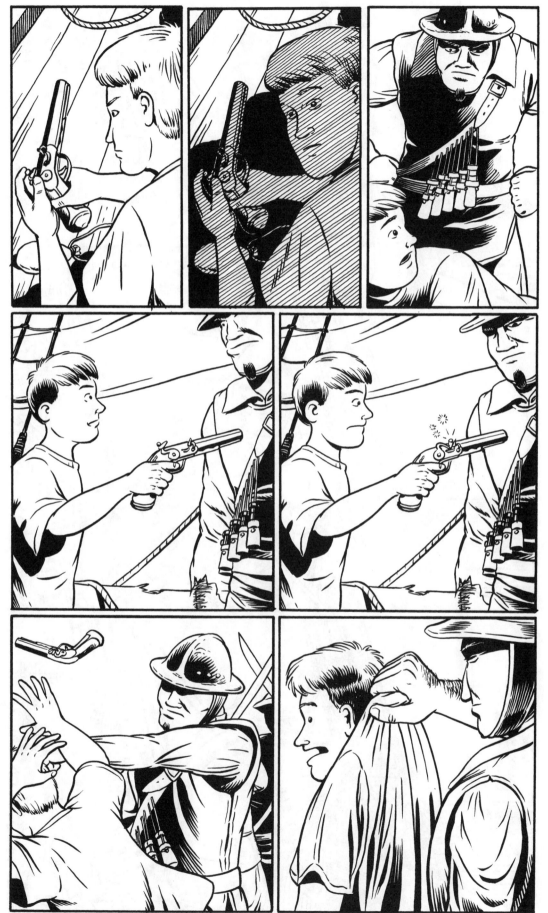

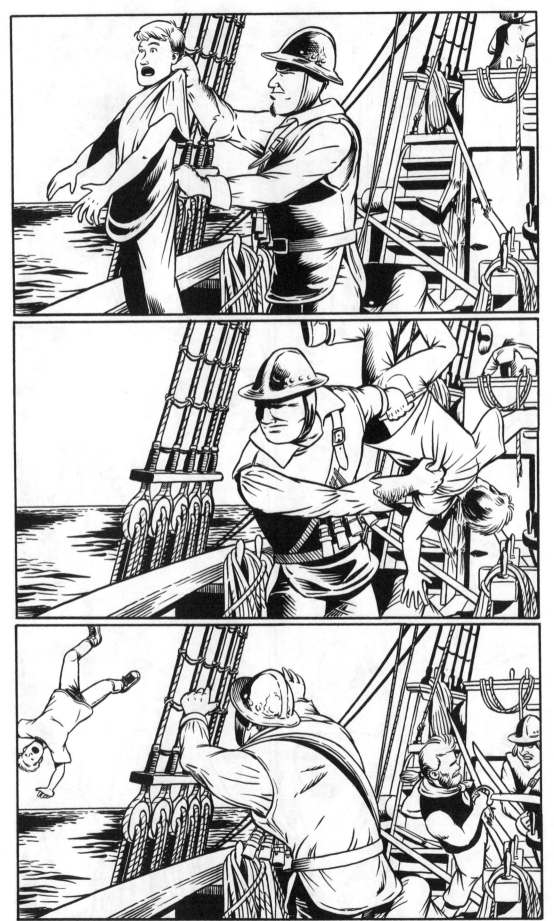

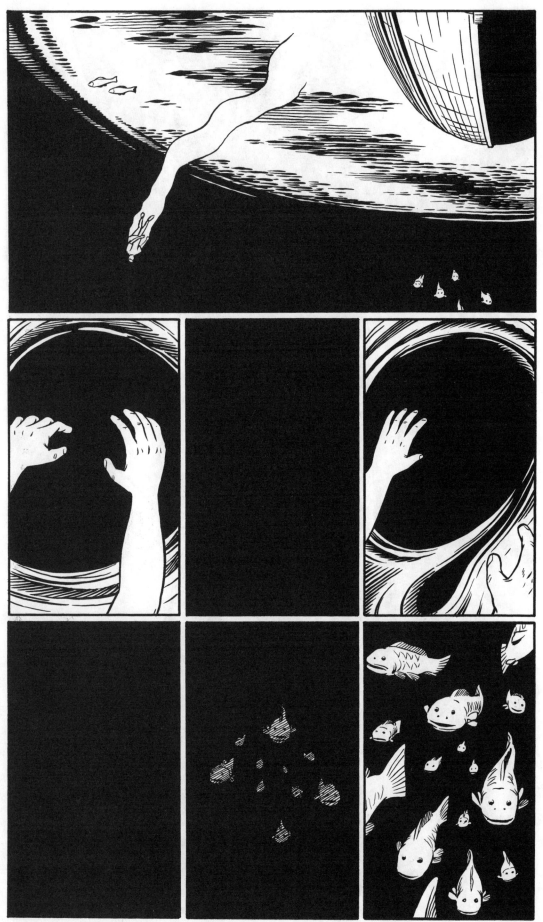

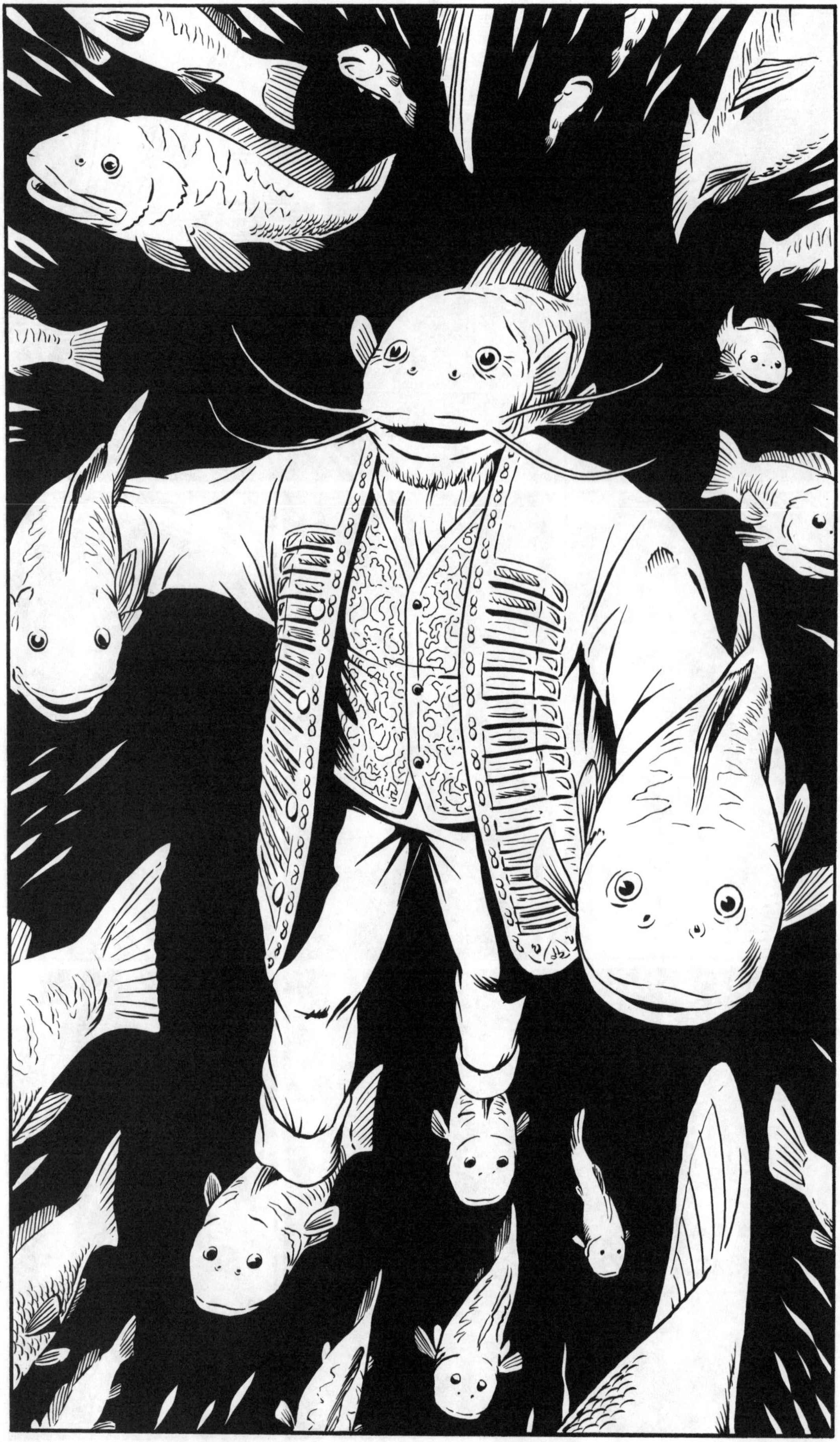

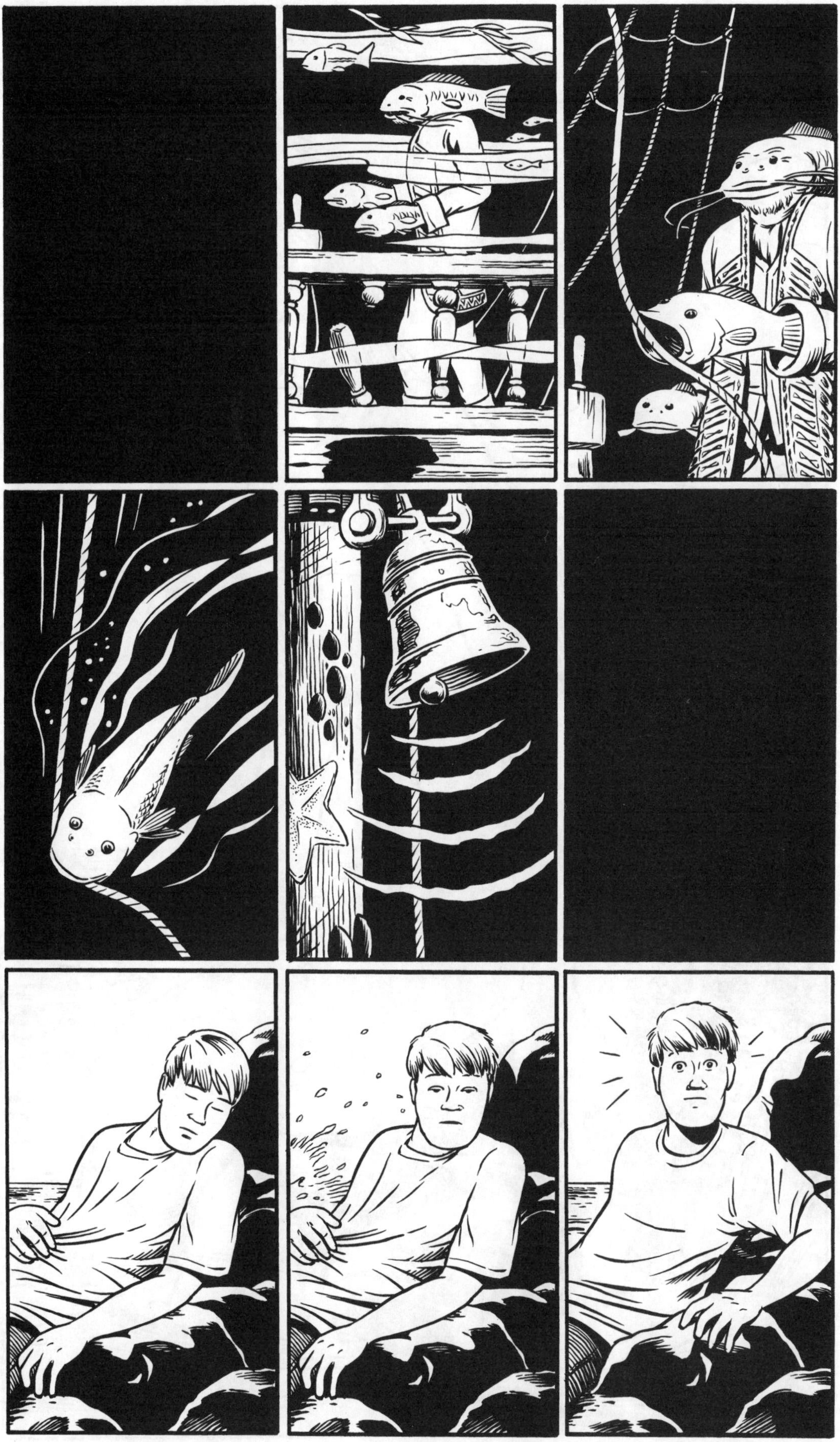

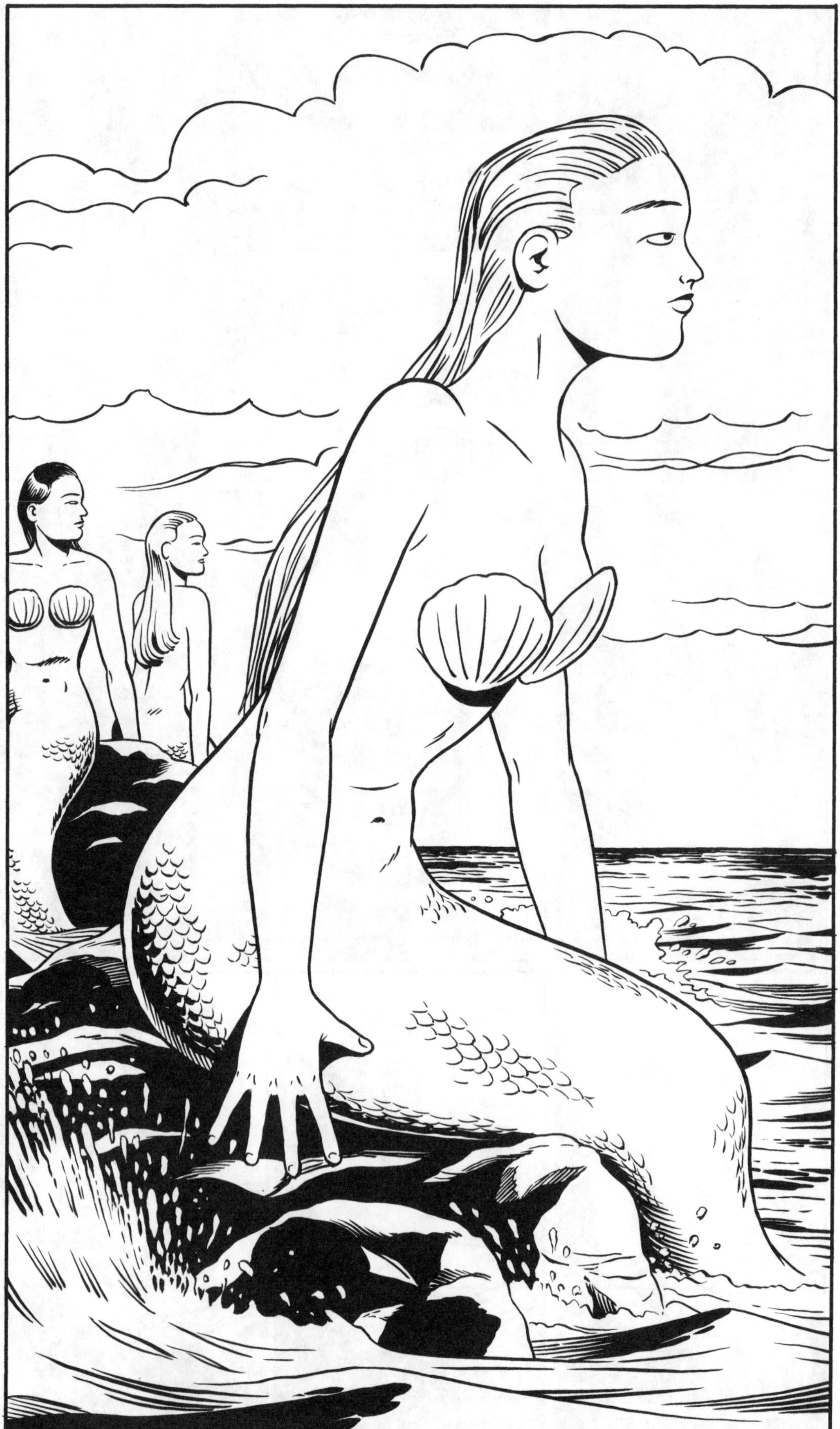

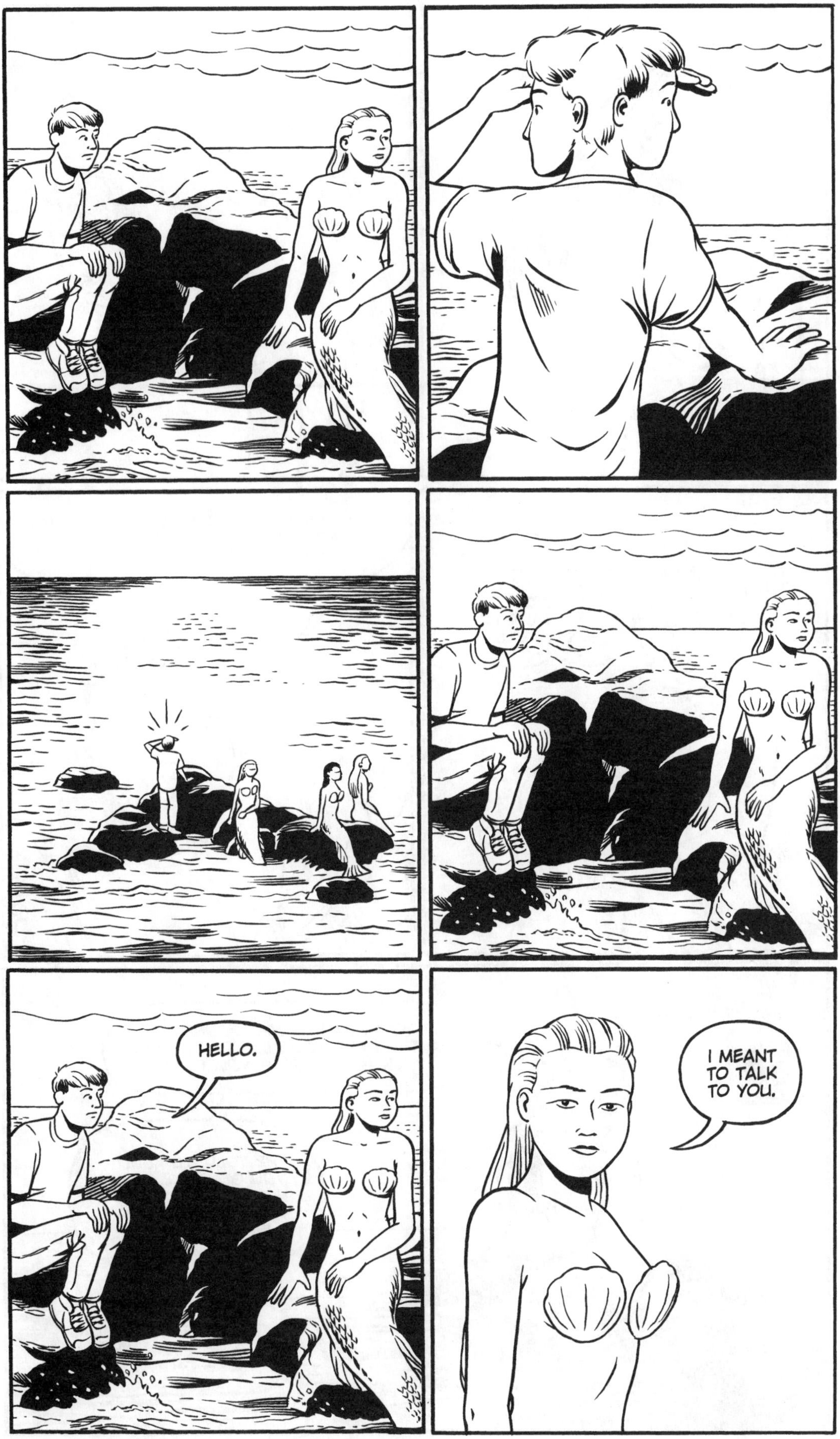
HELLO.
I MEANT TO TALK TO YOU.

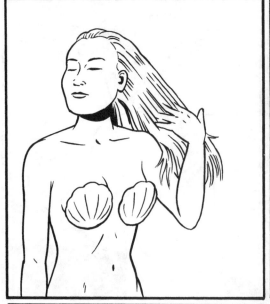

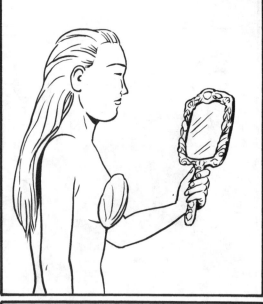

THEN I MEANT *NOT* TO TALK TO YOU.

WE CAN TALK. OR WE DON'T HAVE TO, EITHER. WHATEVER YOU WANT. THANKS FOR SAVING ME.

IT WAS ADARRO WHO FOUND YOU AND PUFFED YOU ALL UP WITH AIR. THEN HE BROUGHT YOU TO ME.

HE TOLD ME ABOUT YOU BEFORE. ABOUT HOW CONNECTED YOU ARE TO THE WAY THE WORLD STREAMS.

THAT'S VERY UNUSUAL FOR A MAN WHO WALKS ON THE LAND.

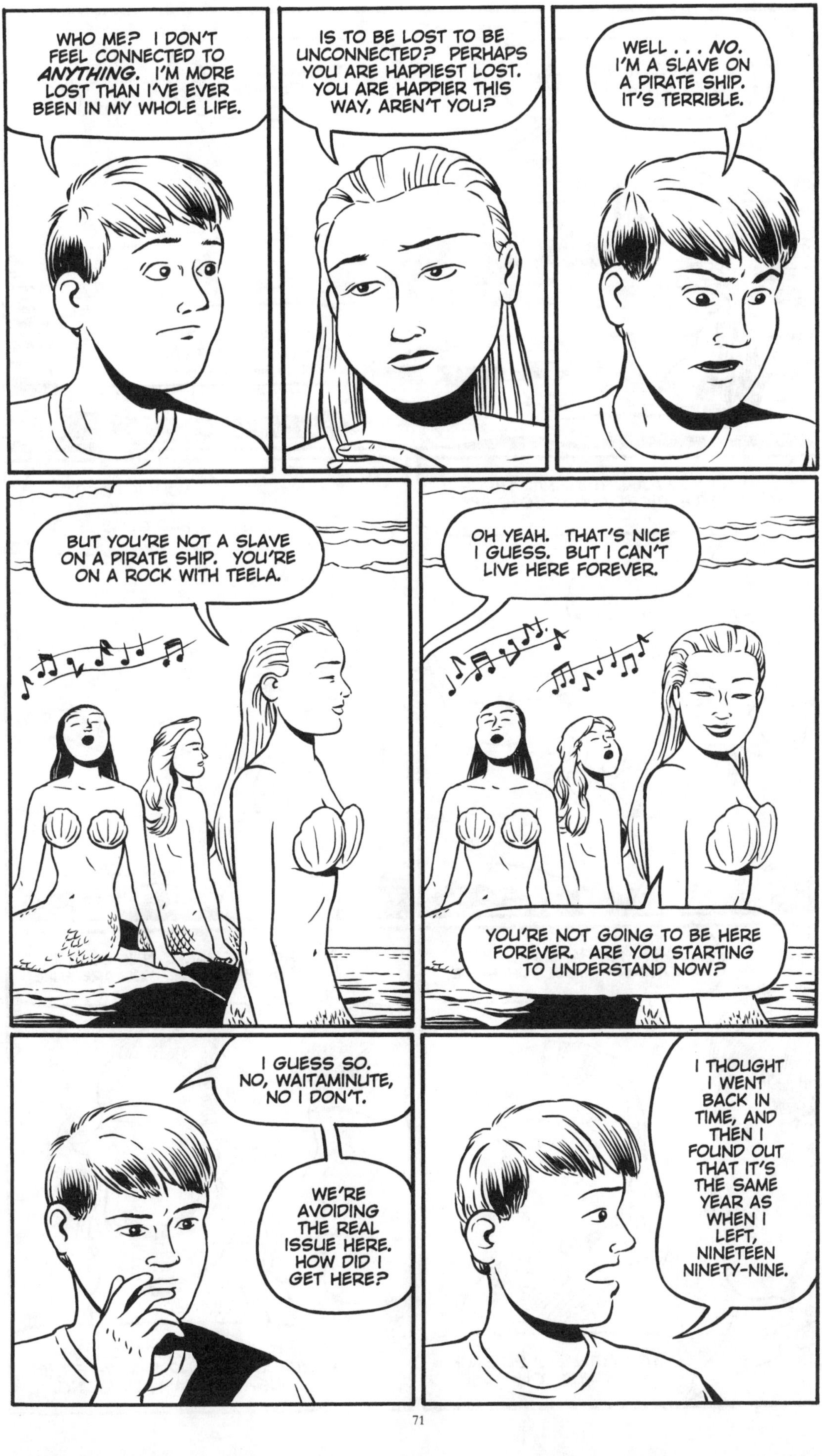
WHO ME? I DON'T FEEL CONNECTED TO *ANYTHING*. I'M MORE LOST THAN I'VE EVER BEEN IN MY WHOLE LIFE.
IS TO BE LOST TO BE UNCONNECTED? PERHAPS YOU ARE HAPPIEST LOST. YOU ARE HAPPIER THIS WAY, AREN'T YOU?
WELL . . . *NO*. I'M A SLAVE ON A PIRATE SHIP. IT'S TERRIBLE.
BUT YOU'RE NOT A SLAVE ON A PIRATE SHIP. YOU'RE ON A ROCK WITH TEELA.
OH YEAH. THAT'S NICE I GUESS. BUT I CAN'T LIVE HERE FOREVER.
YOU'RE NOT GOING TO BE HERE FOREVER. ARE YOU STARTING TO UNDERSTAND NOW?
I GUESS SO. NO, WAITAMINUTE, NO I DON'T.
WE'RE AVOIDING THE REAL ISSUE HERE. HOW DID I GET HERE?
I THOUGHT I WENT BACK IN TIME, AND THEN I FOUND OUT THAT IT'S THE SAME YEAR AS WHEN I LEFT, NINETEEN NINETY-NINE.

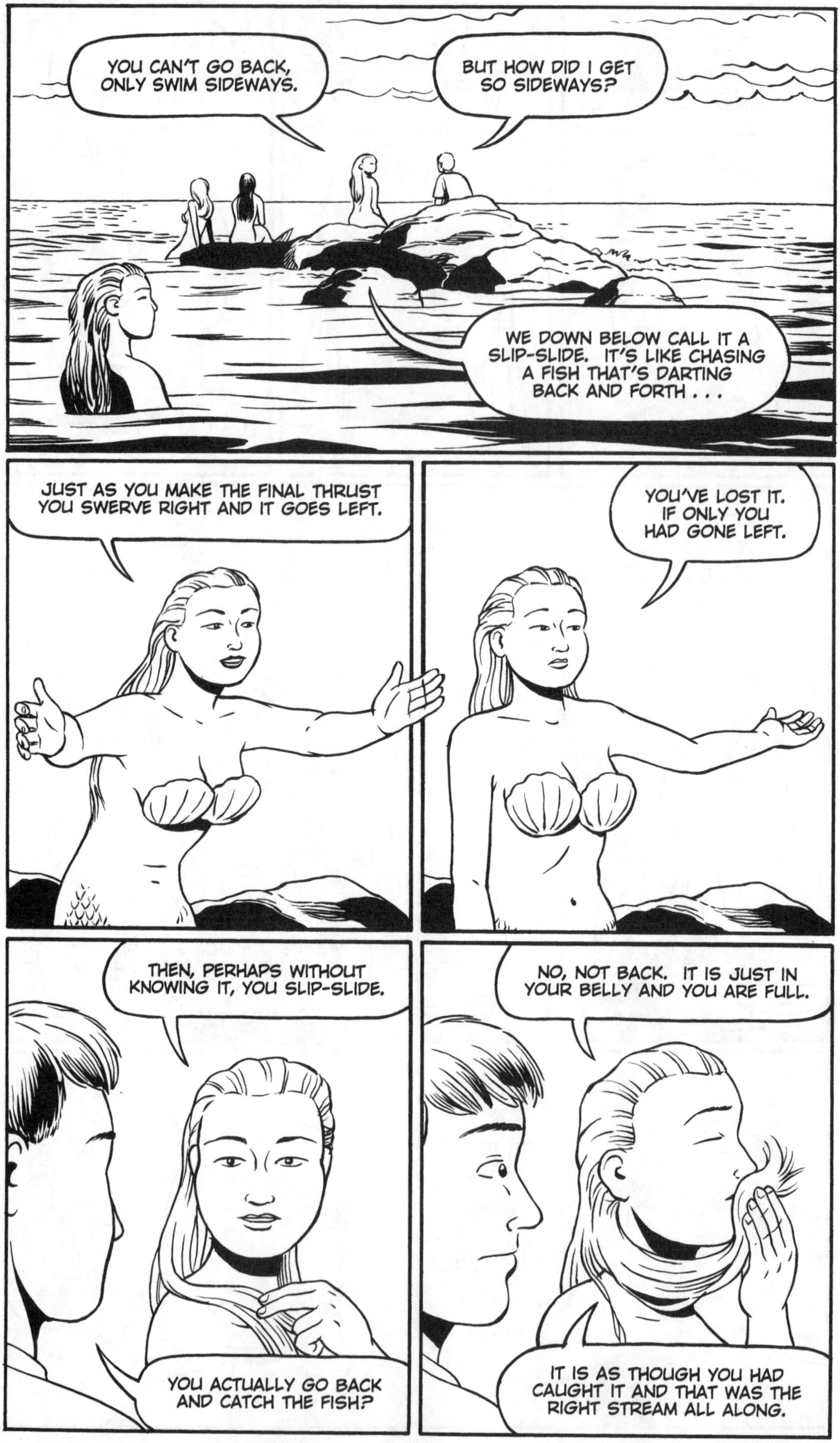
YOU CAN'T GO BACK, ONLY SWIM SIDEWAYS.
BUT HOW DID I GET SO SIDEWAYS?
WE DOWN BELOW CALL IT A SLIP-SLIDE. IT'S LIKE CHASING A FISH THAT'S DARTING BACK AND FORTH . . .
JUST AS YOU MAKE THE FINAL THRUST YOU SWERVE RIGHT AND IT GOES LEFT.
YOU'VE LOST IT. IF ONLY YOU HAD GONE LEFT.
THEN, PERHAPS WITHOUT KNOWING IT, YOU SLIP-SLIDE.
YOU ACTUALLY GO BACK AND CATCH THE FISH?
NO, NOT BACK. IT IS JUST IN YOUR BELLY AND YOU ARE FULL.
IT IS AS THOUGH YOU HAD CAUGHT IT AND THAT WAS THE RIGHT STREAM ALL ALONG.

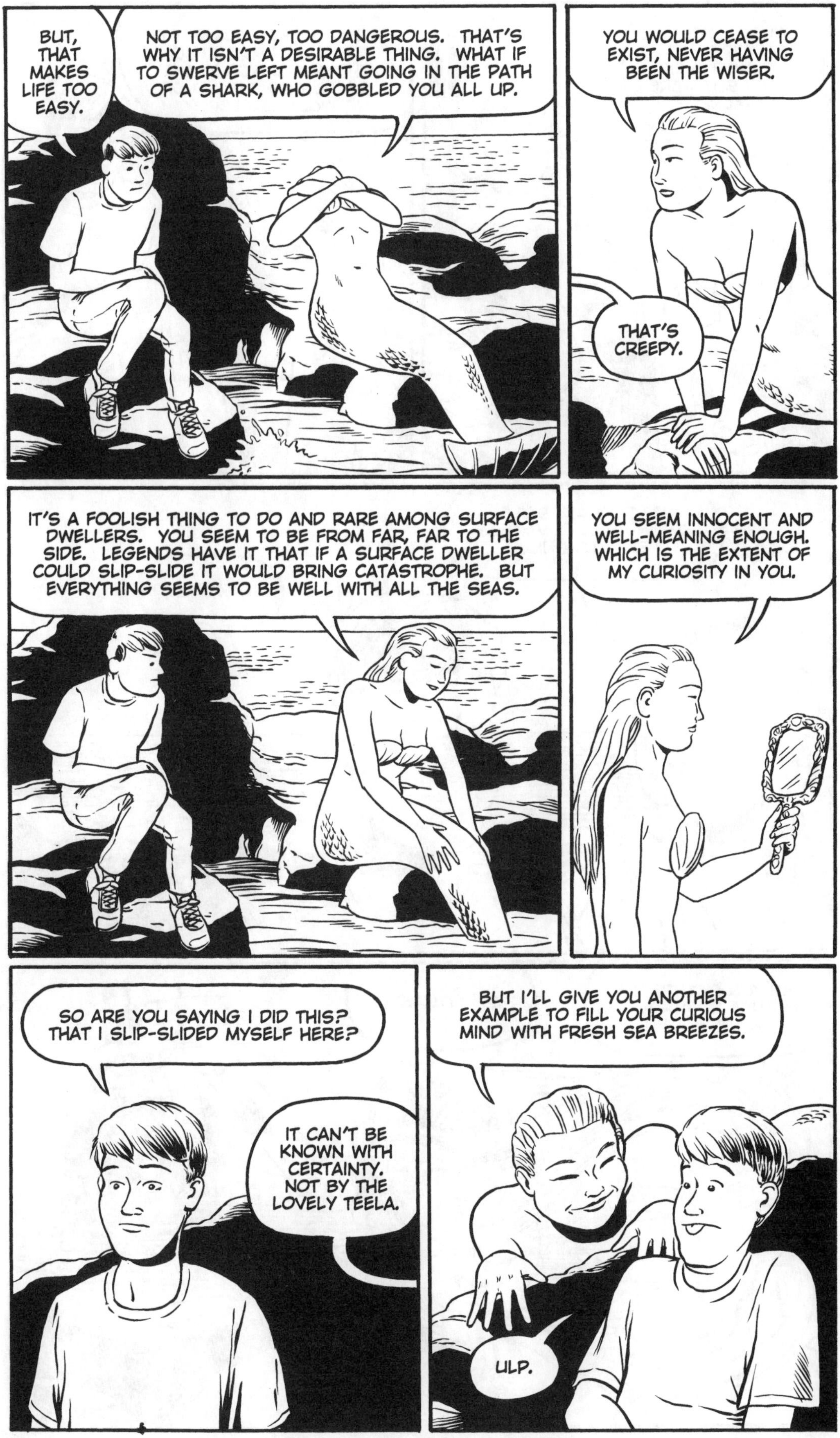
BUT, THAT MAKES LIFE TOO EASY.
NOT TOO EASY, TOO DANGEROUS. THAT'S WHY IT ISN'T A DESIRABLE THING. WHAT IF TO SWERVE LEFT MEANT GOING IN THE PATH OF A SHARK, WHO GOBBLED YOU ALL UP.
YOU WOULD CEASE TO EXIST, NEVER HAVING BEEN THE WISER.
THAT'S CREEPY.
IT'S A FOOLISH THING TO DO AND RARE AMONG SURFACE DWELLERS. YOU SEEM TO BE FROM FAR, FAR TO THE SIDE. LEGENDS HAVE IT THAT IF A SURFACE DWELLER COULD SLIP-SLIDE IT WOULD BRING CATASTROPHE. BUT EVERYTHING SEEMS TO BE WELL WITH ALL THE SEAS.
YOU SEEM INNOCENT AND WELL-MEANING ENOUGH. WHICH IS THE EXTENT OF MY CURIOSITY IN YOU.
SO ARE YOU SAYING I DID THIS? THAT I SLIP-SLIDED MYSELF HERE?
IT CAN'T BE KNOWN WITH CERTAINTY. NOT BY THE LOVELY TEELA.
BUT I'LL GIVE YOU ANOTHER EXAMPLE TO FILL YOUR CURIOUS MIND WITH FRESH SEA BREEZES.
ULP.

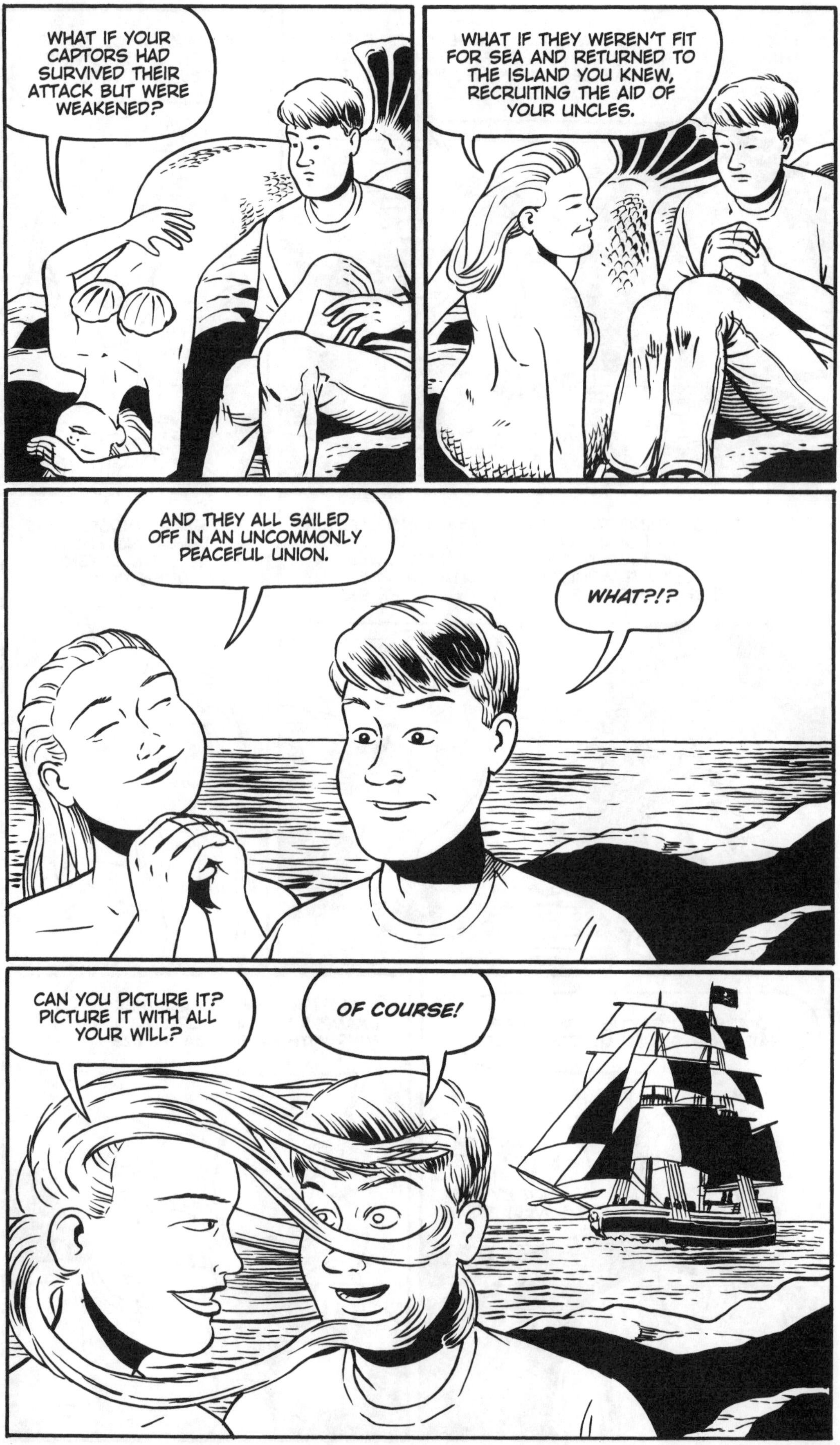
WHAT IF YOUR CAPTORS HAD SURVIVED THEIR ATTACK BUT WERE WEAKENED?
WHAT IF THEY WEREN'T FIT FOR SEA AND RETURNED TO THE ISLAND YOU KNEW, RECRUITING THE AID OF YOUR UNCLES.
AND THEY ALL SAILED OFF IN AN UNCOMMONLY PEACEFUL UNION.
WHAT?!?
CAN YOU PICTURE IT? PICTURE IT WITH ALL YOUR WILL?
OF COURSE!

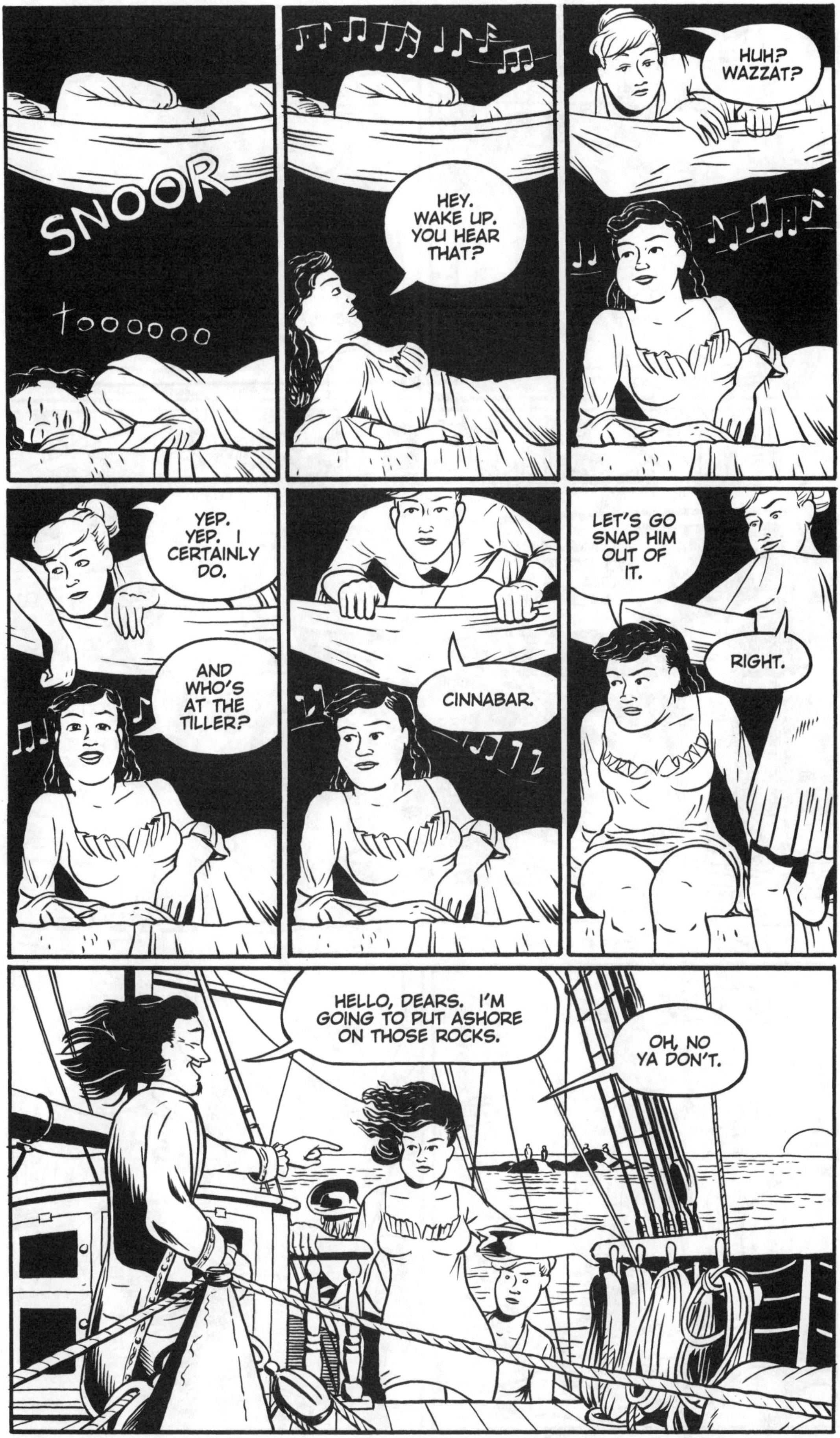
SNOOR
tooooooo
HEY. WAKE UP. YOU HEAR THAT?
HUH? WAZZAT?
YEP. YEP. I CERTAINLY DO.
AND WHO'S AT THE TILLER?
CINNABAR.
LET'S GO SNAP HIM OUT OF IT.
RIGHT.
HELLO, DEARS. I'M GOING TO PUT ASHORE ON THOSE ROCKS.
OH, NO YA DON'T.

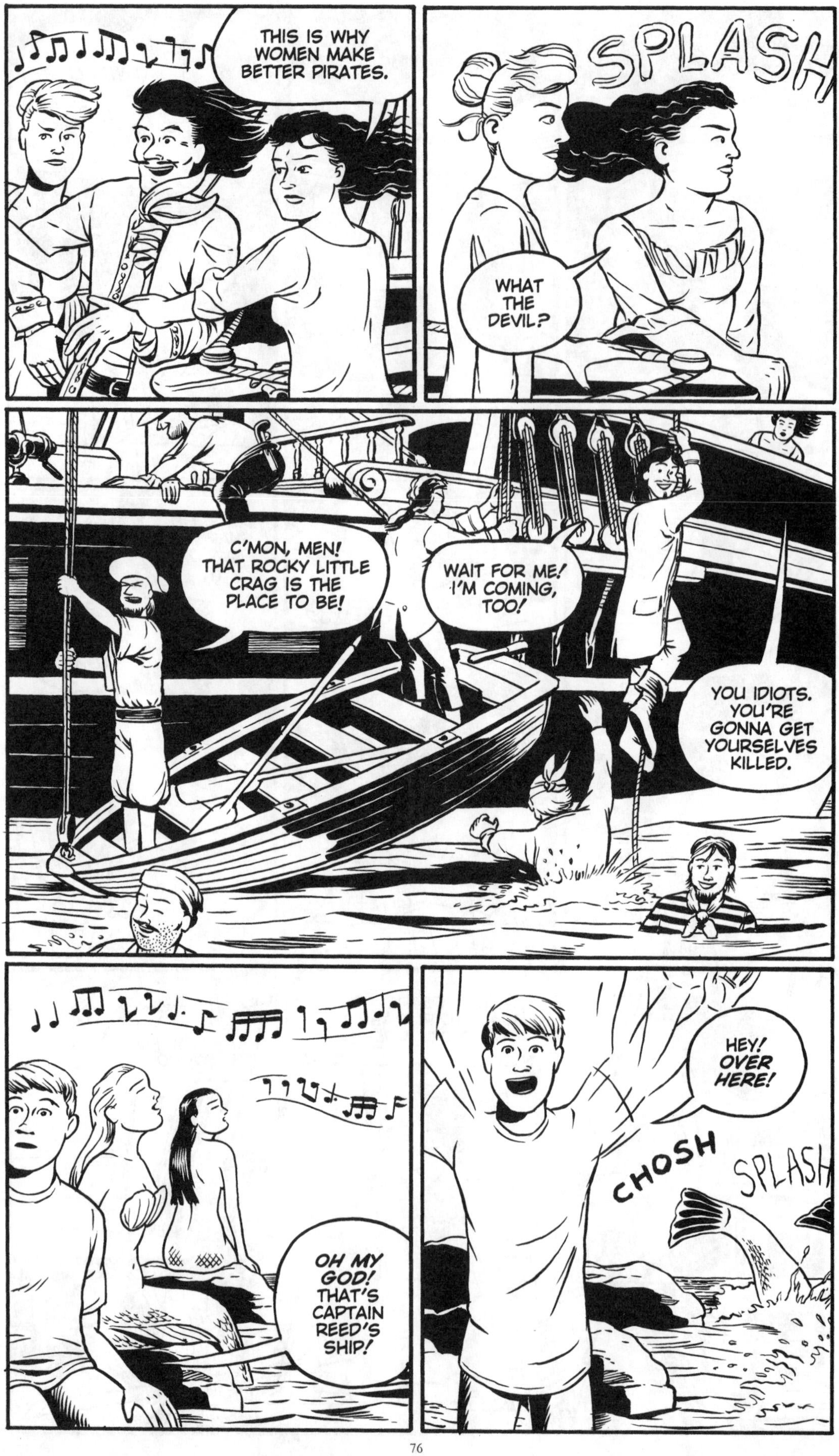
THIS IS WHY WOMEN MAKE BETTER PIRATES.
SPLASH
WHAT THE DEVIL?
C'MON, MEN! THAT ROCKY LITTLE CRAG IS THE PLACE TO BE!
WAIT FOR ME! I'M COMING, TOO!
YOU IDIOTS. YOU'RE GONNA GET YOURSELVES KILLED.
OH MY GOD! THAT'S CAPTAIN REED'S SHIP!
HEY! OVER HERE!
CHOSH
SPLASH

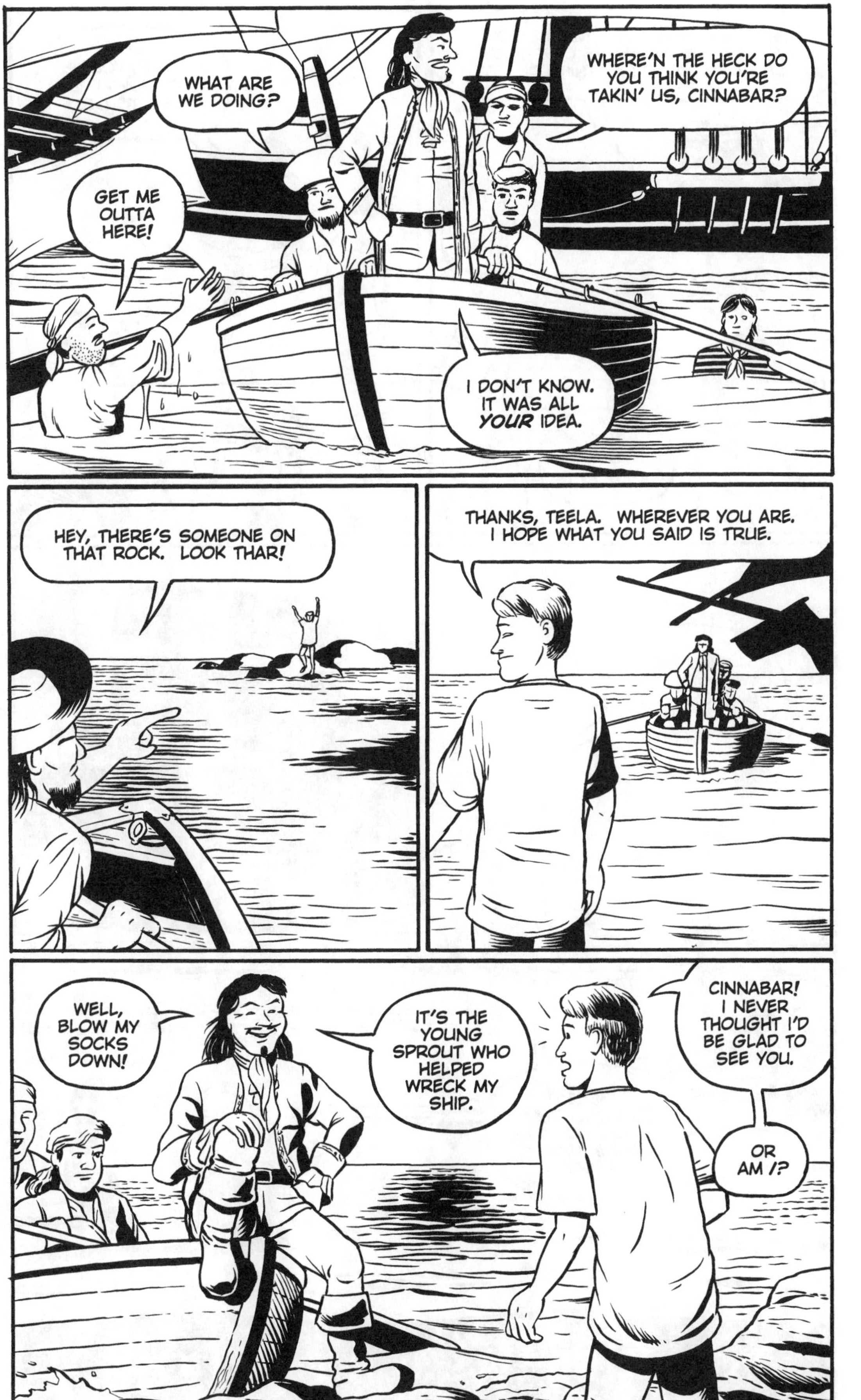
WHAT ARE WE DOING?
WHERE'N THE HECK DO YOU THINK YOU'RE TAKIN' US, CINNABAR?
GET ME OUTTA HERE!
I DON'T KNOW. IT WAS ALL *YOUR* IDEA.
HEY, THERE'S SOMEONE ON THAT ROCK. LOOK THAR!
THANKS, TEELA. WHEREVER YOU ARE. I HOPE WHAT YOU SAID IS TRUE.
WELL, BLOW MY SOCKS DOWN!
IT'S THE YOUNG SPROUT WHO HELPED WRECK MY SHIP.
CINNABAR! I NEVER THOUGHT I'D BE GLAD TO SEE YOU.
OR AM *I*?

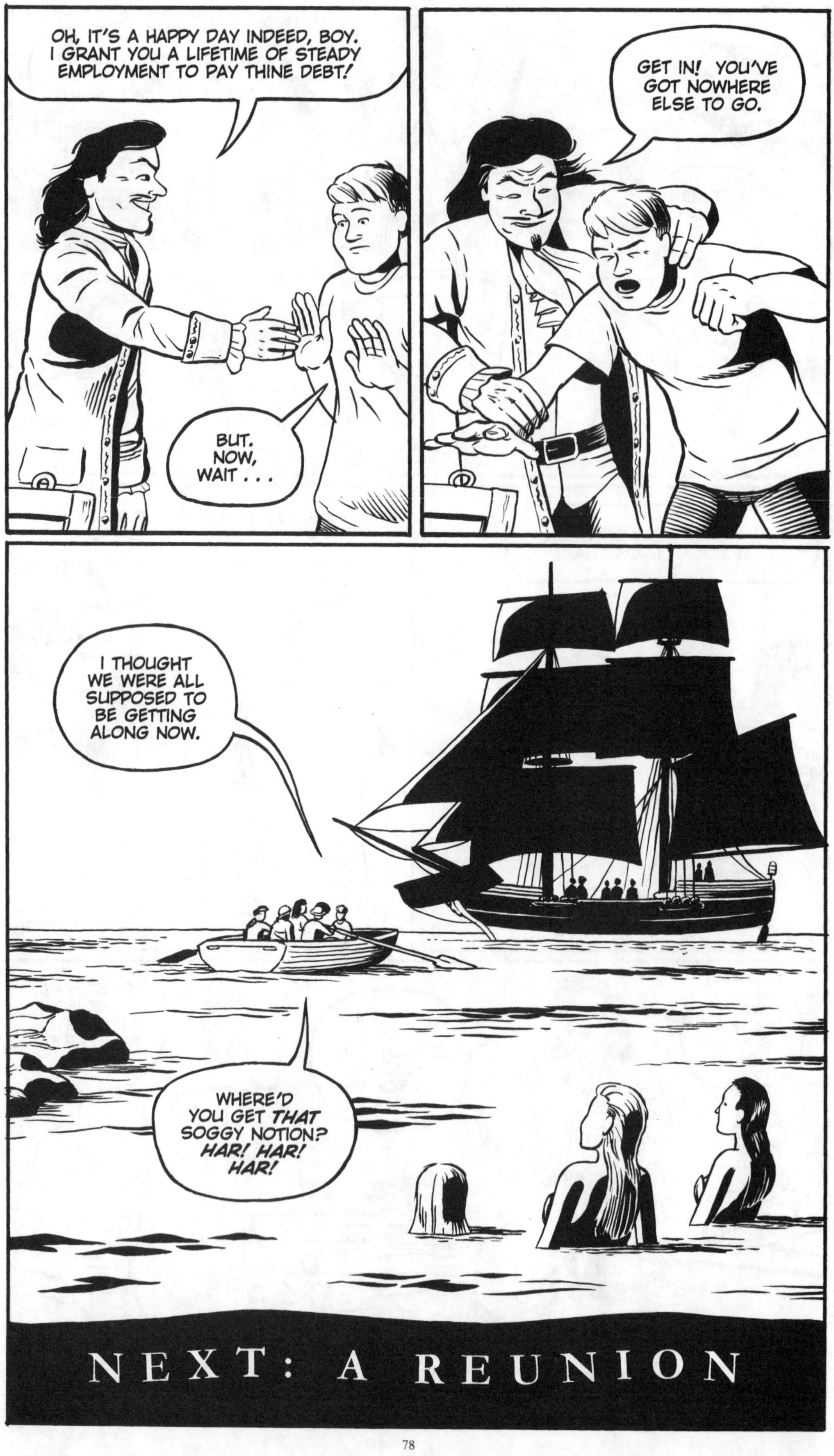
OH, IT'S A HAPPY DAY INDEED, BOY. I GRANT YOU A LIFETIME OF STEADY EMPLOYMENT TO PAY THINE DEBT!
BUT. NOW, WAIT . . .
GET IN! YOU'VE GOT NOWHERE ELSE TO GO.
I THOUGHT WE WERE ALL SUPPOSED TO BE GETTING ALONG NOW.
WHERE'D YOU GET *THAT* SOGGY NOTION? ***HAR! HAR! HAR!***
NEXT: A REUNION

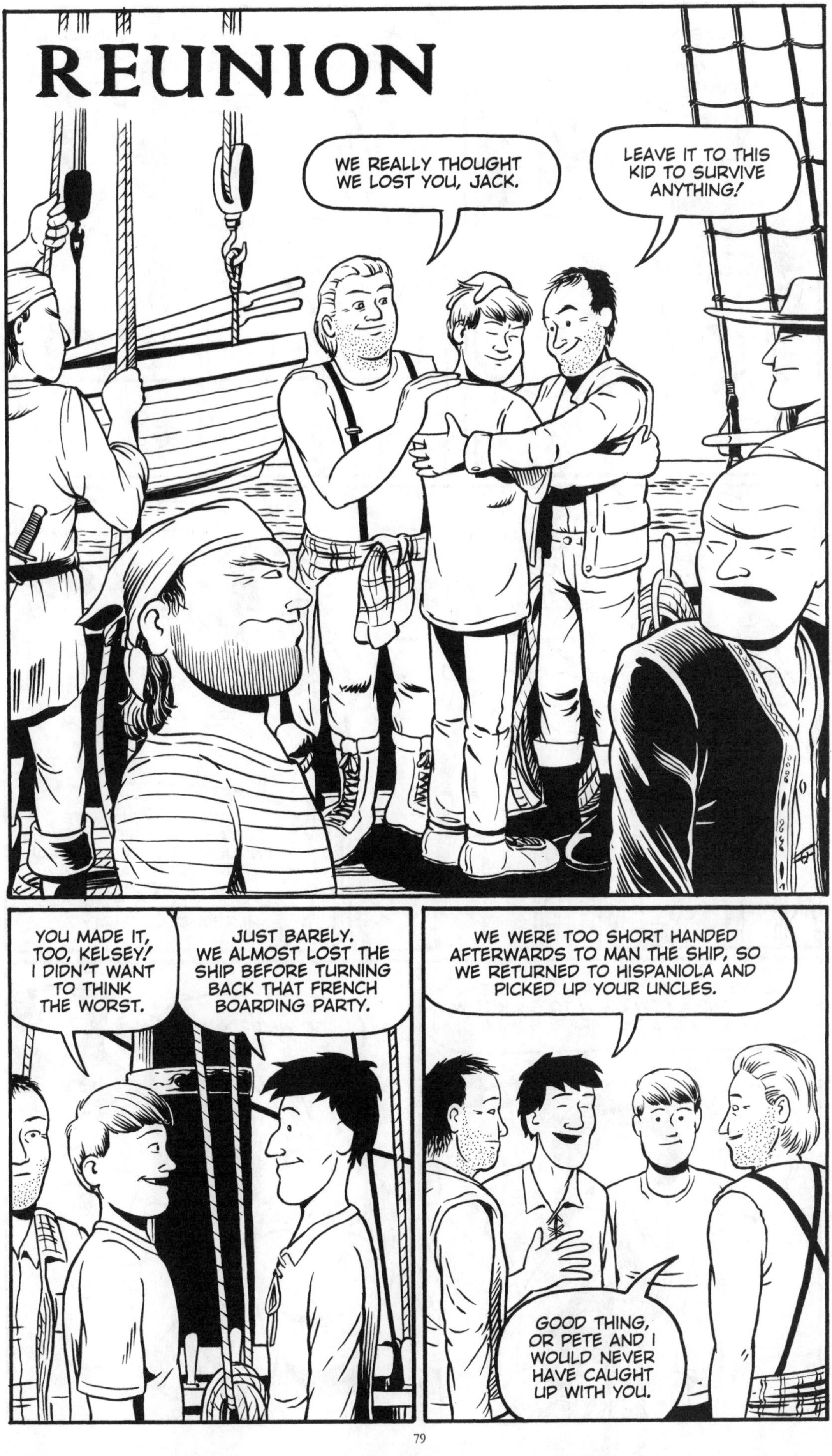
REUNION
WE REALLY THOUGHT WE LOST YOU, JACK.
LEAVE IT TO THIS KID TO SURVIVE ANYTHING!
YOU MADE IT, TOO, KELSEY! I DIDN'T WANT TO THINK THE WORST.
JUST BARELY. WE ALMOST LOST THE SHIP BEFORE TURNING BACK THAT FRENCH BOARDING PARTY.
WE WERE TOO SHORT HANDED AFTERWARDS TO MAN THE SHIP, SO WE RETURNED TO HISPANIOLA AND PICKED UP YOUR UNCLES.
GOOD THING, OR PETE AND I WOULD NEVER HAVE CAUGHT UP WITH YOU.

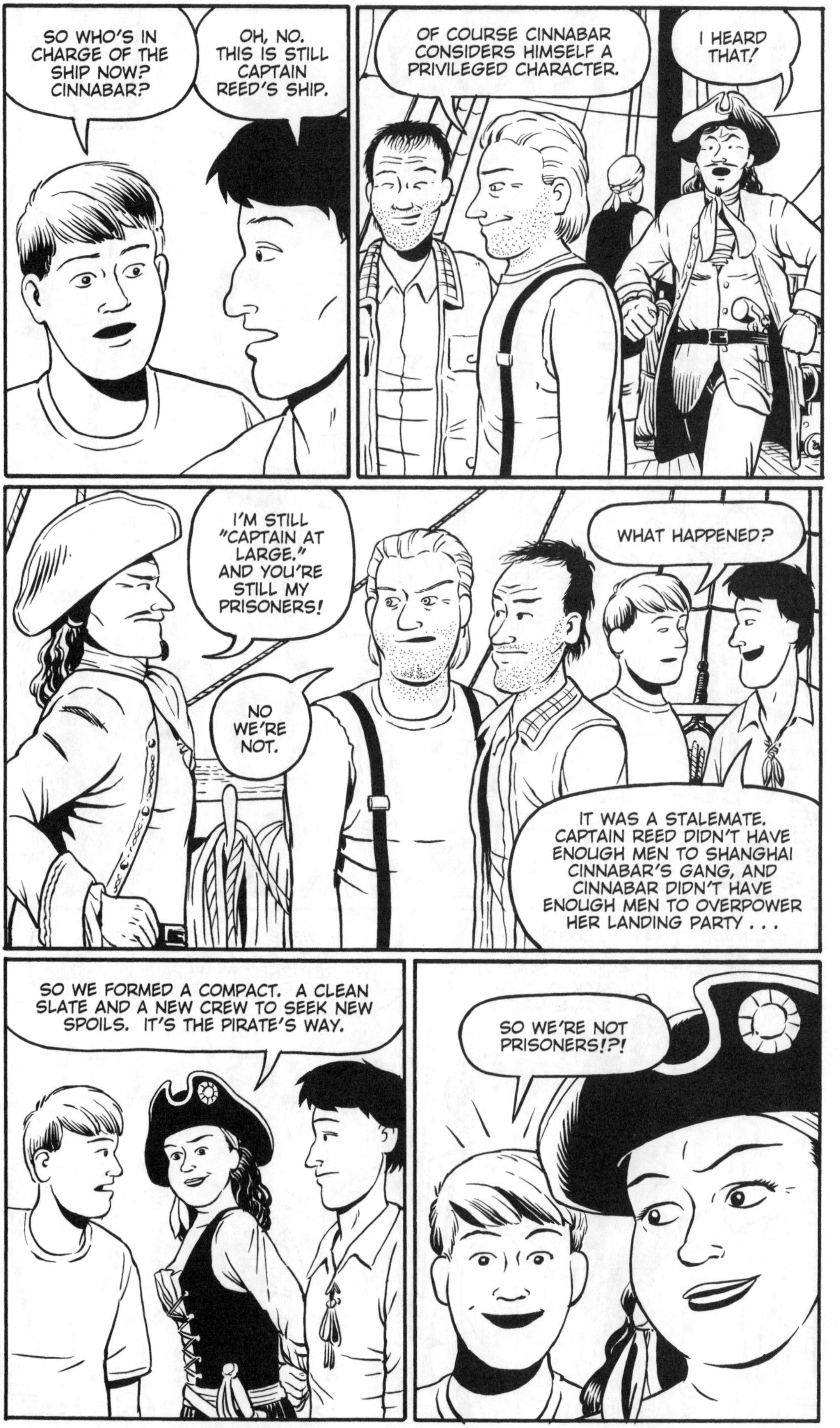
SO WHO'S IN CHARGE OF THE SHIP NOW? CINNABAR?
OH, NO. THIS IS STILL CAPTAIN REED'S SHIP.
OF COURSE CINNABAR CONSIDERS HIMSELF A PRIVILEGED CHARACTER.
I HEARD THAT!
I'M STILL "CAPTAIN AT LARGE." AND YOU'RE STILL MY PRISONERS!
NO WE'RE NOT.
WHAT HAPPENED?
IT WAS A STALEMATE. CAPTAIN REED DIDN'T HAVE ENOUGH MEN TO SHANGHAI CINNABAR'S GANG, AND CINNABAR DIDN'T HAVE ENOUGH MEN TO OVERPOWER HER LANDING PARTY . . .
SO WE FORMED A COMPACT. A CLEAN SLATE AND A NEW CREW TO SEEK NEW SPOILS. IT'S THE PIRATE'S WAY.
SO WE'RE NOT PRISONERS!?!

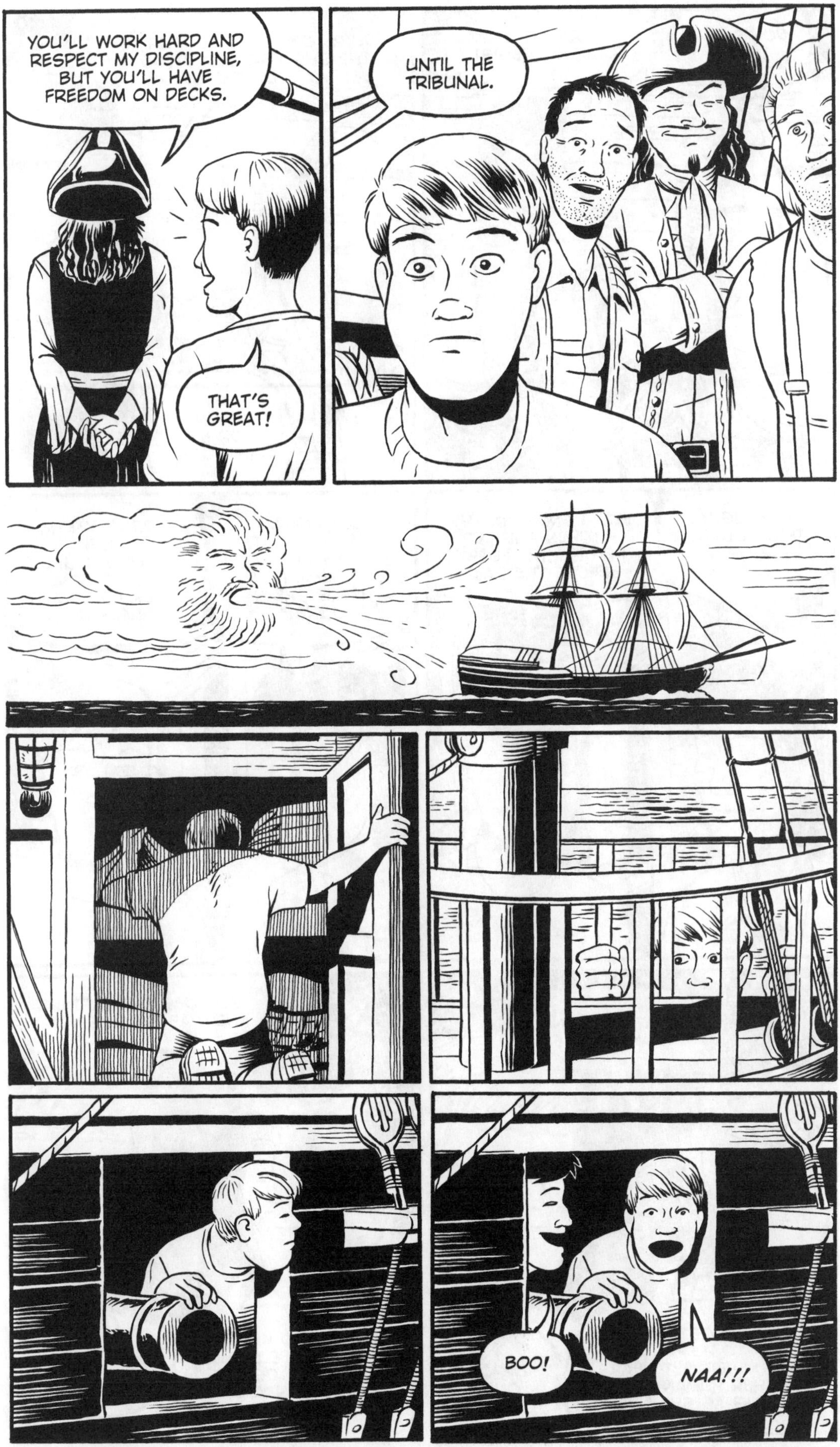
YOU'LL WORK HARD AND RESPECT MY DISCIPLINE, BUT YOU'LL HAVE FREEDOM ON DECKS.
THAT'S GREAT!
UNTIL THE TRIBUNAL.
BOO!
NAA!!!

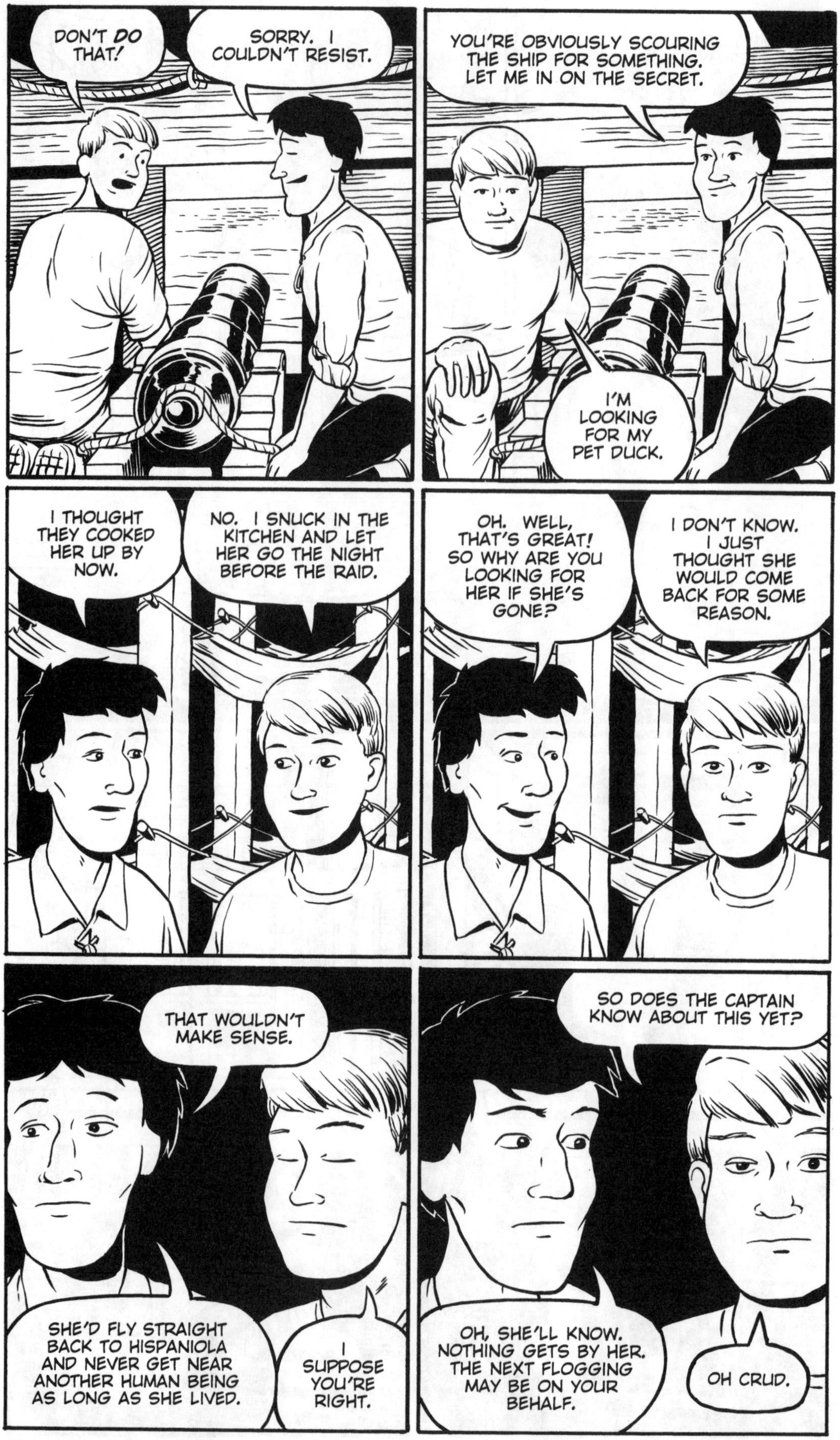
DON'T DO THAT!
SORRY. I COULDN'T RESIST.
YOU'RE OBVIOUSLY SCOURING THE SHIP FOR SOMETHING. LET ME IN ON THE SECRET.
I'M LOOKING FOR MY PET DUCK.
I THOUGHT THEY COOKED HER UP BY NOW.
NO. I SNUCK IN THE KITCHEN AND LET HER GO THE NIGHT BEFORE THE RAID.
OH. WELL, THAT'S GREAT! SO WHY ARE YOU LOOKING FOR HER IF SHE'S GONE?
I DON'T KNOW. I JUST THOUGHT SHE WOULD COME BACK FOR SOME REASON.
THAT WOULDN'T MAKE SENSE.
SHE'D FLY STRAIGHT BACK TO HISPANIOLA AND NEVER GET NEAR ANOTHER HUMAN BEING AS LONG AS SHE LIVED.
I SUPPOSE YOU'RE RIGHT.
SO DOES THE CAPTAIN KNOW ABOUT THIS YET?
OH, SHE'LL KNOW. NOTHING GETS BY HER. THE NEXT FLOGGING MAY BE ON YOUR BEHALF.
OH CRUD.

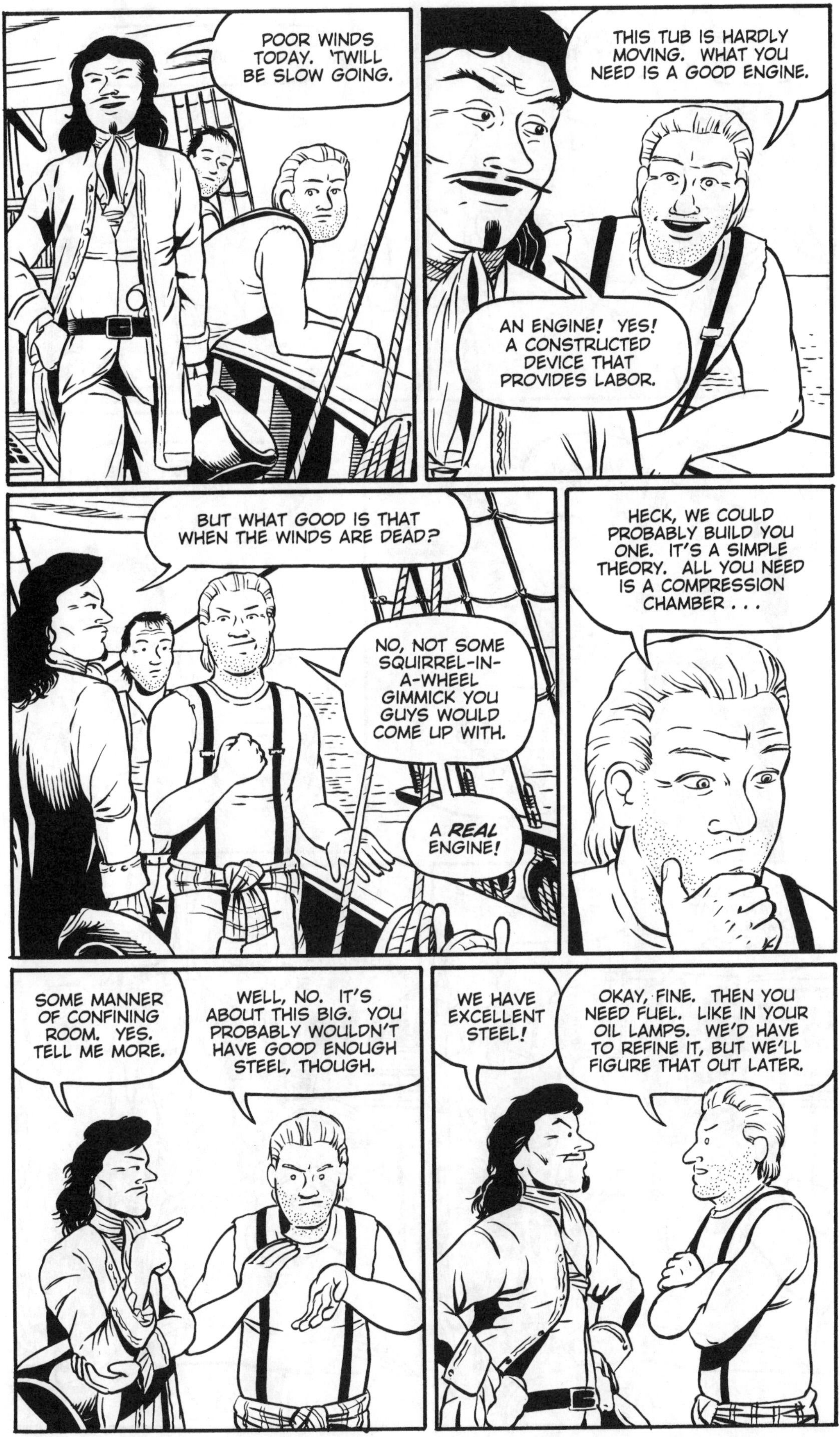
POOR WINDS TODAY. 'TWILL BE SLOW GOING.
THIS TUB IS HARDLY MOVING. WHAT YOU NEED IS A GOOD ENGINE.
AN ENGINE! YES! A CONSTRUCTED DEVICE THAT PROVIDES LABOR.
BUT WHAT GOOD IS THAT WHEN THE WINDS ARE DEAD?
NO, NOT SOME SQUIRREL-IN-A-WHEEL GIMMICK YOU GUYS WOULD COME UP WITH.
A *REAL* ENGINE!
HECK, WE COULD PROBABLY BUILD YOU ONE. IT'S A SIMPLE THEORY. ALL YOU NEED IS A COMPRESSION CHAMBER . . .
SOME MANNER OF CONFINING ROOM. YES. TELL ME MORE.
WELL, NO. IT'S ABOUT THIS BIG. YOU PROBABLY WOULDN'T HAVE GOOD ENOUGH STEEL, THOUGH.
WE HAVE EXCELLENT STEEL!
OKAY, FINE. THEN YOU NEED FUEL. LIKE IN YOUR OIL LAMPS. WE'D HAVE TO REFINE IT, BUT WE'LL FIGURE THAT OUT LATER.

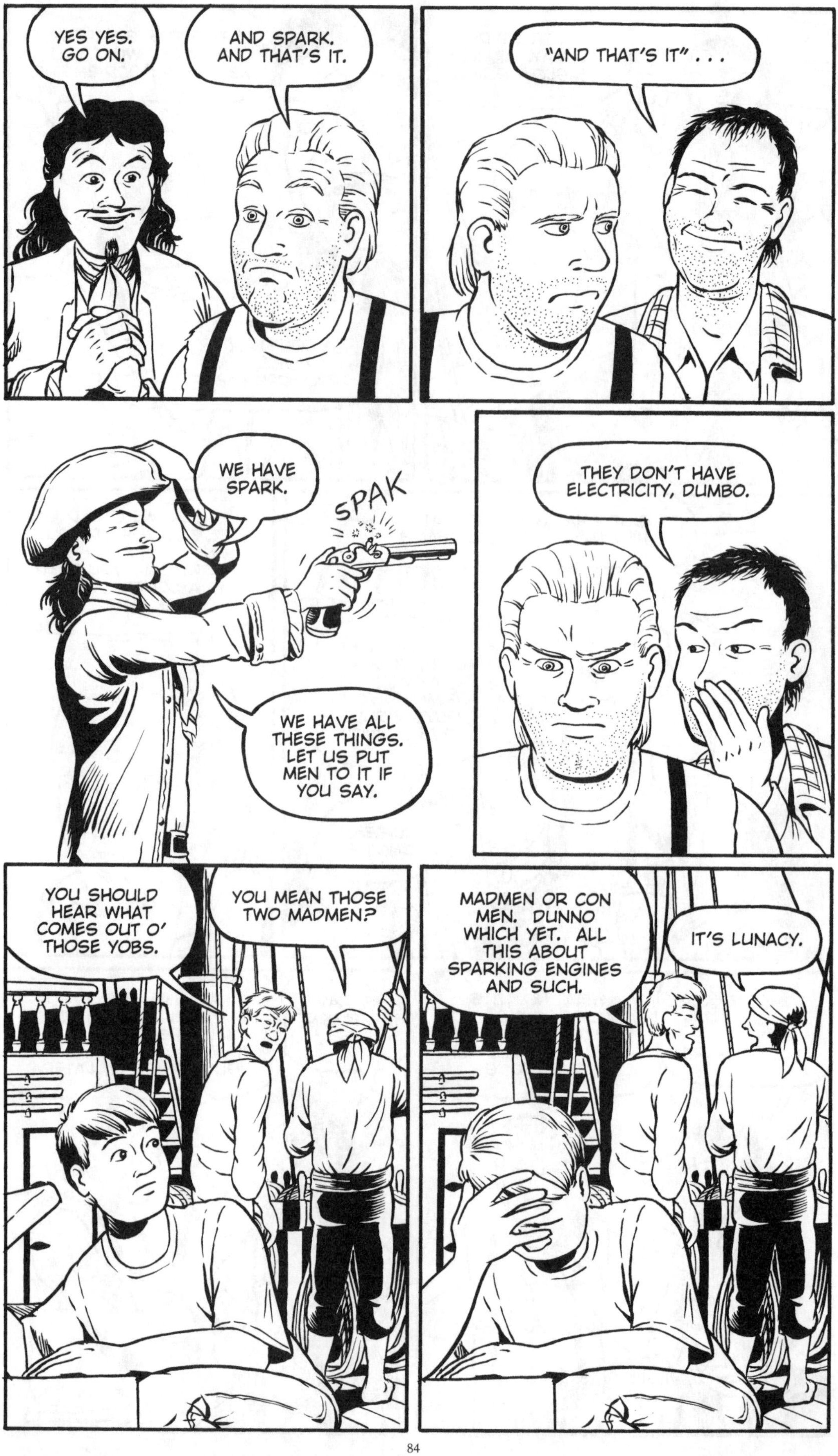
YES YES. GO ON.
AND SPARK. AND THAT'S IT.
"AND THAT'S IT" . . .
WE HAVE SPARK.
SPAK
WE HAVE ALL THESE THINGS. LET US PUT MEN TO IT IF YOU SAY.
THEY DON'T HAVE ELECTRICITY, DUMBO.
YOU SHOULD HEAR WHAT COMES OUT O' THOSE YOBS.
YOU MEAN THOSE TWO MADMEN?
MADMEN OR CON MEN. DUNNO WHICH YET. ALL THIS ABOUT SPARKING ENGINES AND SUCH.
IT'S LUNACY.

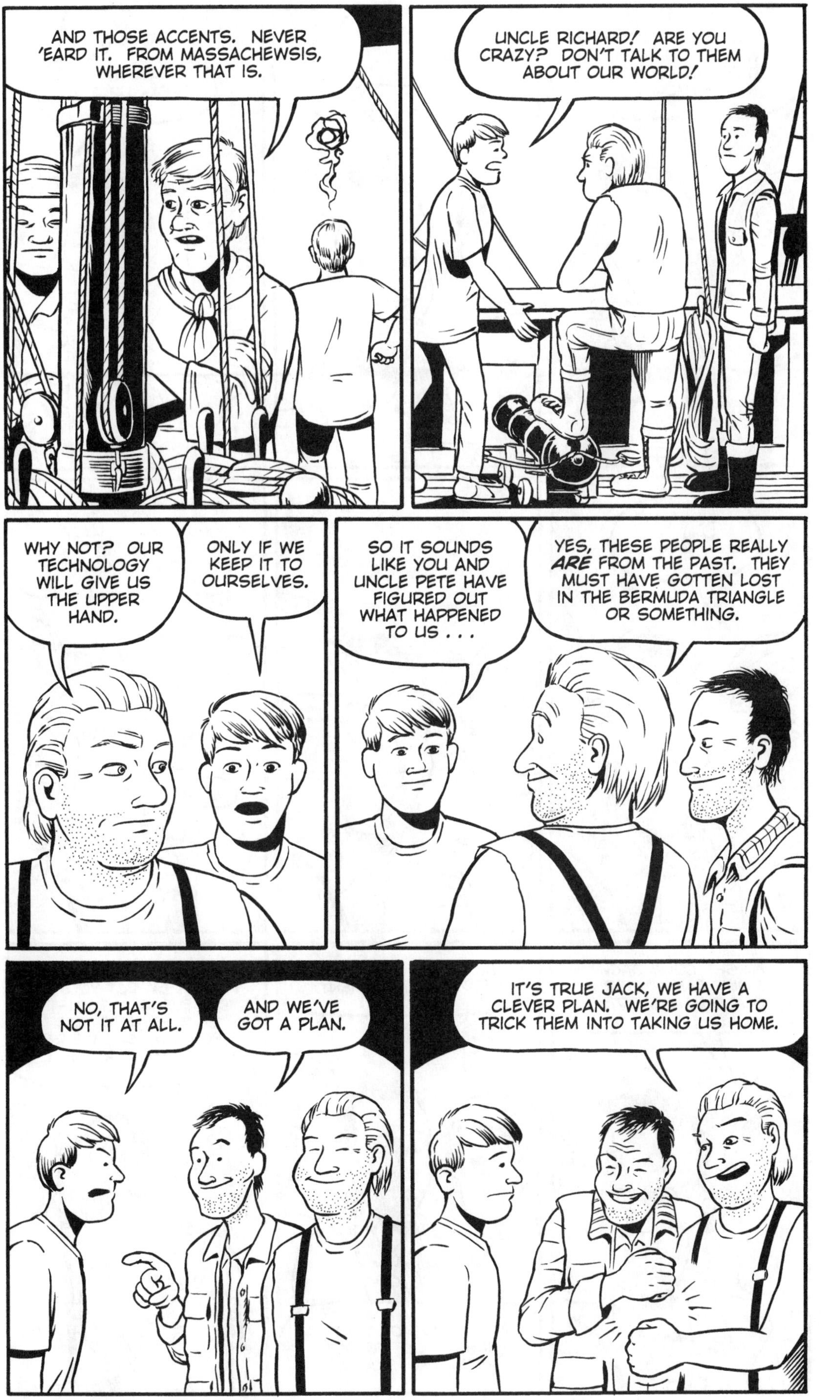
AND THOSE ACCENTS. NEVER 'EARD IT. FROM MASSACHEWSIS, WHEREVER THAT IS.
UNCLE RICHARD! ARE YOU CRAZY? DON'T TALK TO THEM ABOUT OUR WORLD!
WHY NOT? OUR TECHNOLOGY WILL GIVE US THE UPPER HAND.
ONLY IF WE KEEP IT TO OURSELVES.
SO IT SOUNDS LIKE YOU AND UNCLE PETE HAVE FIGURED OUT WHAT HAPPENED TO US . . .
YES, THESE PEOPLE REALLY *ARE* FROM THE PAST. THEY MUST HAVE GOTTEN LOST IN THE BERMUDA TRIANGLE OR SOMETHING.
NO, THAT'S NOT IT AT ALL.
AND WE'VE GOT A PLAN.
IT'S TRUE JACK, WE HAVE A CLEVER PLAN. WE'RE GOING TO TRICK THEM INTO TAKING US HOME.

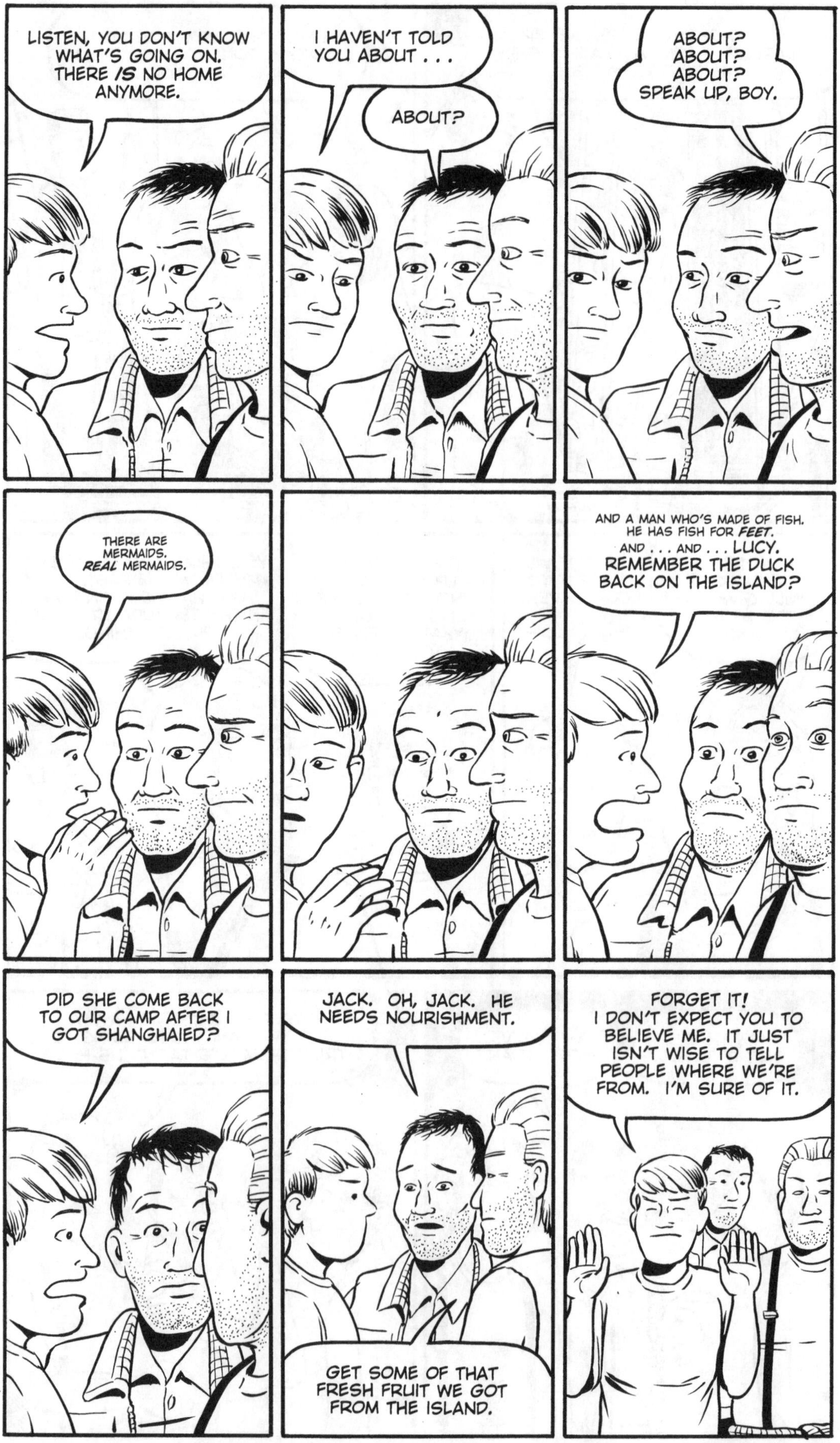
LISTEN, YOU DON'T KNOW WHAT'S GOING ON. THERE *IS* NO HOME ANYMORE.
I HAVEN'T TOLD YOU ABOUT . . .
ABOUT?
ABOUT? ABOUT? ABOUT? SPEAK UP, BOY.
THERE ARE MERMAIDS. *REAL* MERMAIDS.
AND A MAN WHO'S MADE OF FISH. HE HAS FISH FOR *FEET*. AND . . . AND . . . LUCY. REMEMBER THE DUCK BACK ON THE ISLAND?
DID SHE COME BACK TO OUR CAMP AFTER I GOT SHANGHAIED?
JACK. OH, JACK. HE NEEDS NOURISHMENT.
GET SOME OF THAT FRESH FRUIT WE GOT FROM THE ISLAND.
FORGET IT! I DON'T EXPECT YOU TO BELIEVE ME. IT JUST ISN'T WISE TO TELL PEOPLE WHERE WE'RE FROM. I'M SURE OF IT.

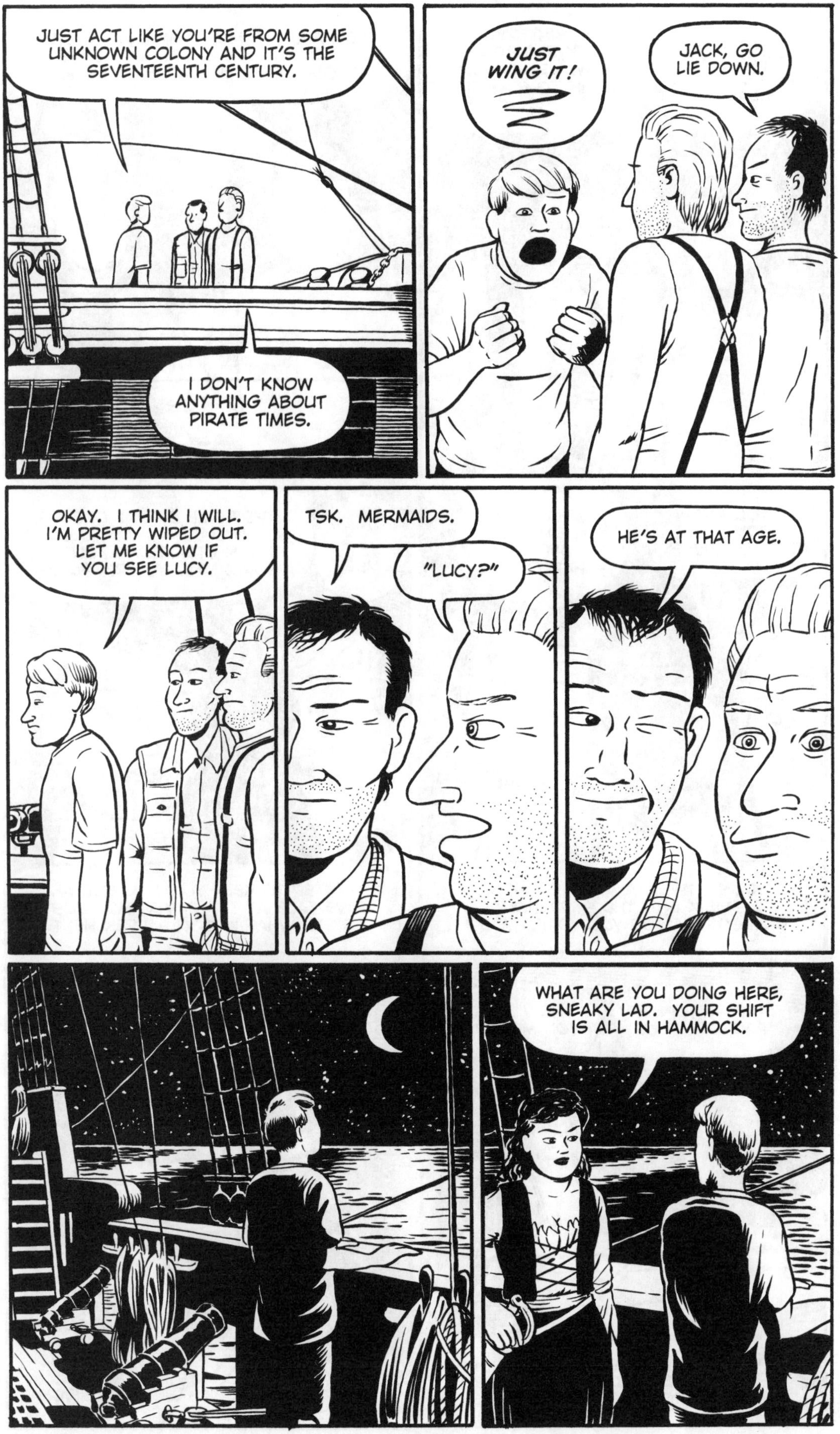
JUST ACT LIKE YOU'RE FROM SOME UNKNOWN COLONY AND IT'S THE SEVENTEENTH CENTURY.
I DON'T KNOW ANYTHING ABOUT PIRATE TIMES.
JUST WING IT!
JACK, GO LIE DOWN.
OKAY. I THINK I WILL. I'M PRETTY WIPED OUT. LET ME KNOW IF YOU SEE LUCY.
TSK. MERMAIDS.
"LUCY?"
HE'S AT THAT AGE.
WHAT ARE YOU DOING HERE, SNEAKY LAD. YOUR SHIFT IS ALL IN HAMMOCK.

I SLEPT THIS AFTERNOON SO I'M NOT TIRED.

YOU SET FREE MY DUCK DINNER AND NOW YOU OPENLY ADMIT TO SLEEPING ON THE JOB?

YOU ARE THE MOST IMPUDENT DECK HAND ON THIS SHIP. I ALMOST BELIEVE IT COMES FROM PURE INNOCENCE.

ALMOST.

SO YOU KNOW ABOUT MY FREEING LUCY?

OF COURSE. I KNEW ABOUT IT BEFORE IT HAPPENED.

YOU *LET* ME?

THE PRICE OF ONE DUCK IS NOTHING COMPARED TO SOME NEW INFORMATION ABOUT THE WORLD AND ITS TREASURES.

YOU DON'T THINK YOU WOULD BE ABLE TO SNEAK INTO THE STOREHOUSE UNLESS I WANTED YOU TO, DO YOU?

I WANTED TO KEEP YOU CONTENT, AND SAVE FACE AT THE SAME TIME. JUST TO SEE WHAT WOULD HAPPEN NEXT.

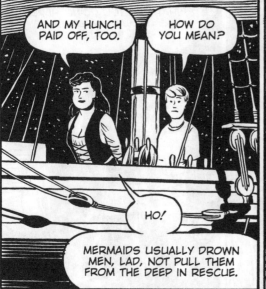

AND MY HUNCH PAID OFF, TOO.

HOW DO YOU MEAN?

THAT I DID NOT EXPECT.

YOU SAW THE MERMAIDS?

HO!

MERMAIDS USUALLY DROWN MEN, LAD, NOT PULL THEM FROM THE DEEP IN RESCUE.

OH YES. MEN'S MEMORIES GO ALL DREAMY-LIKE BUT WE WOMEN SEE THEM ALL TOO CLEAR.

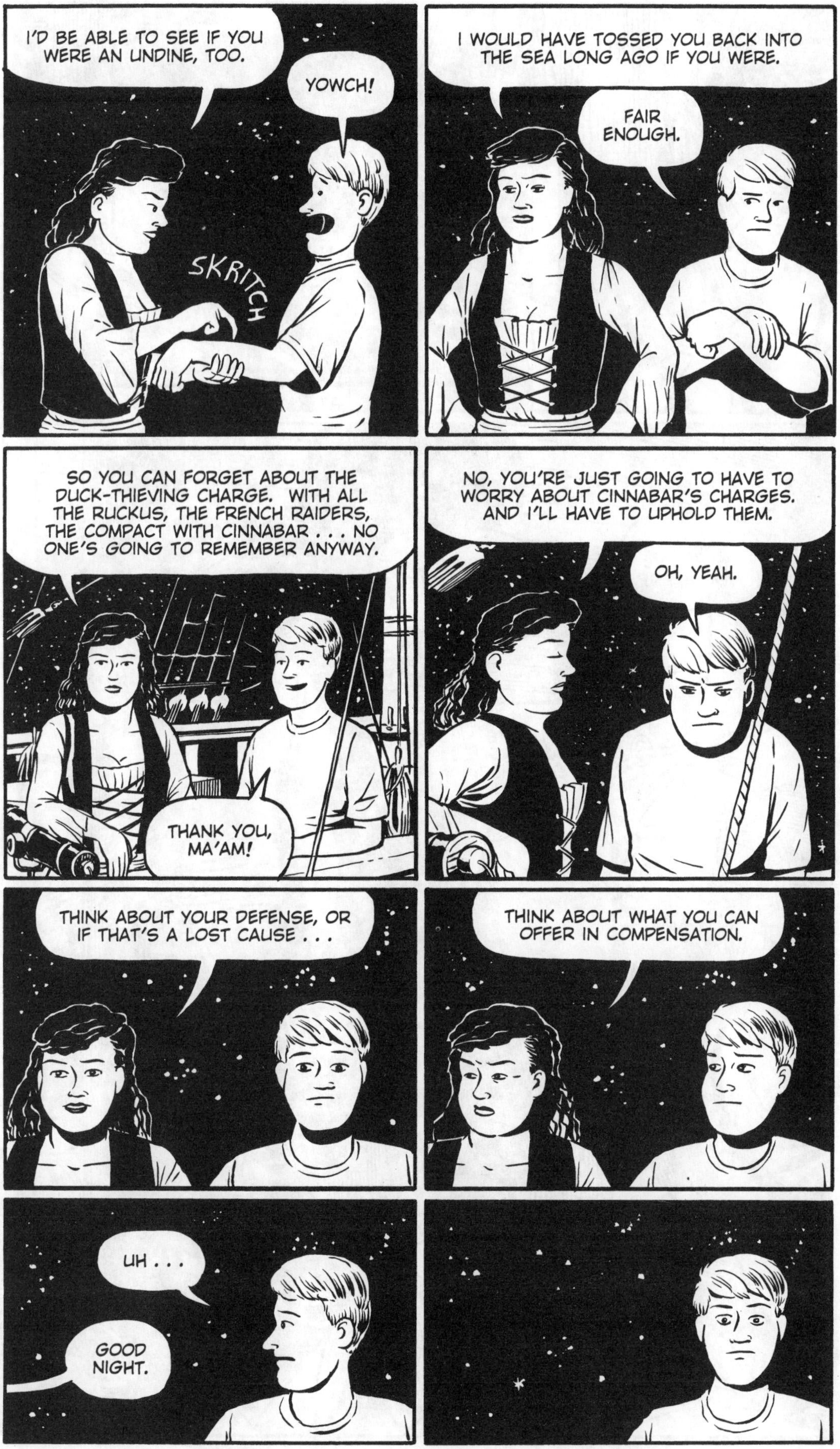
I'D BE ABLE TO SEE IF YOU WERE AN UNDINE, TOO.
YOWCH!
SKRITCH
I WOULD HAVE TOSSED YOU BACK INTO THE SEA LONG AGO IF YOU WERE.
FAIR ENOUGH.
SO YOU CAN FORGET ABOUT THE DUCK-THIEVING CHARGE. WITH ALL THE RUCKUS, THE FRENCH RAIDERS, THE COMPACT WITH CINNABAR . . . NO ONE'S GOING TO REMEMBER ANYWAY.
THANK YOU, MA'AM!
NO, YOU'RE JUST GOING TO HAVE TO WORRY ABOUT CINNABAR'S CHARGES. AND I'LL HAVE TO UPHOLD THEM.
OH, YEAH.
THINK ABOUT YOUR DEFENSE, OR IF THAT'S A LOST CAUSE . . .
THINK ABOUT WHAT YOU CAN OFFER IN COMPENSATION.
UH . . .
GOOD NIGHT.

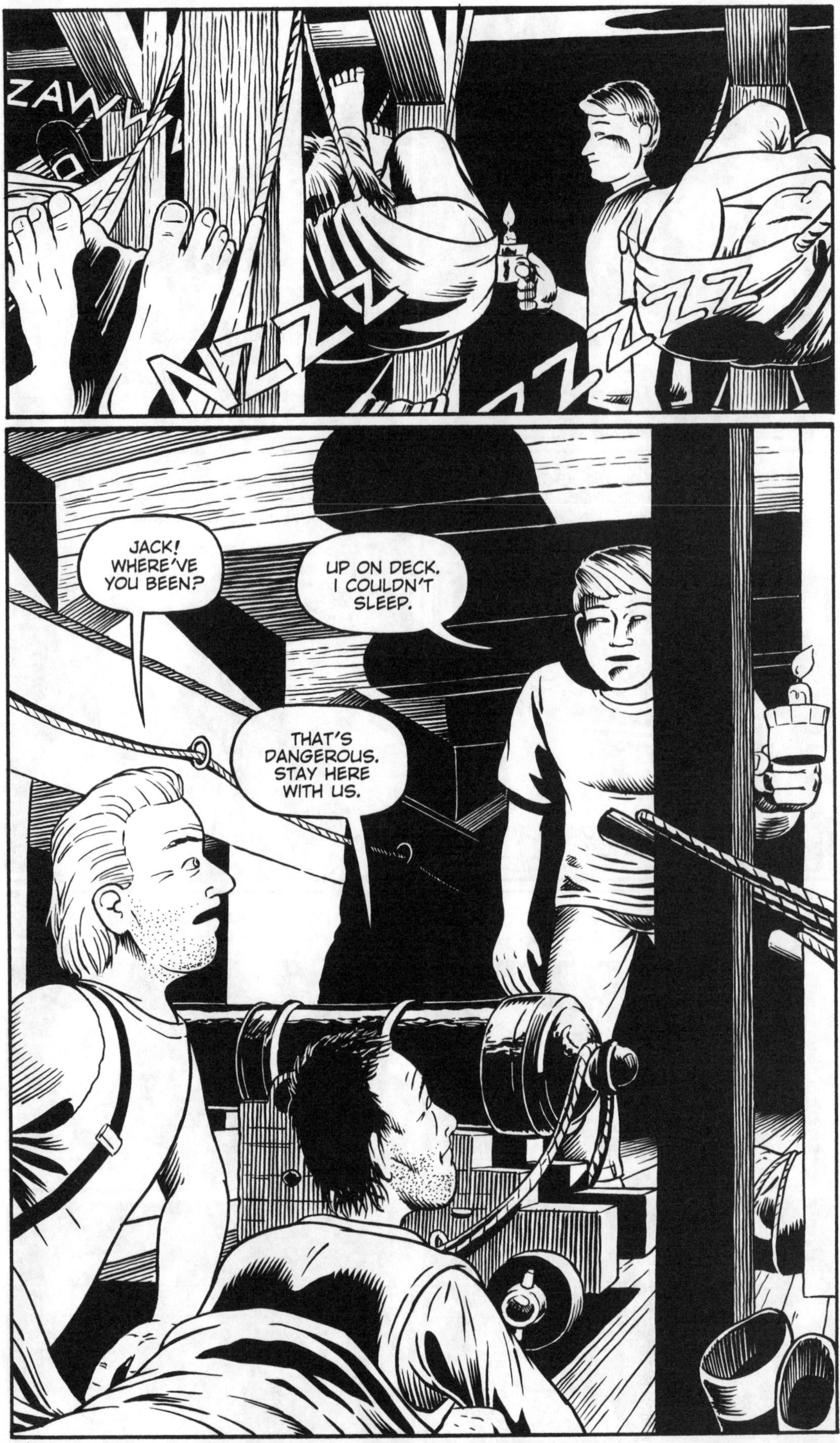

JACK! WHERE'VE YOU BEEN?
UP ON DECK. I COULDN'T SLEEP.
THAT'S DANGEROUS. STAY HERE WITH US.

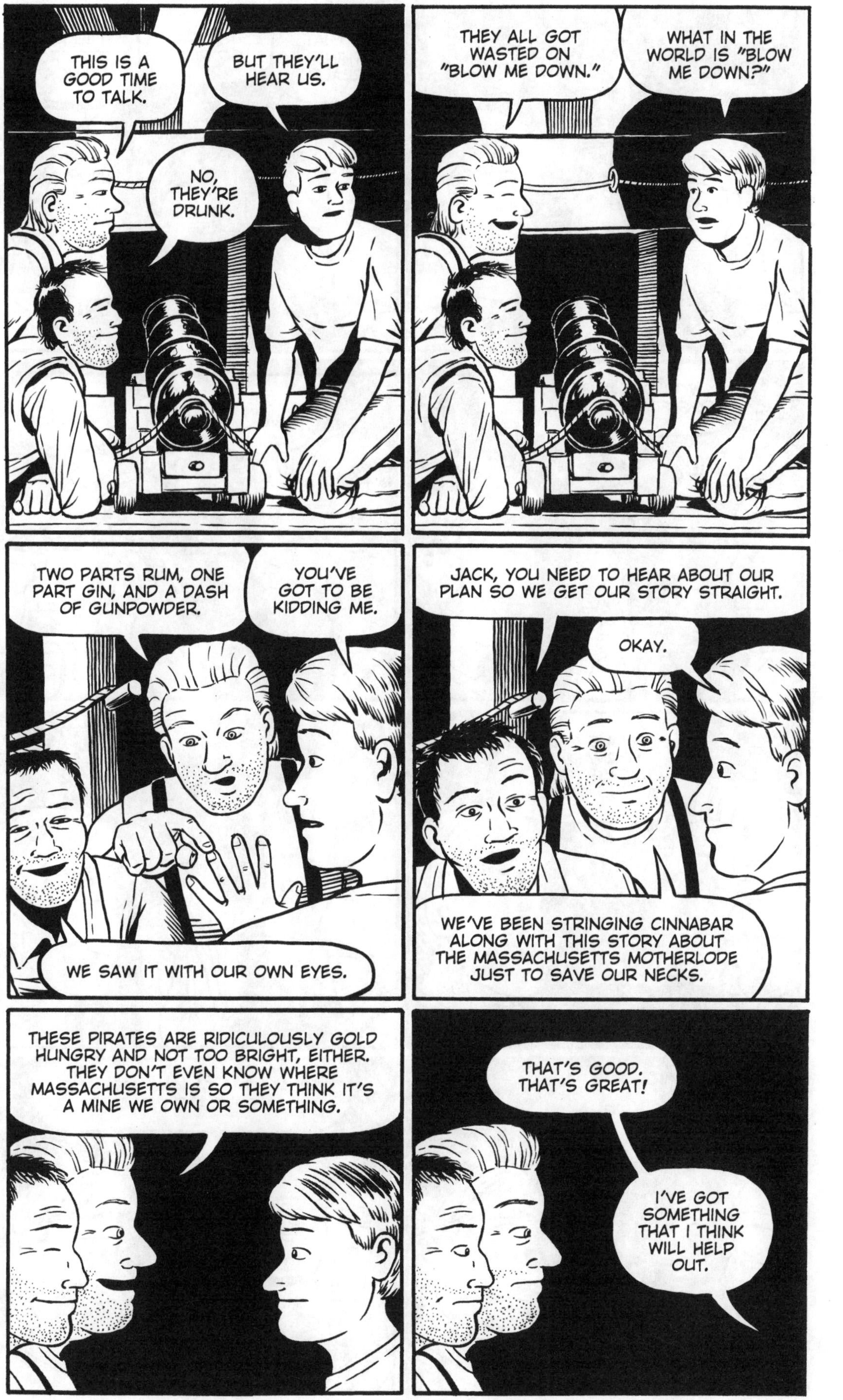
THIS IS A GOOD TIME TO TALK.
BUT THEY'LL HEAR US.
NO, THEY'RE DRUNK.
THEY ALL GOT WASTED ON "BLOW ME DOWN."
WHAT IN THE WORLD IS "BLOW ME DOWN?"
TWO PARTS RUM, ONE PART GIN, AND A DASH OF GUNPOWDER.
YOU'VE GOT TO BE KIDDING ME.
WE SAW IT WITH OUR OWN EYES.
JACK, YOU NEED TO HEAR ABOUT OUR PLAN SO WE GET OUR STORY STRAIGHT.
OKAY.
WE'VE BEEN STRINGING CINNABAR ALONG WITH THIS STORY ABOUT THE MASSACHUSETTS MOTHERLODE JUST TO SAVE OUR NECKS.
THESE PIRATES ARE RIDICULOUSLY GOLD HUNGRY AND NOT TOO BRIGHT, EITHER. THEY DON'T EVEN KNOW WHERE MASSACHUSETTS IS SO THEY THINK IT'S A MINE WE OWN OR SOMETHING.
THAT'S GOOD. THAT'S GREAT!
I'VE GOT SOMETHING THAT I THINK WILL HELP OUT.

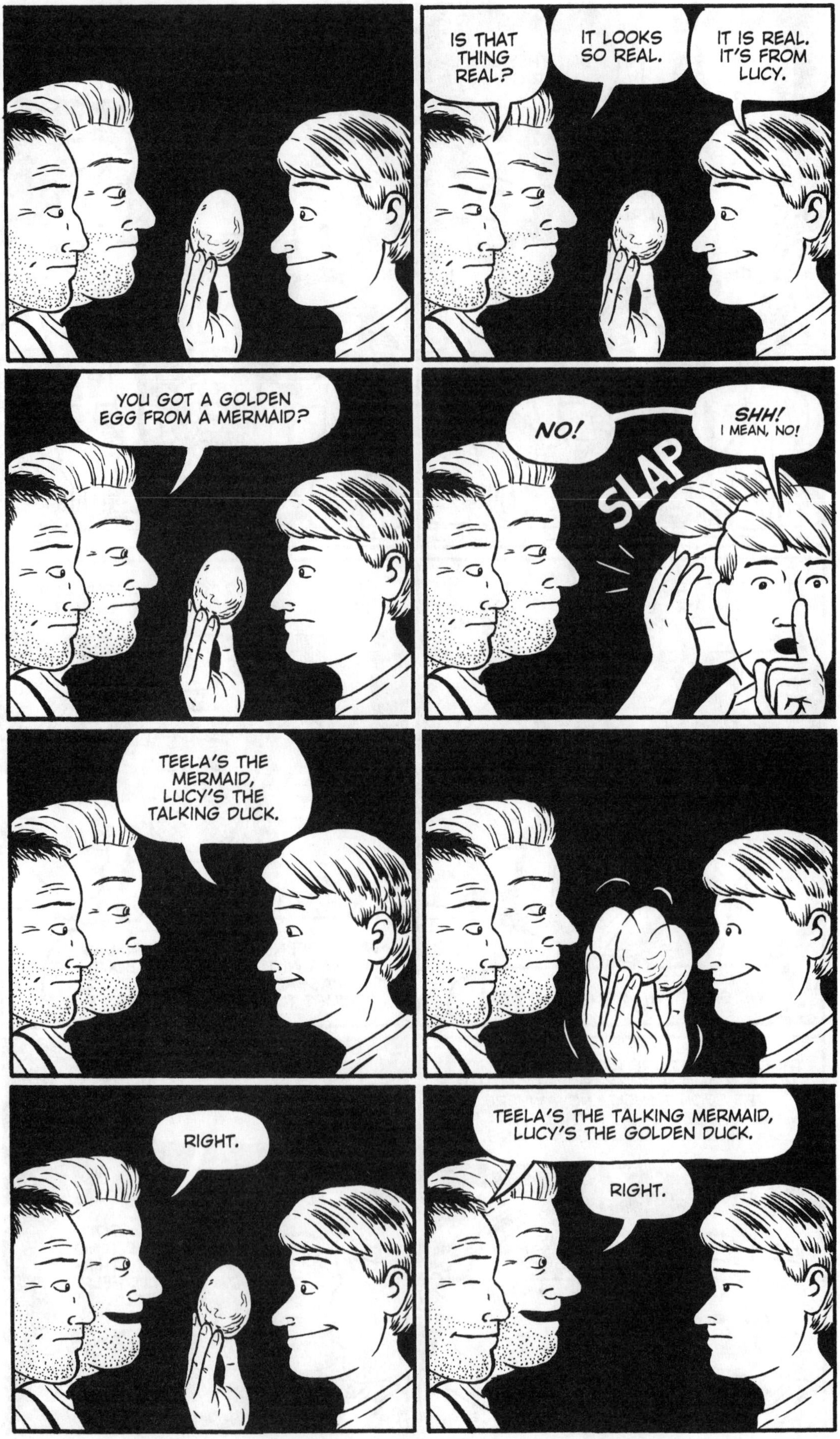
IS THAT THING REAL?
IT LOOKS SO REAL.
IT IS REAL. IT'S FROM LUCY.
YOU GOT A GOLDEN EGG FROM A MERMAID?
NO!
SLAP
SHH! I MEAN, NO!
TEELA'S THE MERMAID, LUCY'S THE TALKING DUCK.
RIGHT.
TEELA'S THE TALKING MERMAID, LUCY'S THE GOLDEN DUCK.
RIGHT.

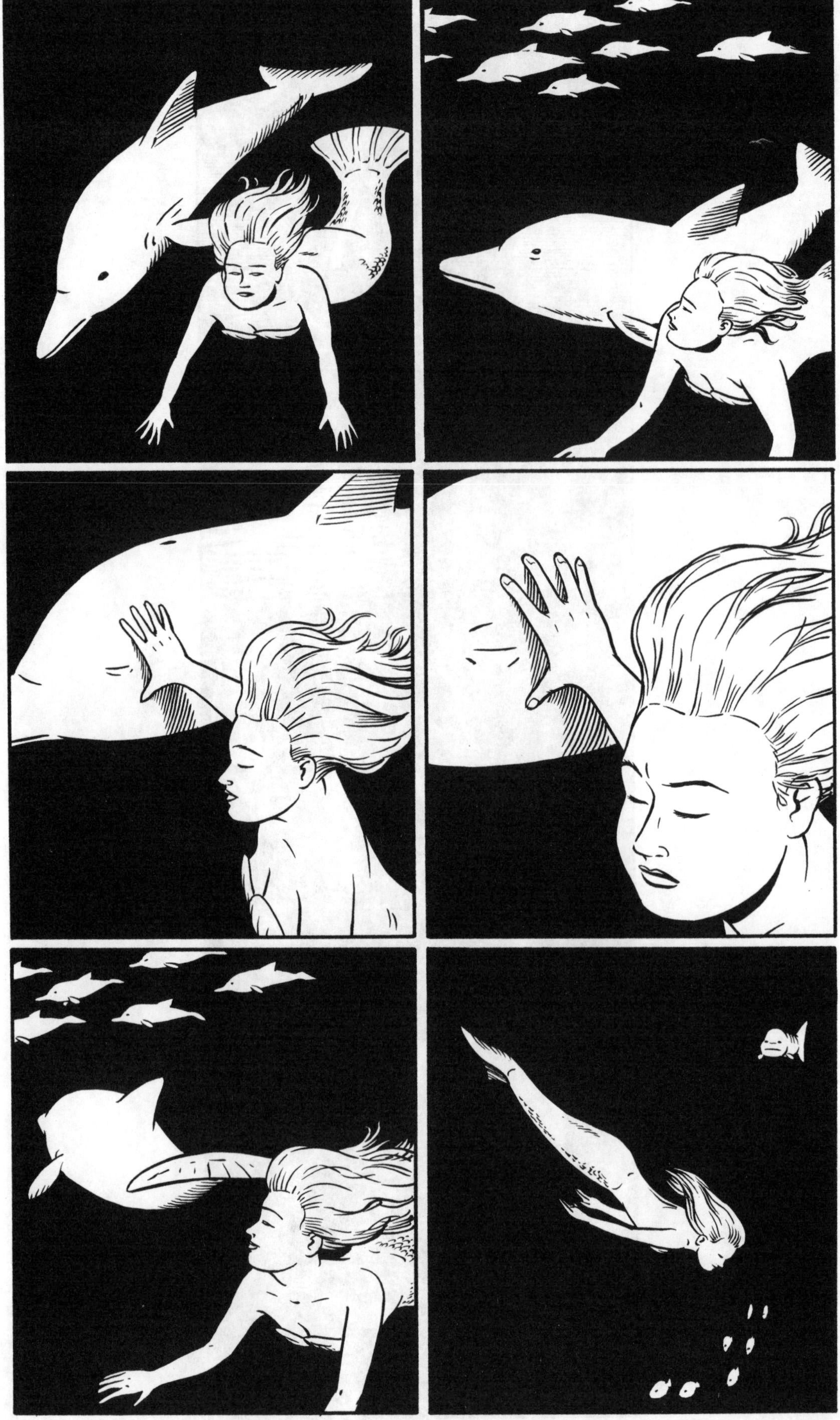

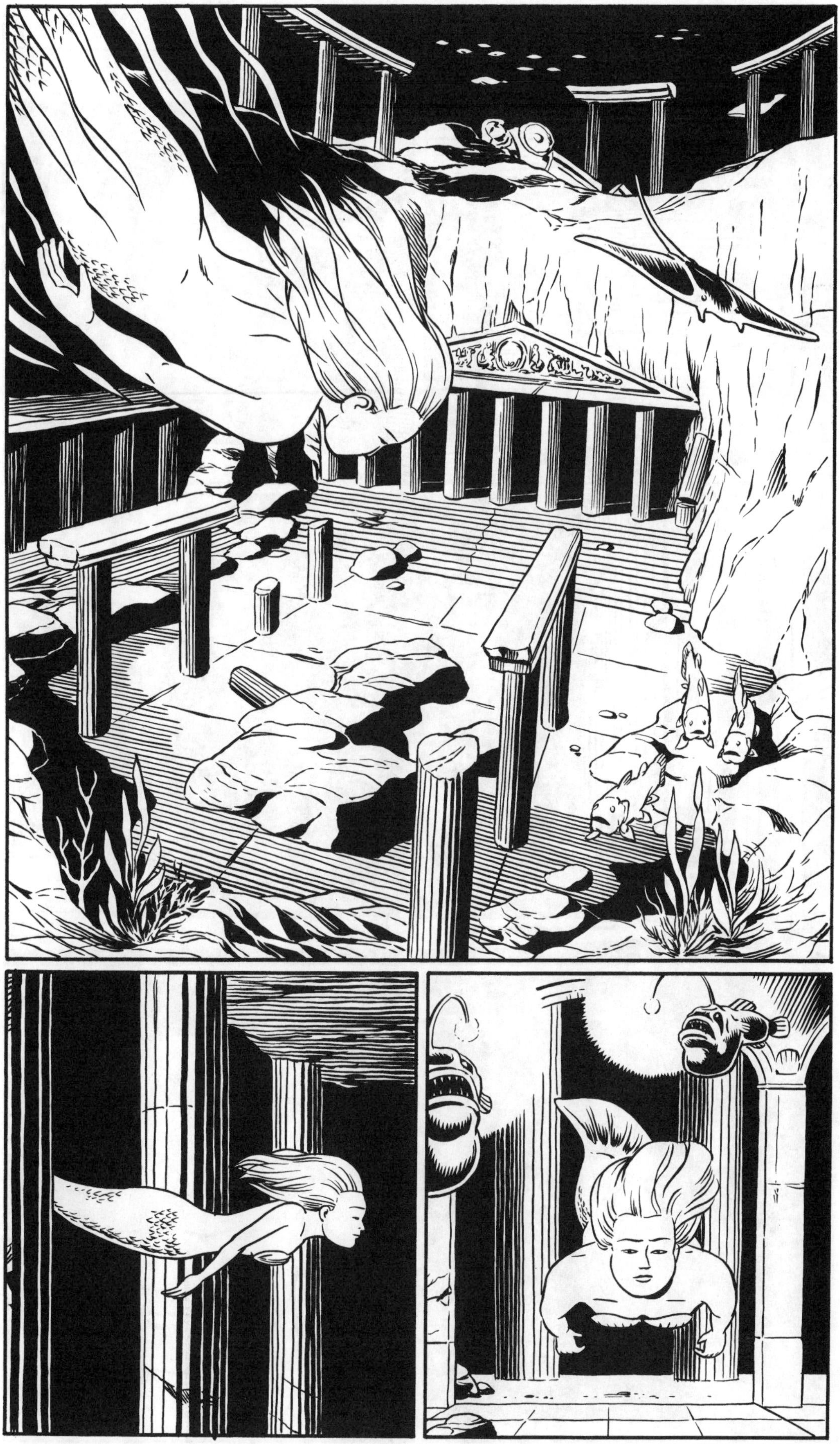

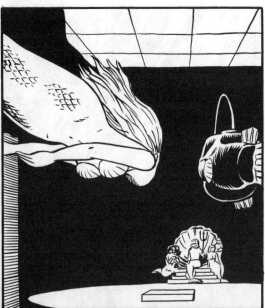

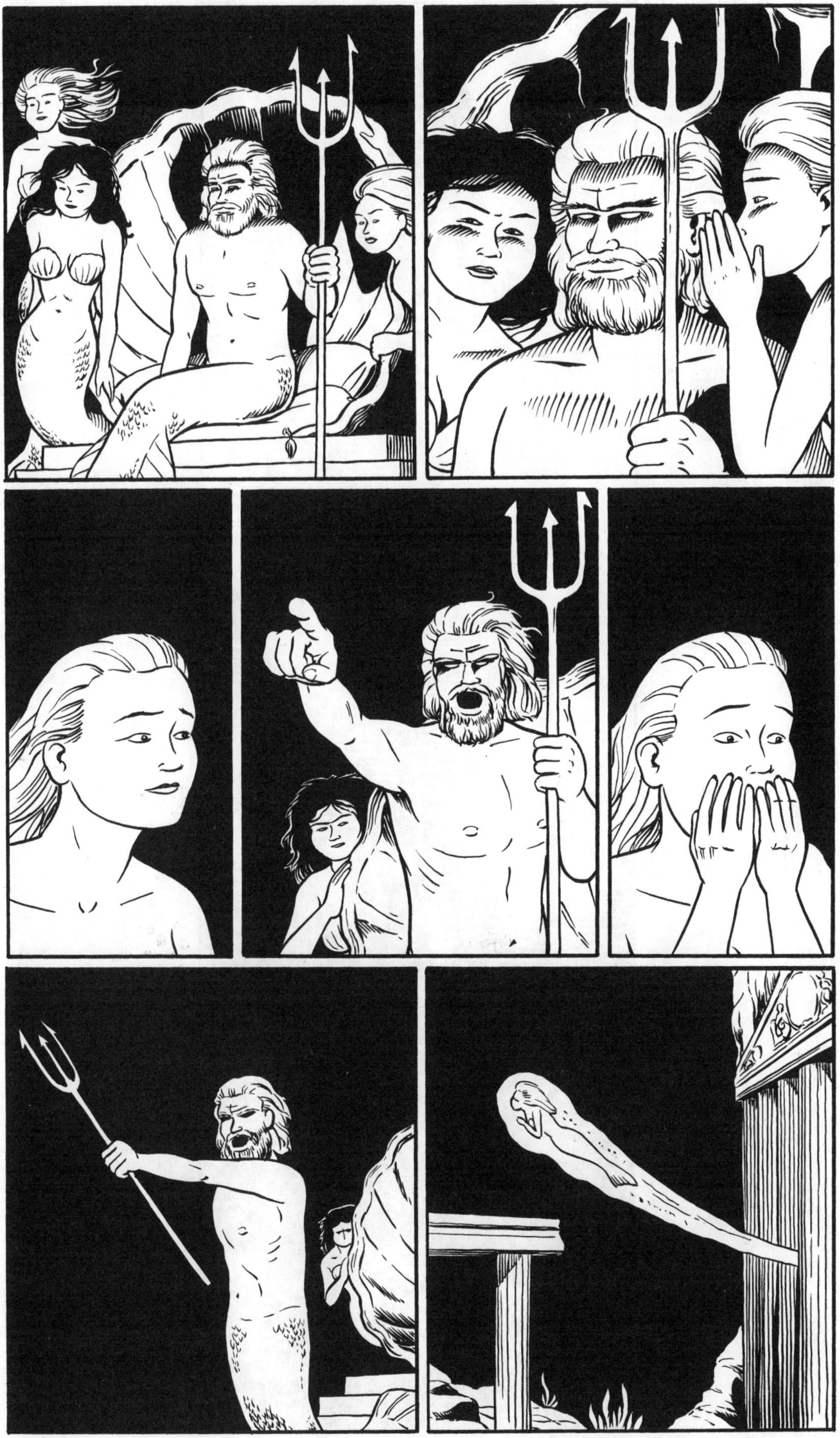

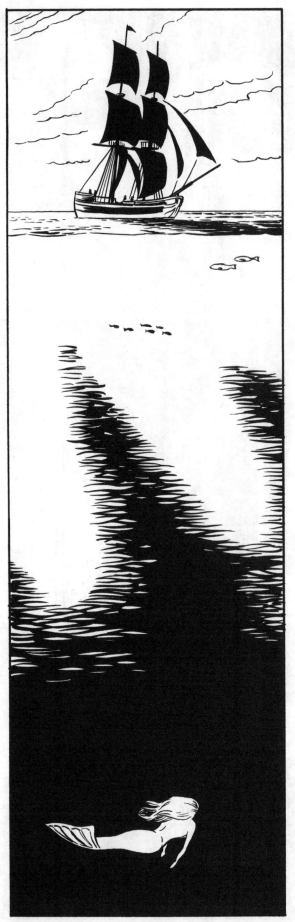

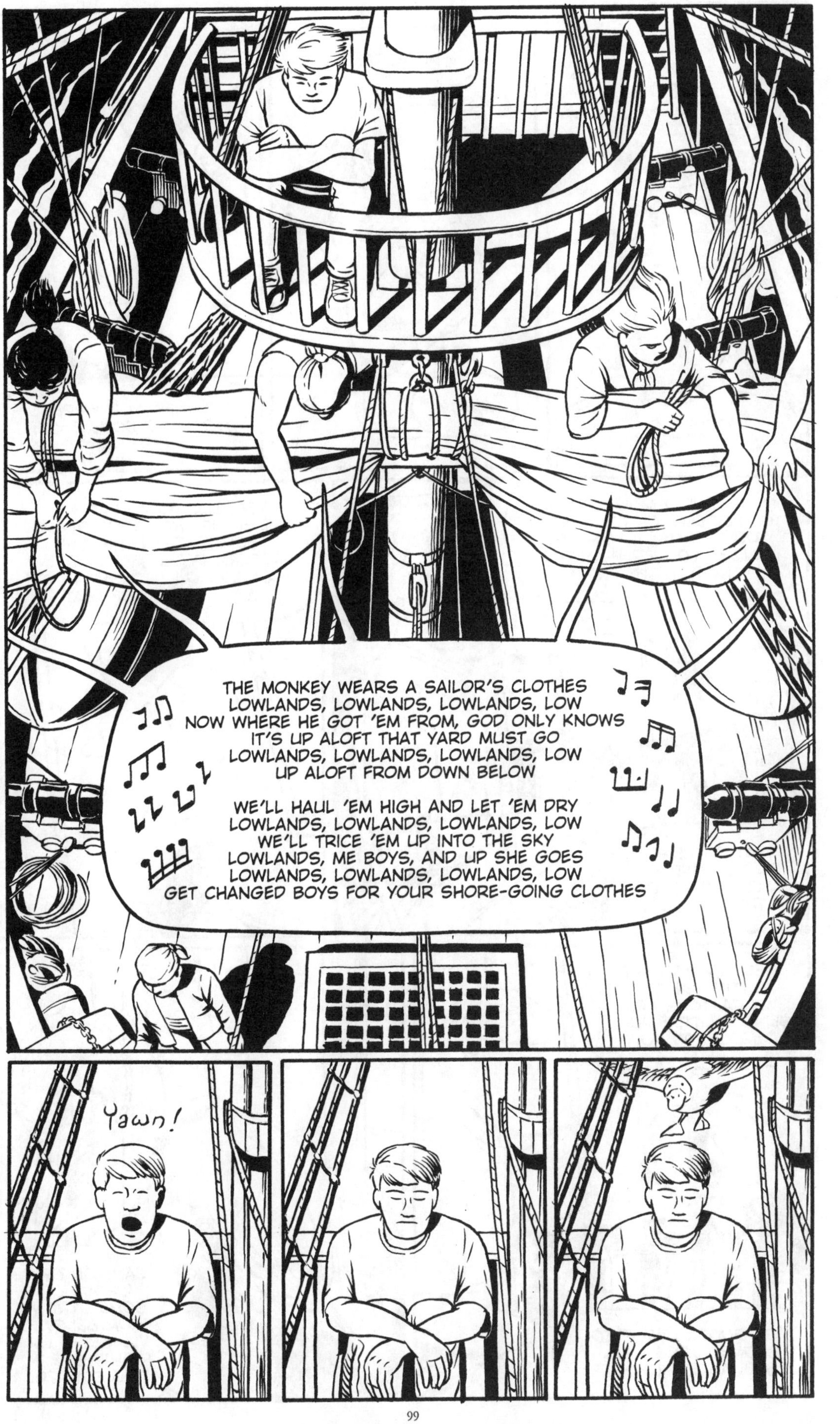
THE MONKEY WEARS A SAILOR'S CLOTHES
LOWLANDS, LOWLANDS, LOWLANDS, LOW
NOW WHERE HE GOT 'EM FROM, GOD ONLY KNOWS
IT'S UP ALOFT THAT YARD MUST GO
LOWLANDS, LOWLANDS, LOWLANDS, LOW
UP ALOFT FROM DOWN BELOW

WE'LL HAUL 'EM HIGH AND LET 'EM DRY
LOWLANDS, LOWLANDS, LOWLANDS, LOW
WE'LL TRICE 'EM UP INTO THE SKY
LOWLANDS, ME BOYS, AND UP SHE GOES
LOWLANDS, LOWLANDS, LOWLANDS, LOW
GET CHANGED BOYS FOR YOUR SHORE-GOING CLOTHES
Yawn!

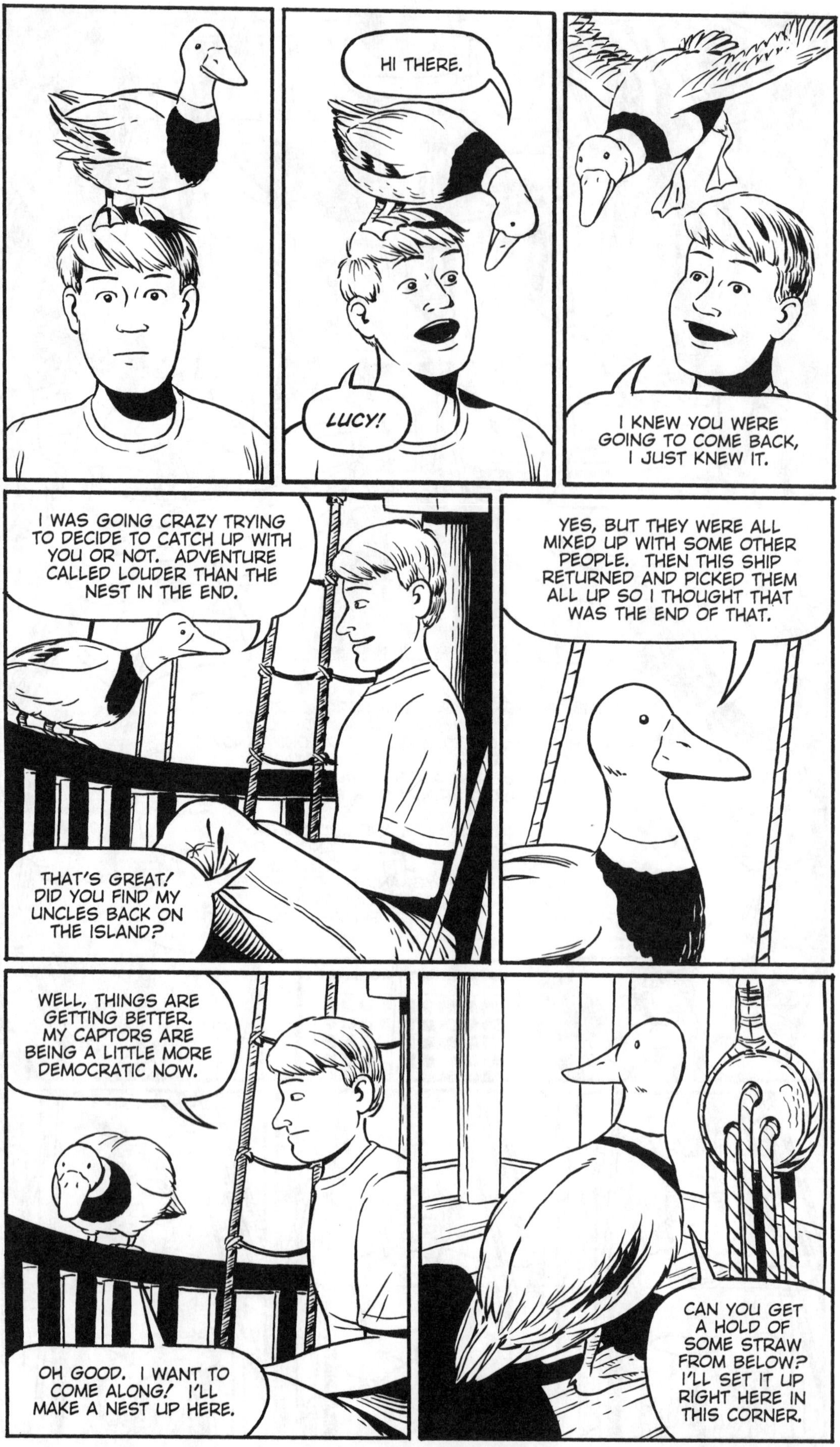
HI THERE.
LUCY!
I KNEW YOU WERE GOING TO COME BACK, I JUST KNEW IT.
I WAS GOING CRAZY TRYING TO DECIDE TO CATCH UP WITH YOU OR NOT. ADVENTURE CALLED LOUDER THAN THE NEST IN THE END.
THAT'S GREAT! DID YOU FIND MY UNCLES BACK ON THE ISLAND?
YES, BUT THEY WERE ALL MIXED UP WITH SOME OTHER PEOPLE. THEN THIS SHIP RETURNED AND PICKED THEM ALL UP SO I THOUGHT THAT WAS THE END OF THAT.
WELL, THINGS ARE GETTING BETTER. MY CAPTORS ARE BEING A LITTLE MORE DEMOCRATIC NOW.
OH GOOD. I WANT TO COME ALONG! I'LL MAKE A NEST UP HERE.
CAN YOU GET A HOLD OF SOME STRAW FROM BELOW? I'LL SET IT UP RIGHT HERE IN THIS CORNER.

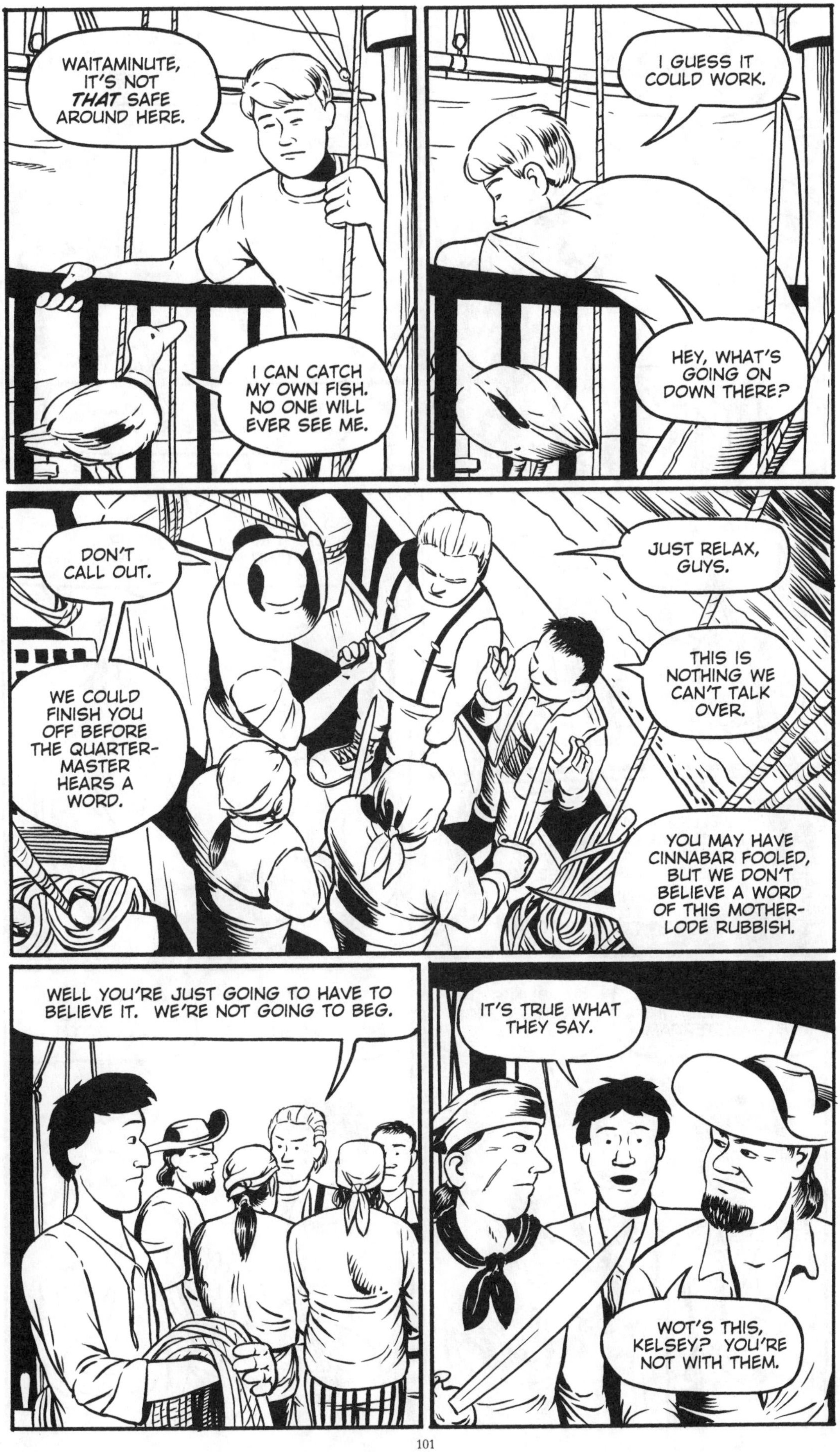
WAITAMINUTE, IT'S NOT *THAT* SAFE AROUND HERE.
I CAN CATCH MY OWN FISH. NO ONE WILL EVER SEE ME.
I GUESS IT COULD WORK.
HEY, WHAT'S GOING ON DOWN THERE?
DON'T CALL OUT.
WE COULD FINISH YOU OFF BEFORE THE QUARTER-MASTER HEARS A WORD.
JUST RELAX, GUYS.
THIS IS NOTHING WE CAN'T TALK OVER.
YOU MAY HAVE CINNABAR FOOLED, BUT WE DON'T BELIEVE A WORD OF THIS MOTHER-LODE RUBBISH.
WELL YOU'RE JUST GOING TO HAVE TO BELIEVE IT. WE'RE NOT GOING TO BEG.
IT'S TRUE WHAT THEY SAY.
WOT'S THIS, KELSEY? YOU'RE NOT WITH THEM.

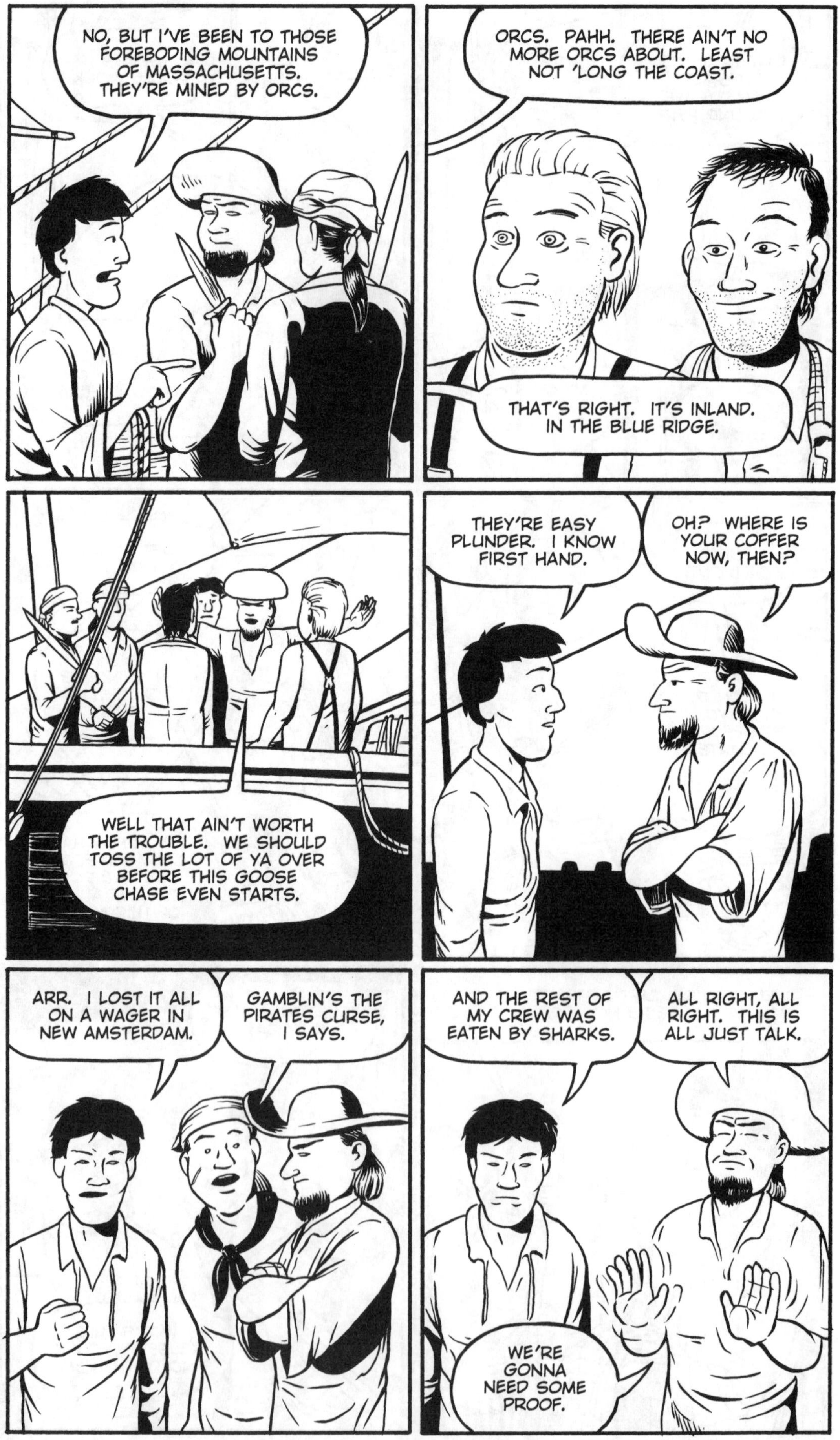
NO, BUT I'VE BEEN TO THOSE FOREBODING MOUNTAINS OF MASSACHUSETTS. THEY'RE MINED BY ORCS.
ORCS. PAHH. THERE AIN'T NO MORE ORCS ABOUT. LEAST NOT 'LONG THE COAST.
THAT'S RIGHT. IT'S INLAND. IN THE BLUE RIDGE.
WELL THAT AIN'T WORTH THE TROUBLE. WE SHOULD TOSS THE LOT OF YA OVER BEFORE THIS GOOSE CHASE EVEN STARTS.
THEY'RE EASY PLUNDER. I KNOW FIRST HAND.
OH? WHERE IS YOUR COFFER NOW, THEN?
ARR. I LOST IT ALL ON A WAGER IN NEW AMSTERDAM.
GAMBLIN'S THE PIRATES CURSE, I SAYS.
AND THE REST OF MY CREW WAS EATEN BY SHARKS.
ALL RIGHT, ALL RIGHT. THIS IS ALL JUST TALK.
WE'RE GONNA NEED SOME PROOF.

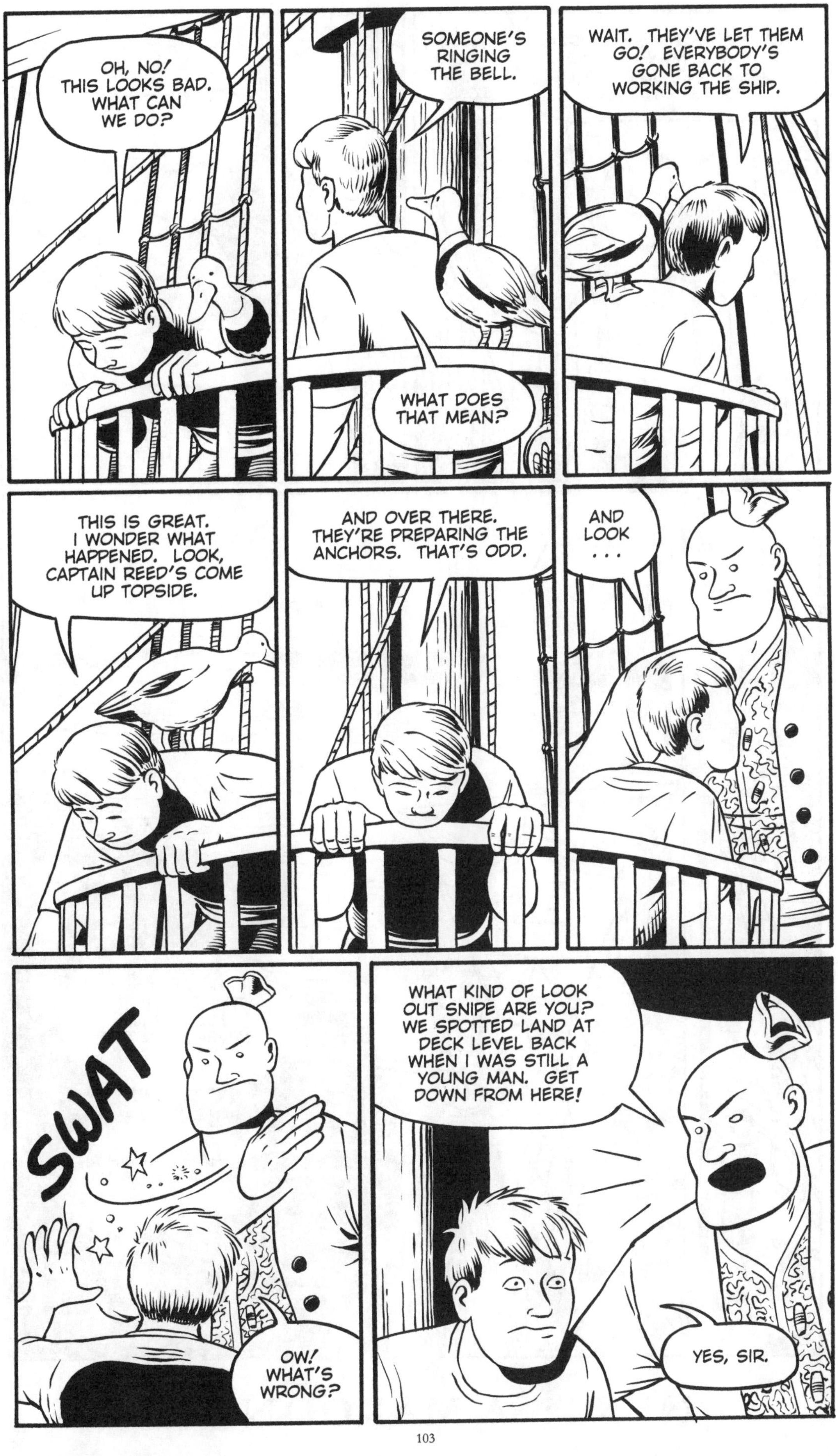
OH, NO! THIS LOOKS BAD. WHAT CAN WE DO?
SOMEONE'S RINGING THE BELL.
WHAT DOES THAT MEAN?
WAIT. THEY'VE LET THEM GO! EVERYBODY'S GONE BACK TO WORKING THE SHIP.
THIS IS GREAT. I WONDER WHAT HAPPENED. LOOK, CAPTAIN REED'S COME UP TOPSIDE.
AND OVER THERE. THEY'RE PREPARING THE ANCHORS. THAT'S ODD.
AND LOOK . . .
SWAT
OW! WHAT'S WRONG?
WHAT KIND OF LOOK OUT SNIPE ARE YOU? WE SPOTTED LAND AT DECK LEVEL BACK WHEN I WAS STILL A YOUNG MAN. GET DOWN FROM HERE!
YES, SIR.

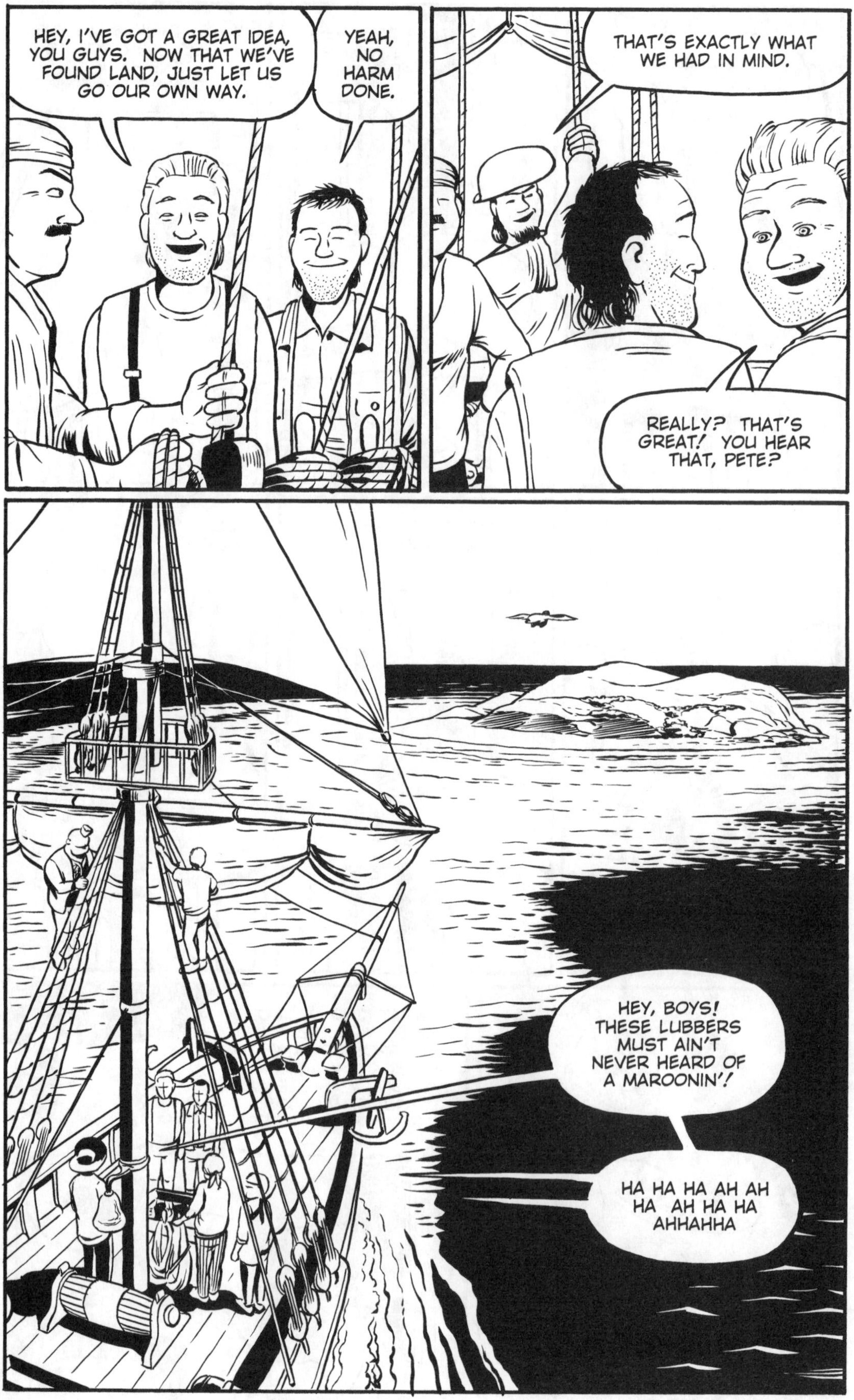
HEY, I'VE GOT A GREAT IDEA, YOU GUYS. NOW THAT WE'VE FOUND LAND, JUST LET US GO OUR OWN WAY.
YEAH, NO HARM DONE.
THAT'S EXACTLY WHAT WE HAD IN MIND.
REALLY? THAT'S GREAT! YOU HEAR THAT, PETE?
HEY, BOYS! THESE LUBBERS MUST AIN'T NEVER HEARD OF A MAROONIN'!
HA HA HA AH AH HA AH HA HA AHHAHHA

NEXT: A MAROONING

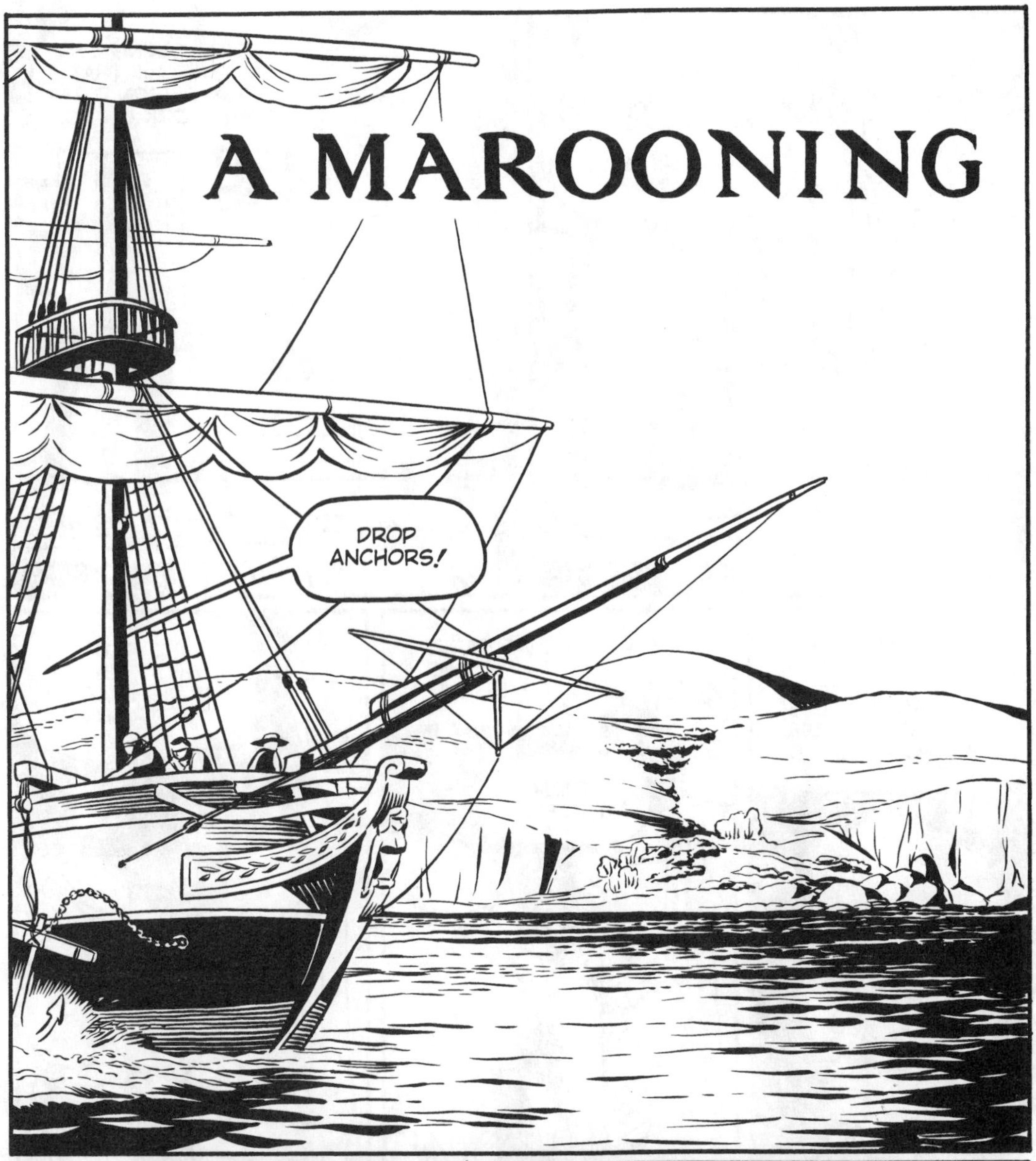
A MAROONING
DROP ANCHORS!

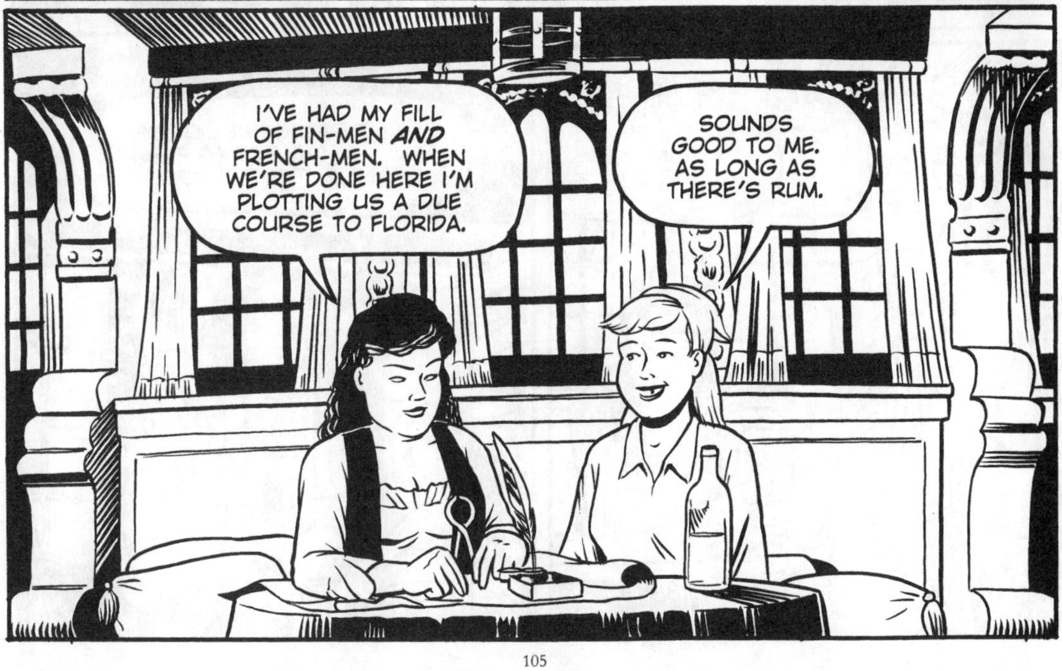
I'VE HAD MY FILL OF FIN-MEN *AND* FRENCH-MEN. WHEN WE'RE DONE HERE I'M PLOTTING US A DUE COURSE TO FLORIDA.
SOUNDS GOOD TO ME. AS LONG AS THERE'S RUM.

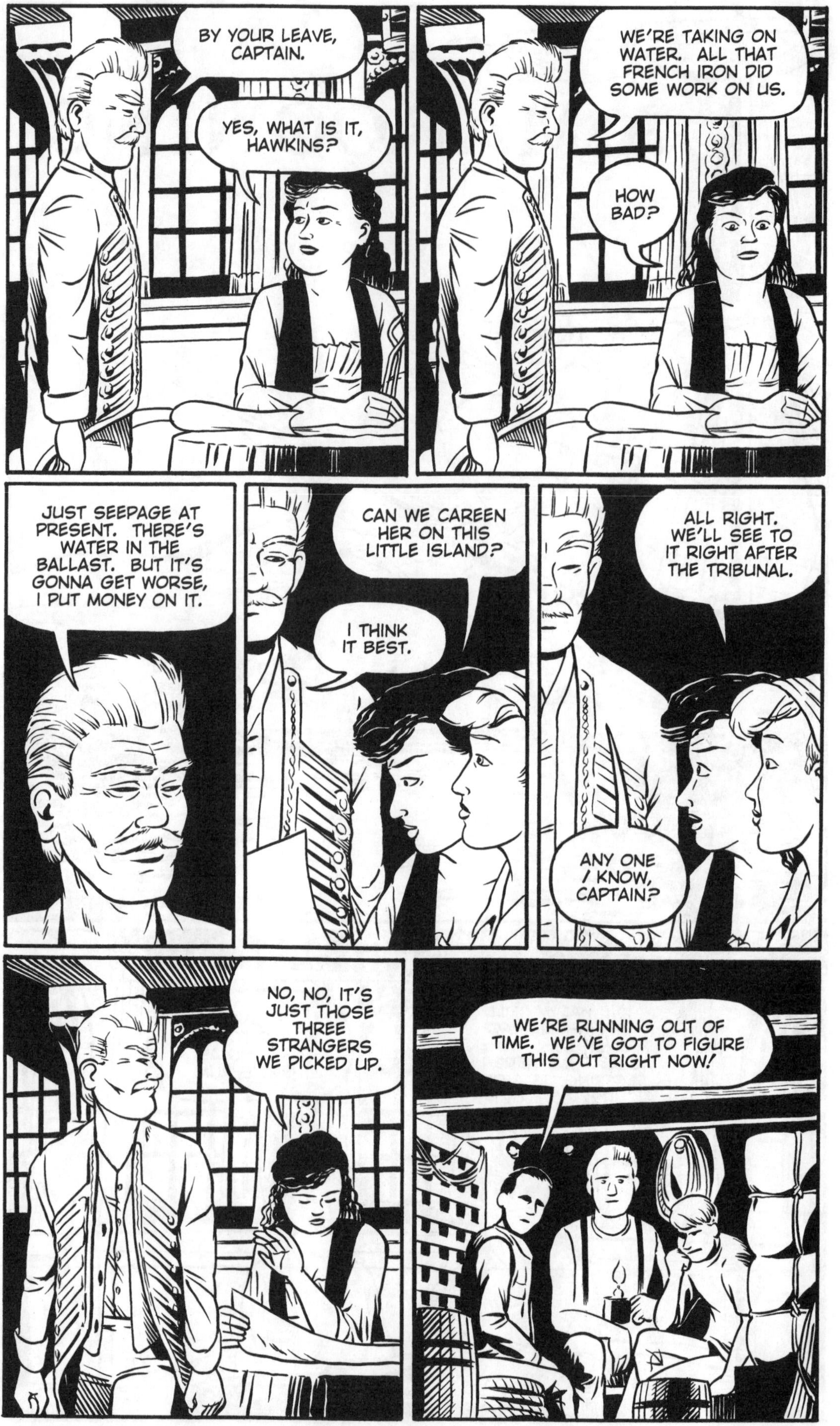
BY YOUR LEAVE, CAPTAIN.
YES, WHAT IS IT, HAWKINS?
WE'RE TAKING ON WATER. ALL THAT FRENCH IRON DID SOME WORK ON US.
HOW BAD?
JUST SEEPAGE AT PRESENT. THERE'S WATER IN THE BALLAST. BUT IT'S GONNA GET WORSE, I PUT MONEY ON IT.
CAN WE CAREEN HER ON THIS LITTLE ISLAND?
I THINK IT BEST.
ALL RIGHT. WE'LL SEE TO IT RIGHT AFTER THE TRIBUNAL.
ANY ONE I KNOW, CAPTAIN?
NO, NO, IT'S JUST THOSE THREE STRANGERS WE PICKED UP.
WE'RE RUNNING OUT OF TIME. WE'VE GOT TO FIGURE THIS OUT RIGHT NOW!

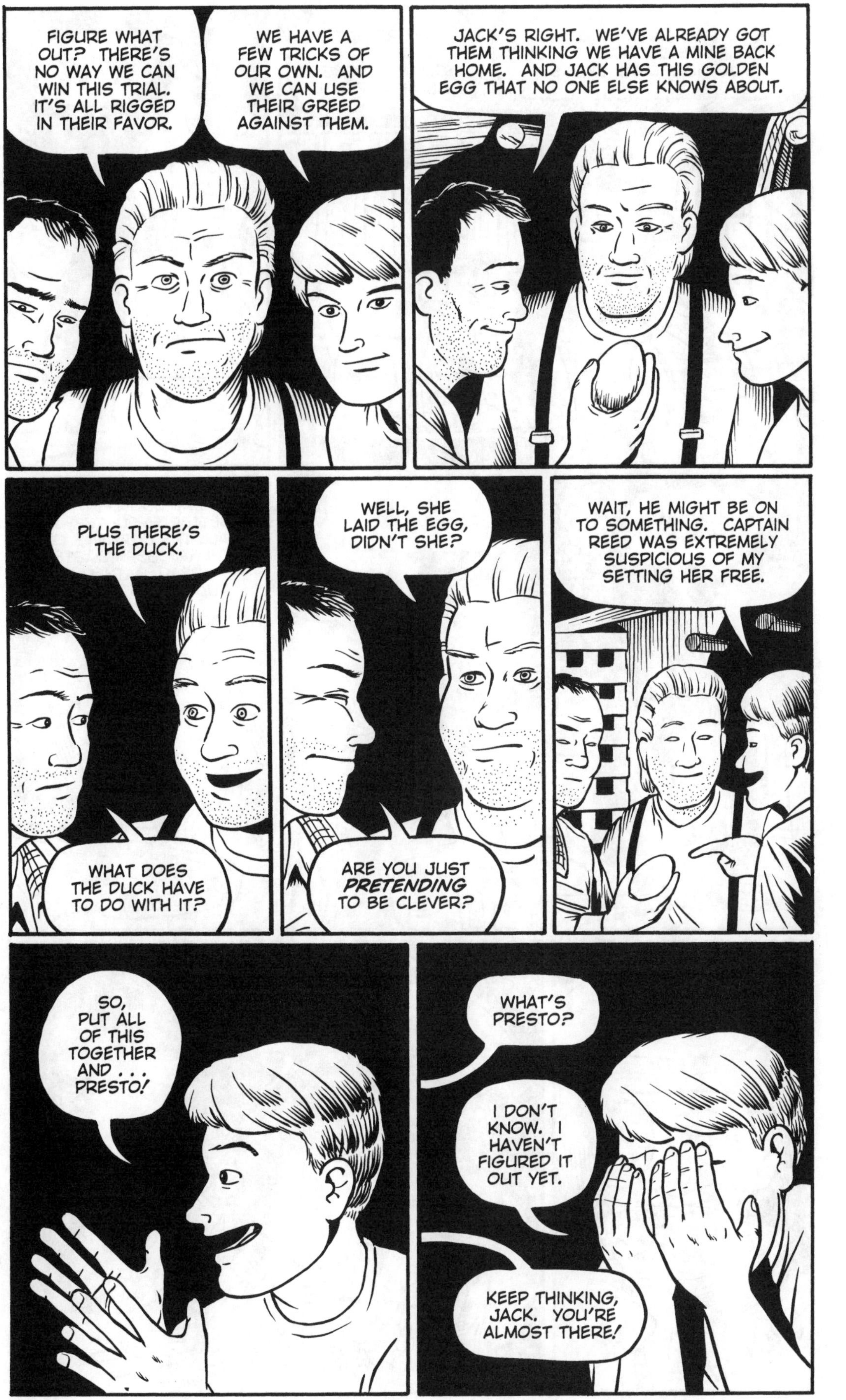
FIGURE WHAT OUT? THERE'S NO WAY WE CAN WIN THIS TRIAL. IT'S ALL RIGGED IN THEIR FAVOR.
WE HAVE A FEW TRICKS OF OUR OWN. AND WE CAN USE THEIR GREED AGAINST THEM.
JACK'S RIGHT. WE'VE ALREADY GOT THEM THINKING WE HAVE A MINE BACK HOME. AND JACK HAS THIS GOLDEN EGG THAT NO ONE ELSE KNOWS ABOUT.
PLUS THERE'S THE DUCK.
WHAT DOES THE DUCK HAVE TO DO WITH IT?
WELL, SHE LAID THE EGG, DIDN'T SHE?
ARE YOU JUST *PRETENDING* TO BE CLEVER?
WAIT, HE MIGHT BE ON TO SOMETHING. CAPTAIN REED WAS EXTREMELY SUSPICIOUS OF MY SETTING HER FREE.
SO, PUT ALL OF THIS TOGETHER AND . . . PRESTO!
WHAT'S PRESTO?
I DON'T KNOW. I HAVEN'T FIGURED IT OUT YET.
KEEP THINKING, JACK. YOU'RE ALMOST THERE!

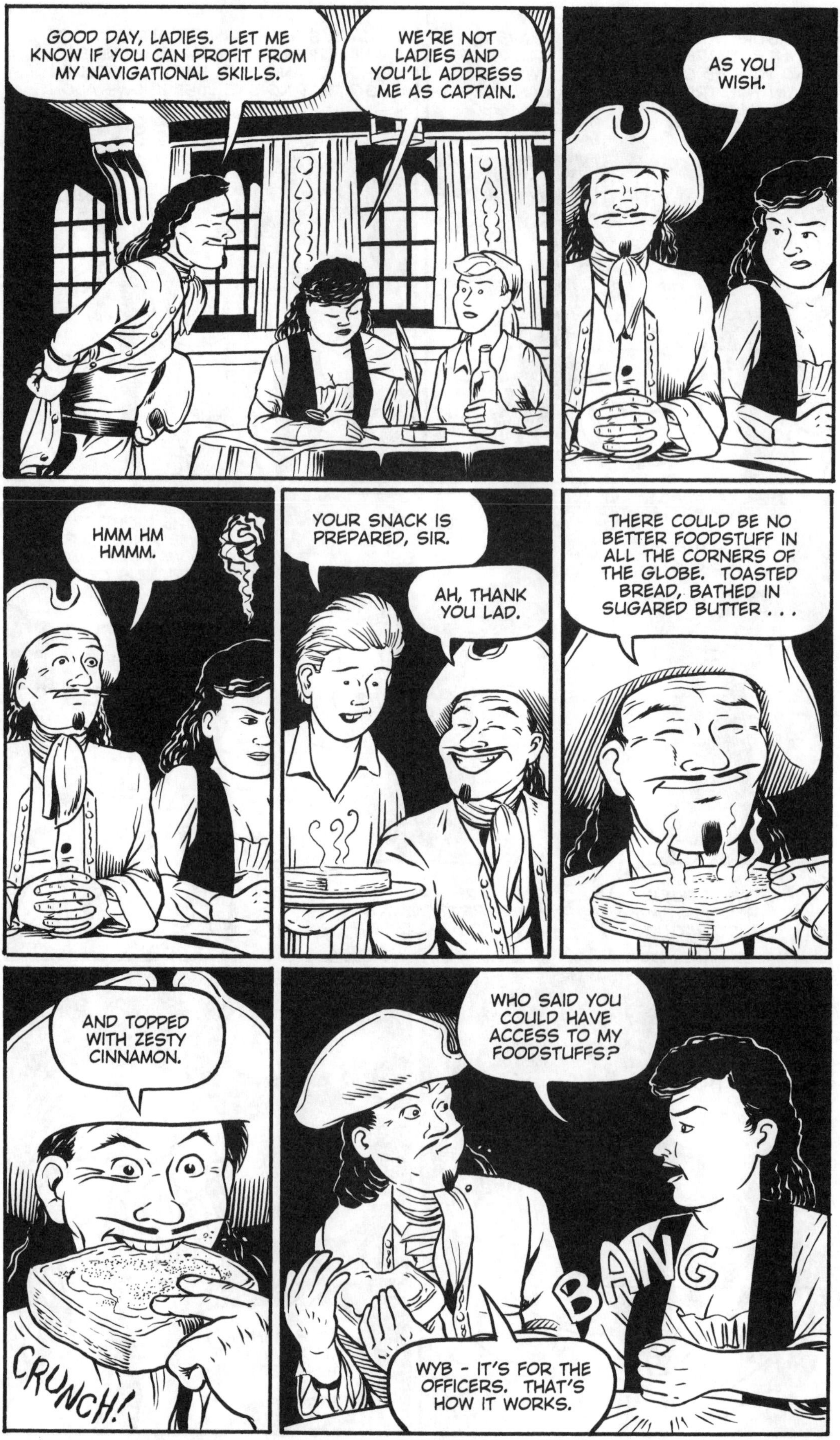
GOOD DAY, LADIES. LET ME KNOW IF YOU CAN PROFIT FROM MY NAVIGATIONAL SKILLS.
WE'RE NOT LADIES AND YOU'LL ADDRESS ME AS CAPTAIN.
AS YOU WISH.
HMM HM HMMM.
YOUR SNACK IS PREPARED, SIR.
AH, THANK YOU LAD.
THERE COULD BE NO BETTER FOODSTUFF IN ALL THE CORNERS OF THE GLOBE. TOASTED BREAD, BATHED IN SUGARED BUTTER . . .
AND TOPPED WITH ZESTY CINNAMON.
CRUNCH!
WHO SAID YOU COULD HAVE ACCESS TO MY FOODSTUFFS?
BANG
WYB - IT'S FOR THE OFFICERS. THAT'S HOW IT WORKS.

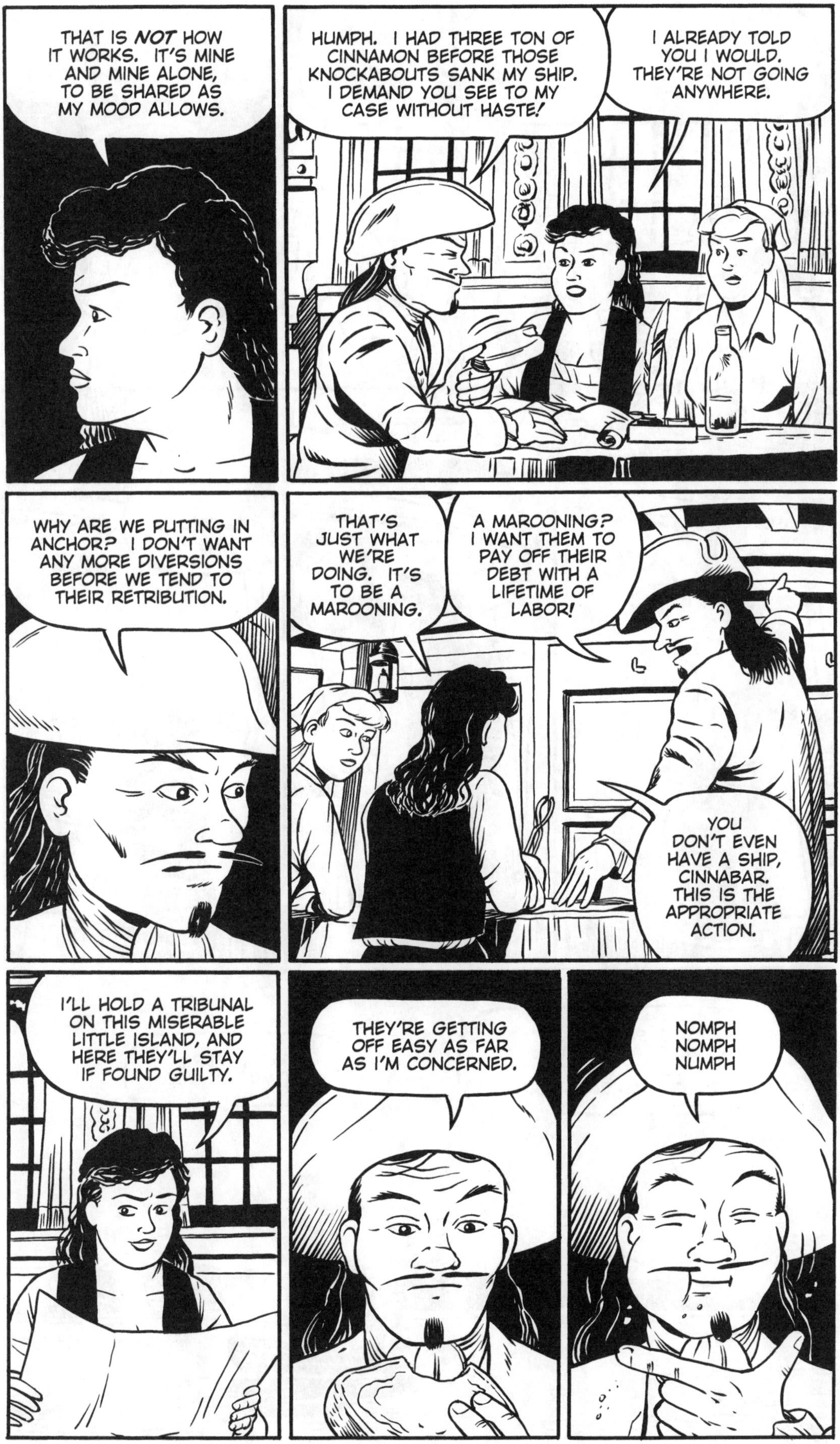
THAT IS *NOT* HOW IT WORKS. IT'S MINE AND MINE ALONE, TO BE SHARED AS MY MOOD ALLOWS.
HUMPH. I HAD THREE TON OF CINNAMON BEFORE THOSE KNOCKABOUTS SANK MY SHIP. I DEMAND YOU SEE TO MY CASE WITHOUT HASTE!
I ALREADY TOLD YOU I WOULD. THEY'RE NOT GOING ANYWHERE.
WHY ARE WE PUTTING IN ANCHOR? I DON'T WANT ANY MORE DIVERSIONS BEFORE WE TEND TO THEIR RETRIBUTION.
THAT'S JUST WHAT WE'RE DOING. IT'S TO BE A MAROONING.
A MAROONING? I WANT THEM TO PAY OFF THEIR DEBT WITH A LIFETIME OF LABOR!
YOU DON'T EVEN HAVE A SHIP, CINNABAR. THIS IS THE APPROPRIATE ACTION.
I'LL HOLD A TRIBUNAL ON THIS MISERABLE LITTLE ISLAND, AND HERE THEY'LL STAY IF FOUND GUILTY.
THEY'RE GETTING OFF EASY AS FAR AS I'M CONCERNED.
NOMPH NOMPH NUMPH

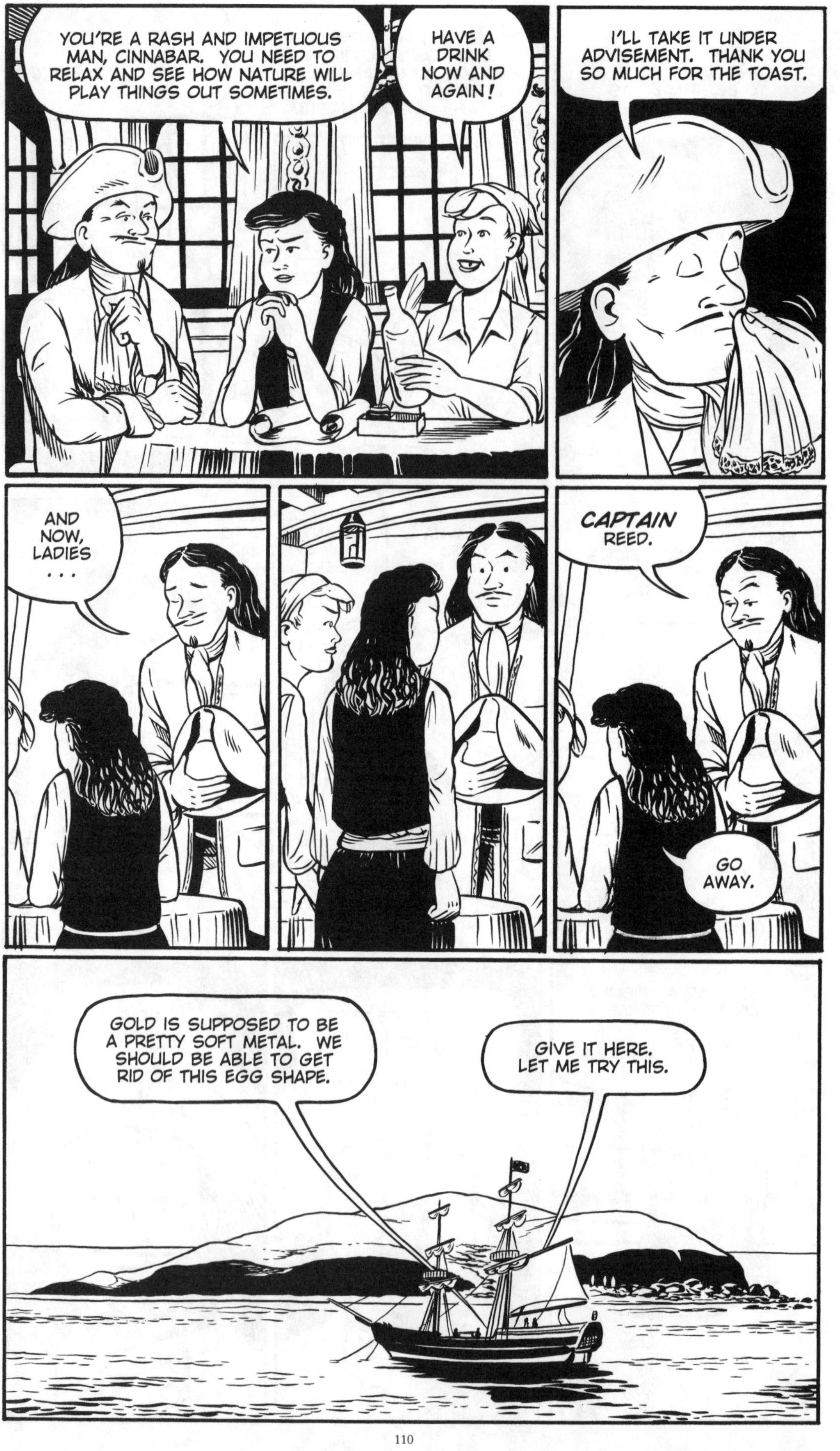
YOU'RE A RASH AND IMPETUOUS MAN, CINNABAR. YOU NEED TO RELAX AND SEE HOW NATURE WILL PLAY THINGS OUT SOMETIMES.
HAVE A DRINK NOW AND AGAIN!
I'LL TAKE IT UNDER ADVISEMENT. THANK YOU SO MUCH FOR THE TOAST.
AND NOW, LADIES . . .
CAPTAIN REED.
GO AWAY.
GOLD IS SUPPOSED TO BE A PRETTY SOFT METAL. WE SHOULD BE ABLE TO GET RID OF THIS EGG SHAPE.
GIVE IT HERE. LET ME TRY THIS.

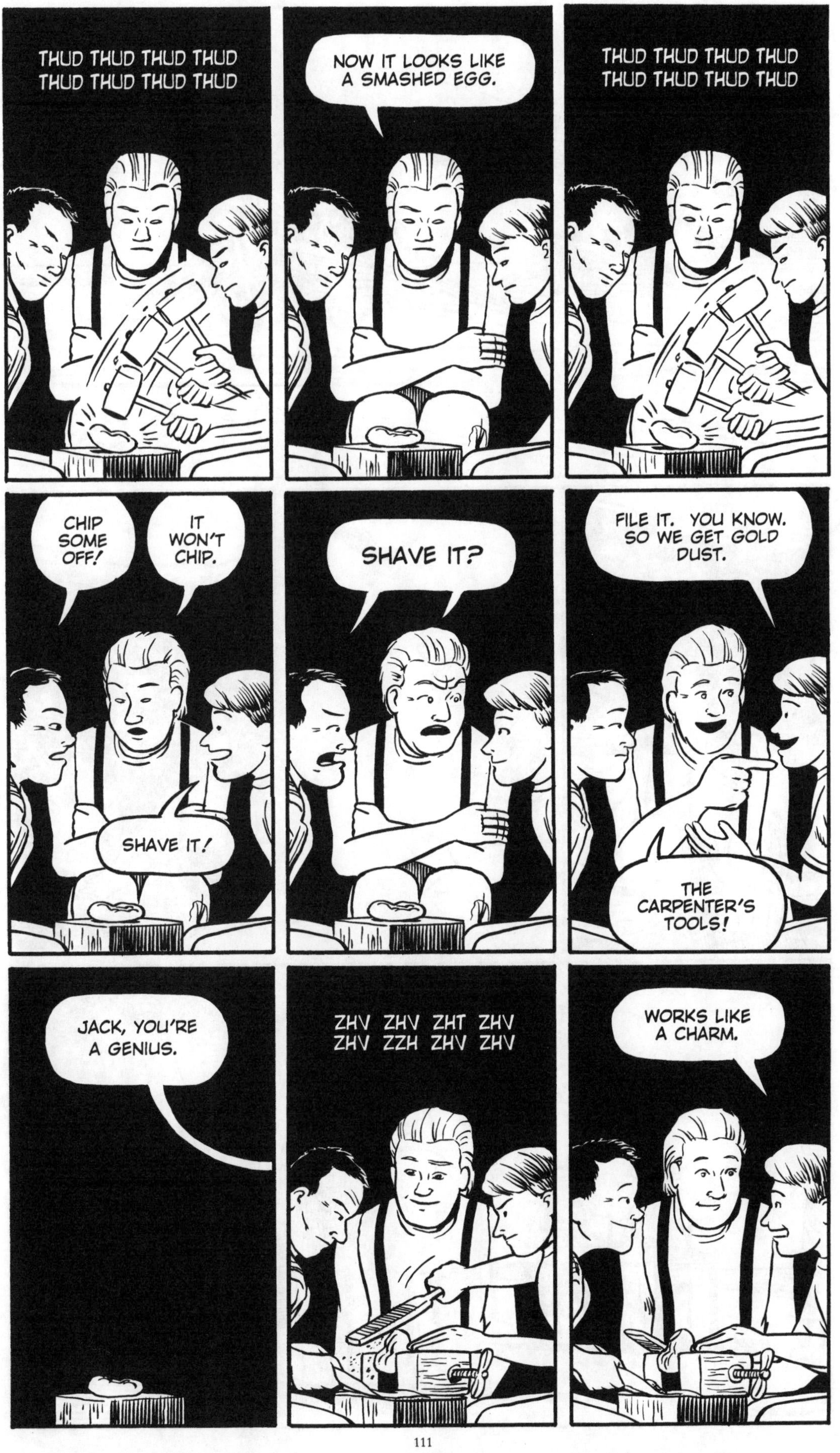
THUD THUD THUD THUD
THUD THUD THUD THUD
NOW IT LOOKS LIKE A SMASHED EGG.
THUD THUD THUD THUD
THUD THUD THUD THUD
CHIP SOME OFF!
IT WON'T CHIP.
SHAVE IT!
SHAVE IT?
FILE IT. YOU KNOW. SO WE GET GOLD DUST.
THE CARPENTER'S TOOLS!
JACK, YOU'RE A GENIUS.
ZHV ZHV ZHT ZHV
ZHV ZZH ZHV ZHV
WORKS LIKE A CHARM.

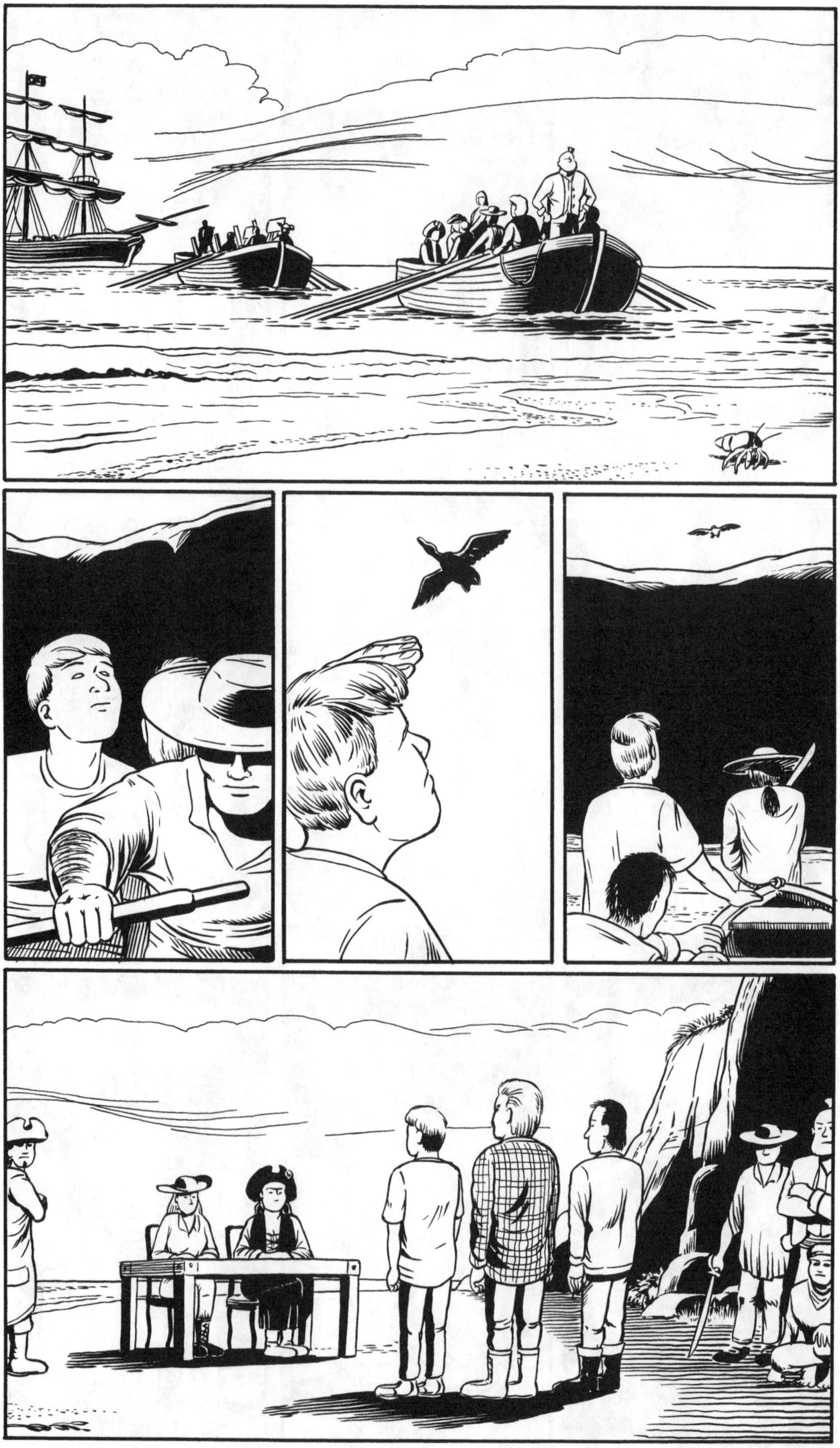

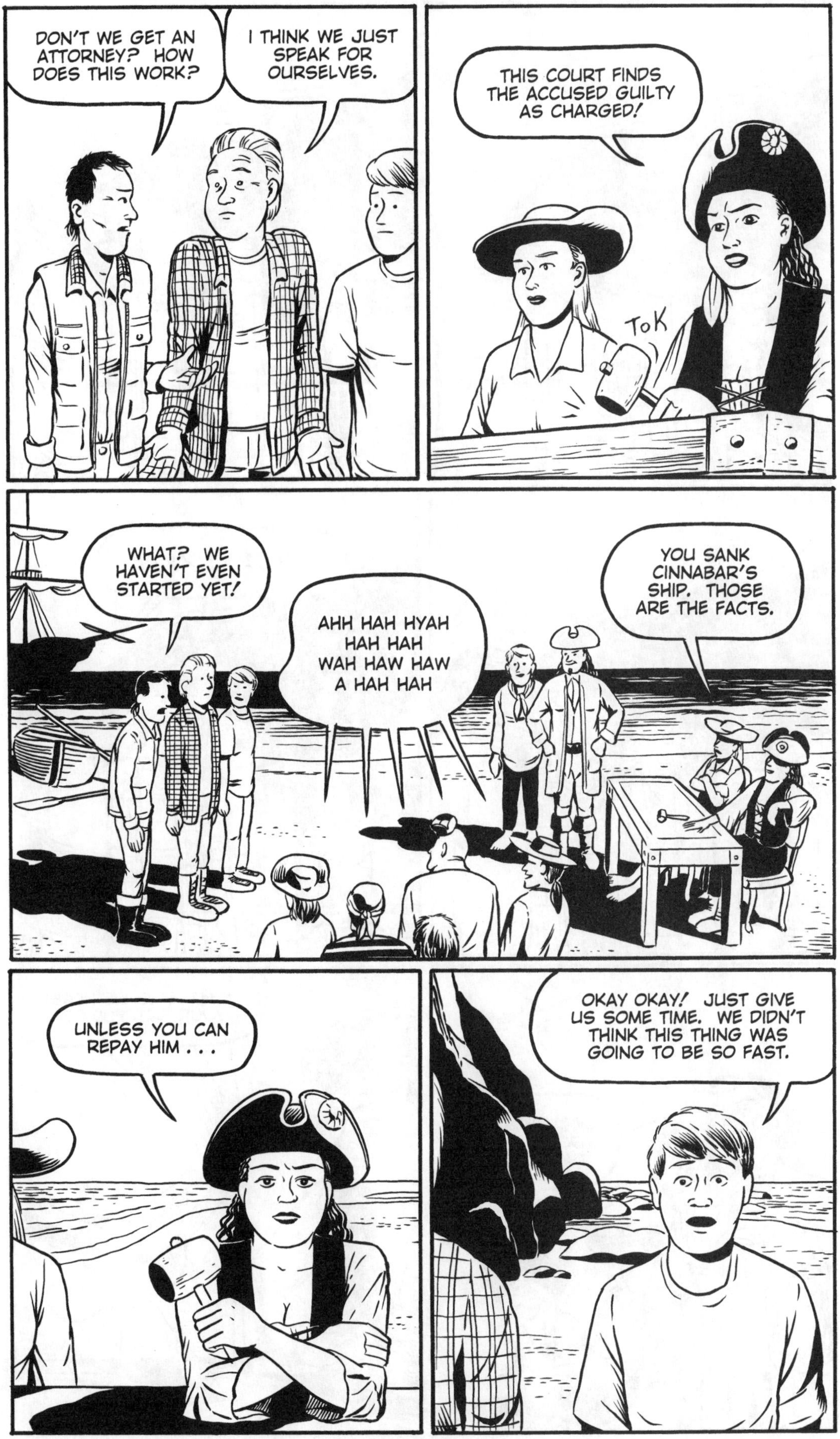
DON'T WE GET AN ATTORNEY? HOW DOES THIS WORK?
I THINK WE JUST SPEAK FOR OURSELVES.
THIS COURT FINDS THE ACCUSED GUILTY AS CHARGED!
TOK
WHAT? WE HAVEN'T EVEN STARTED YET!
AHH HAH HYAH HAH HAH WAH HAW HAW A HAH HAH
YOU SANK CINNABAR'S SHIP. THOSE ARE THE FACTS.
UNLESS YOU CAN REPAY HIM . . .
OKAY OKAY! JUST GIVE US SOME TIME. WE DIDN'T THINK THIS THING WAS GOING TO BE SO FAST.

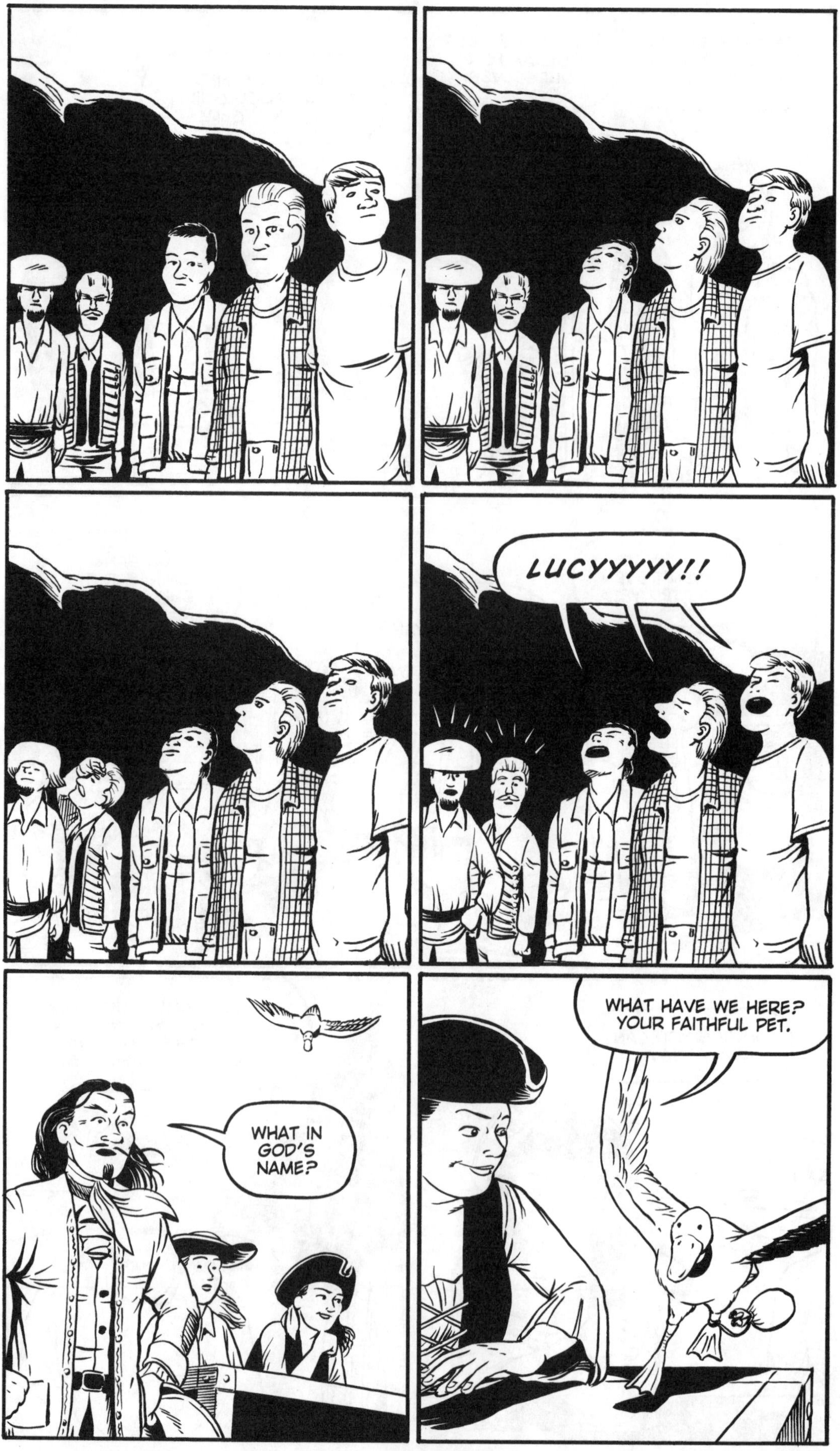
LUCYYYYY!!
WHAT IN GOD'S NAME?
WHAT HAVE WE HERE? YOUR FAITHFUL PET.

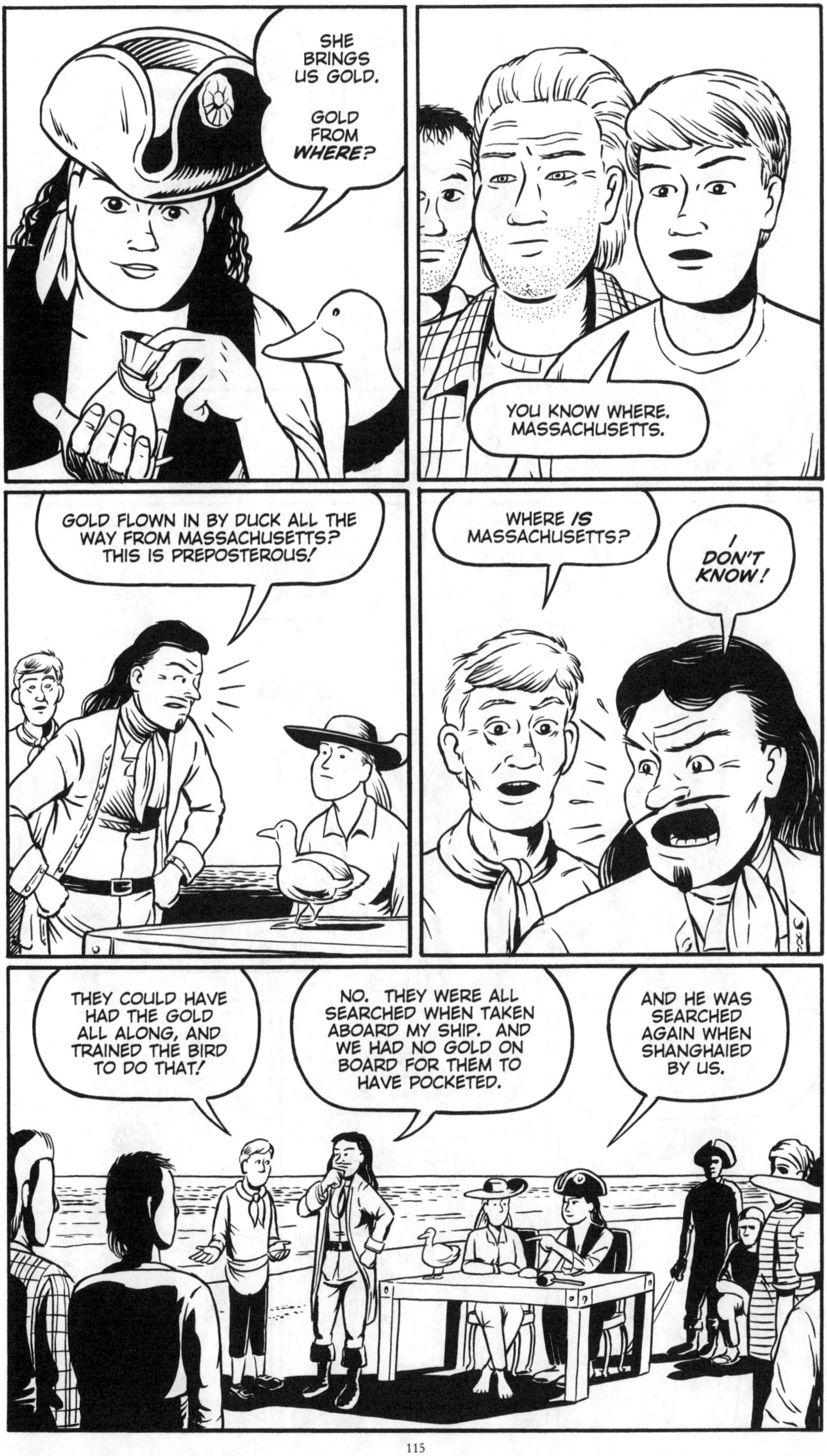
SHE BRINGS US GOLD.
GOLD FROM *WHERE?*
YOU KNOW WHERE. MASSACHUSETTS.
GOLD FLOWN IN BY DUCK ALL THE WAY FROM MASSACHUSETTS? THIS IS PREPOSTEROUS!
WHERE *IS* MASSACHUSETTS?
I DON'T KNOW!
THEY COULD HAVE HAD THE GOLD ALL ALONG, AND TRAINED THE BIRD TO DO THAT!
NO. THEY WERE ALL SEARCHED WHEN TAKEN ABOARD MY SHIP. AND WE HAD NO GOLD ON BOARD FOR THEM TO HAVE POCKETED.
AND HE WAS SEARCHED AGAIN WHEN SHANGHAIED BY US.

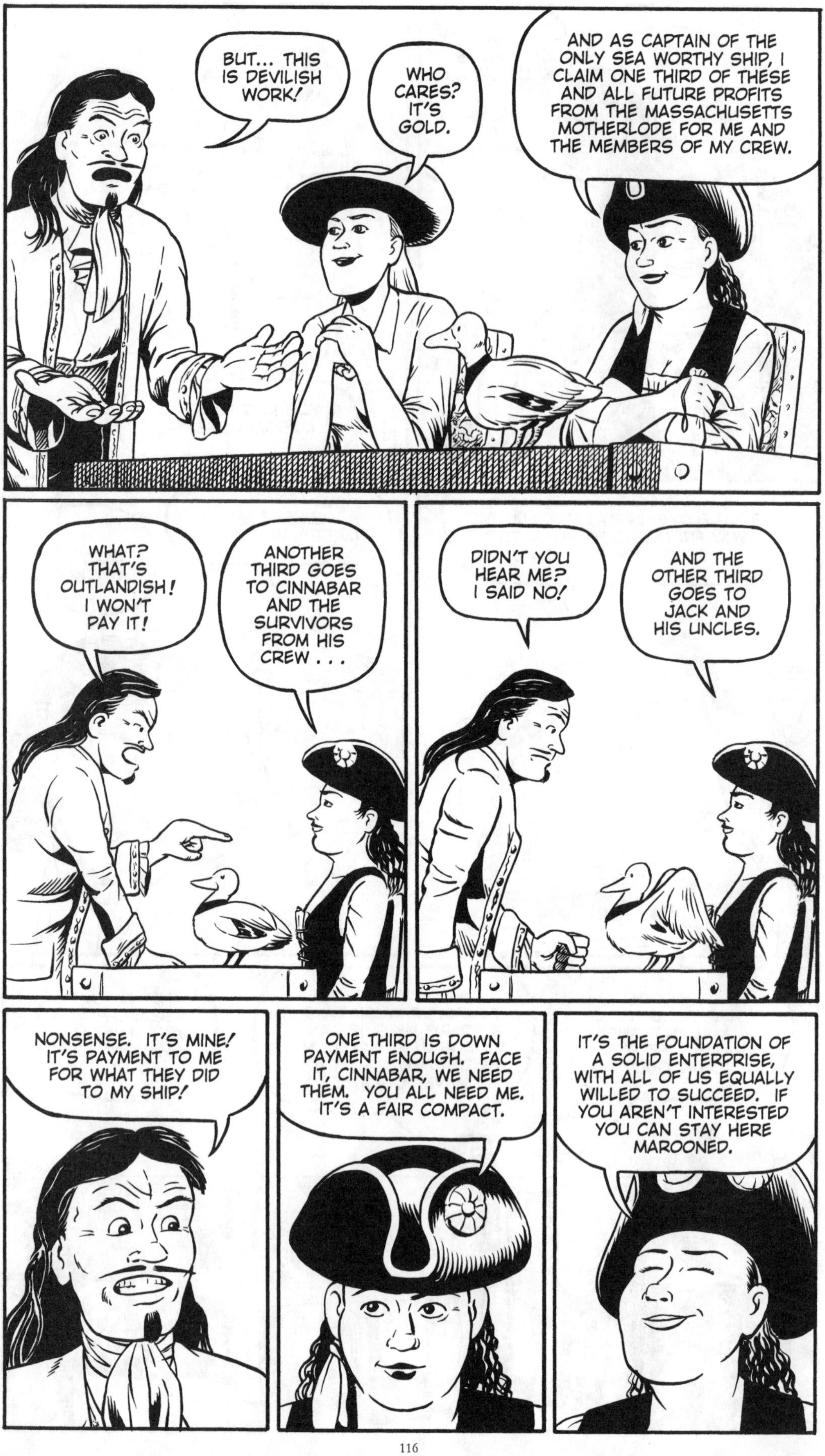
BUT... THIS IS DEVILISH WORK!
WHO CARES? IT'S GOLD.
AND AS CAPTAIN OF THE ONLY SEA WORTHY SHIP, I CLAIM ONE THIRD OF THESE AND ALL FUTURE PROFITS FROM THE MASSACHUSETTS MOTHERLODE FOR ME AND THE MEMBERS OF MY CREW.
WHAT? THAT'S OUTLANDISH! I WON'T PAY IT!
ANOTHER THIRD GOES TO CINNABAR AND THE SURVIVORS FROM HIS CREW . . .
DIDN'T YOU HEAR ME? I SAID NO!
AND THE OTHER THIRD GOES TO JACK AND HIS UNCLES.
NONSENSE. IT'S MINE! IT'S PAYMENT TO ME FOR WHAT THEY DID TO MY SHIP!
ONE THIRD IS DOWN PAYMENT ENOUGH. FACE IT, CINNABAR, WE NEED THEM. YOU ALL NEED ME. IT'S A FAIR COMPACT.
IT'S THE FOUNDATION OF A SOLID ENTERPRISE, WITH ALL OF US EQUALLY WILLED TO SUCCEED. IF YOU AREN'T INTERESTED YOU CAN STAY HERE MAROONED.

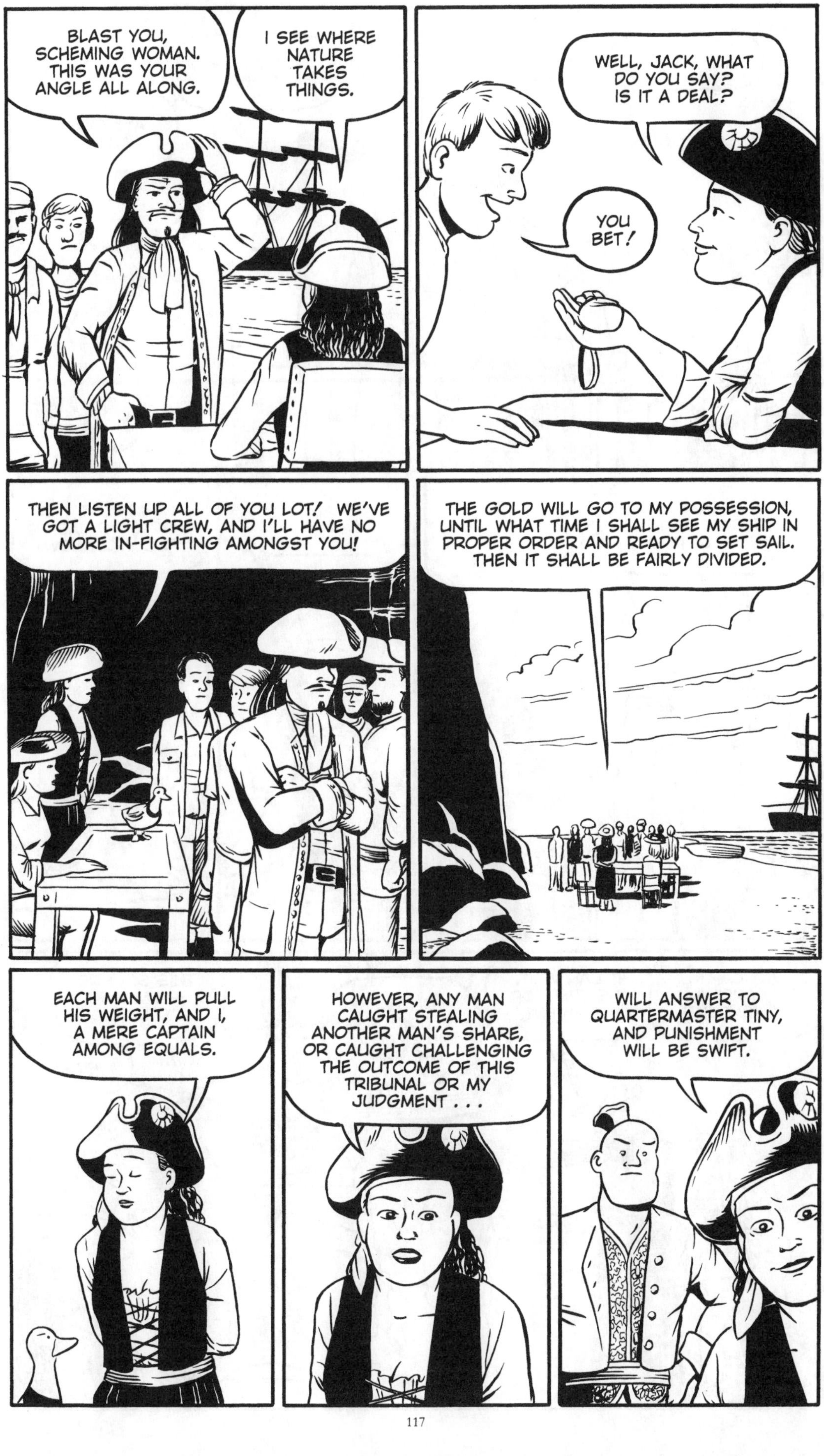
BLAST YOU, SCHEMING WOMAN. THIS WAS YOUR ANGLE ALL ALONG.
I SEE WHERE NATURE TAKES THINGS.
WELL, JACK, WHAT DO YOU SAY? IS IT A DEAL?
YOU BET!
THEN LISTEN UP ALL OF YOU LOT! WE'VE GOT A LIGHT CREW, AND I'LL HAVE NO MORE IN-FIGHTING AMONGST YOU!
THE GOLD WILL GO TO MY POSSESSION, UNTIL WHAT TIME I SHALL SEE MY SHIP IN PROPER ORDER AND READY TO SET SAIL. THEN IT SHALL BE FAIRLY DIVIDED.
EACH MAN WILL PULL HIS WEIGHT, AND I, A MERE CAPTAIN AMONG EQUALS.
HOWEVER, ANY MAN CAUGHT STEALING ANOTHER MAN'S SHARE, OR CAUGHT CHALLENGING THE OUTCOME OF THIS TRIBUNAL OR MY JUDGMENT . . .
WILL ANSWER TO QUARTERMASTER TINY, AND PUNISHMENT WILL BE SWIFT.

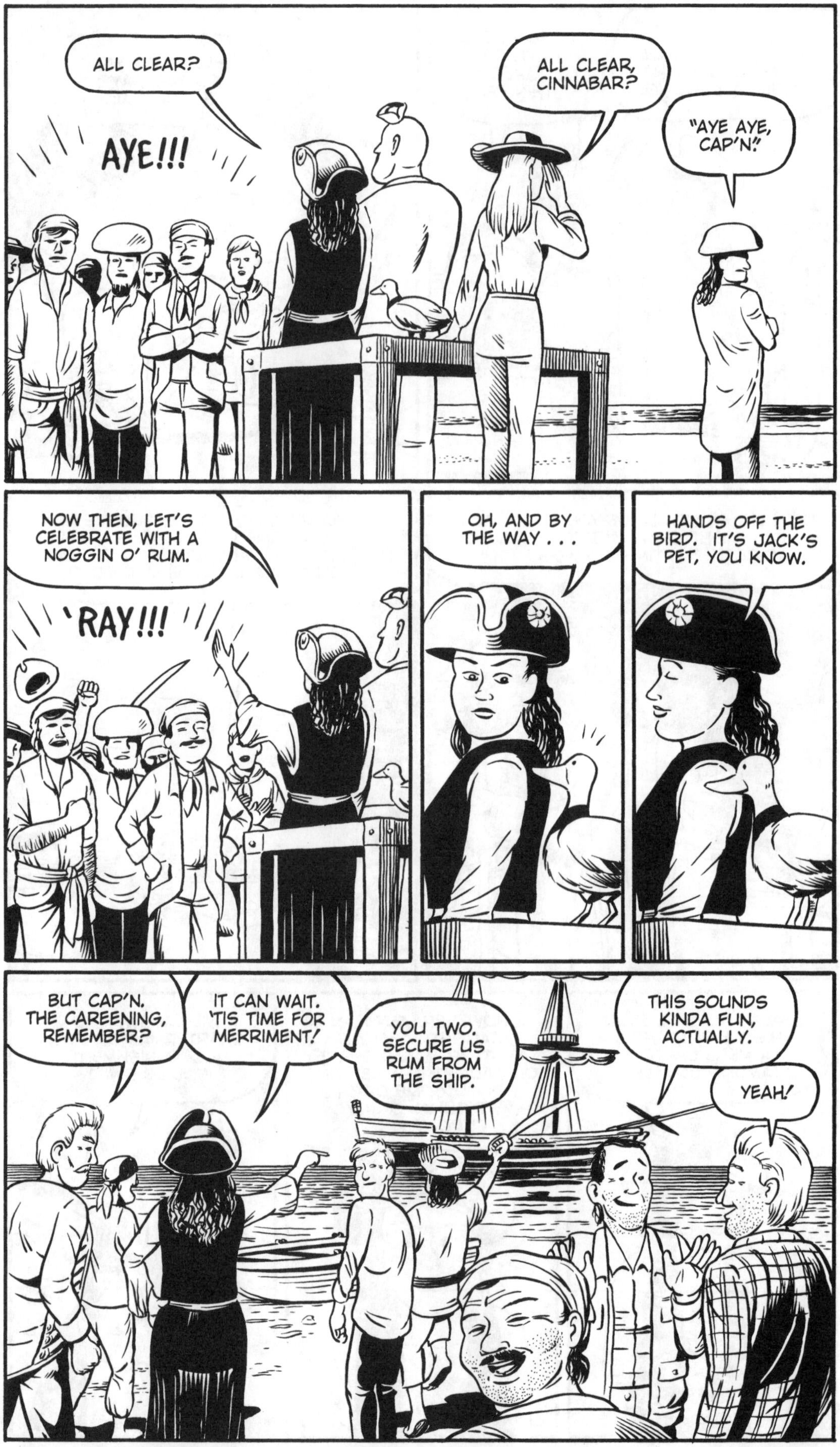
ALL CLEAR?
AYE!!!
ALL CLEAR, CINNABAR?
"AYE AYE, CAP'N."
NOW THEN, LET'S CELEBRATE WITH A NOGGIN O' RUM.
'RAY!!!
OH, AND BY THE WAY . . .
HANDS OFF THE BIRD. IT'S JACK'S PET, YOU KNOW.
BUT CAP'N. THE CAREENING, REMEMBER?
IT CAN WAIT. 'TIS TIME FOR MERRIMENT!
YOU TWO. SECURE US RUM FROM THE SHIP.
THIS SOUNDS KINDA FUN, ACTUALLY.
YEAH!

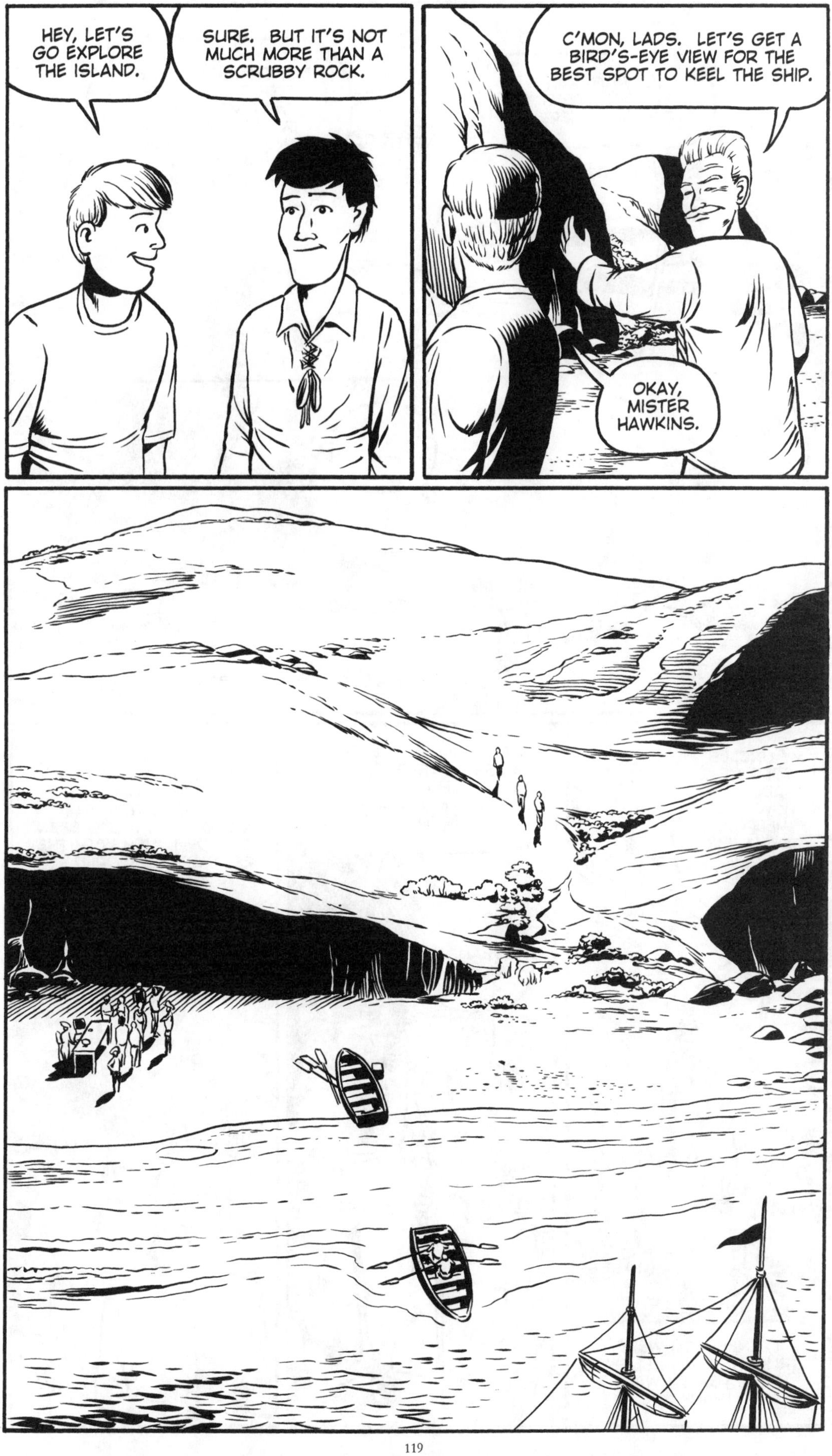
HEY, LET'S GO EXPLORE THE ISLAND.
SURE. BUT IT'S NOT MUCH MORE THAN A SCRUBBY ROCK.
C'MON, LADS. LET'S GET A BIRD'S-EYE VIEW FOR THE BEST SPOT TO KEEL THE SHIP.
OKAY, MISTER HAWKINS.

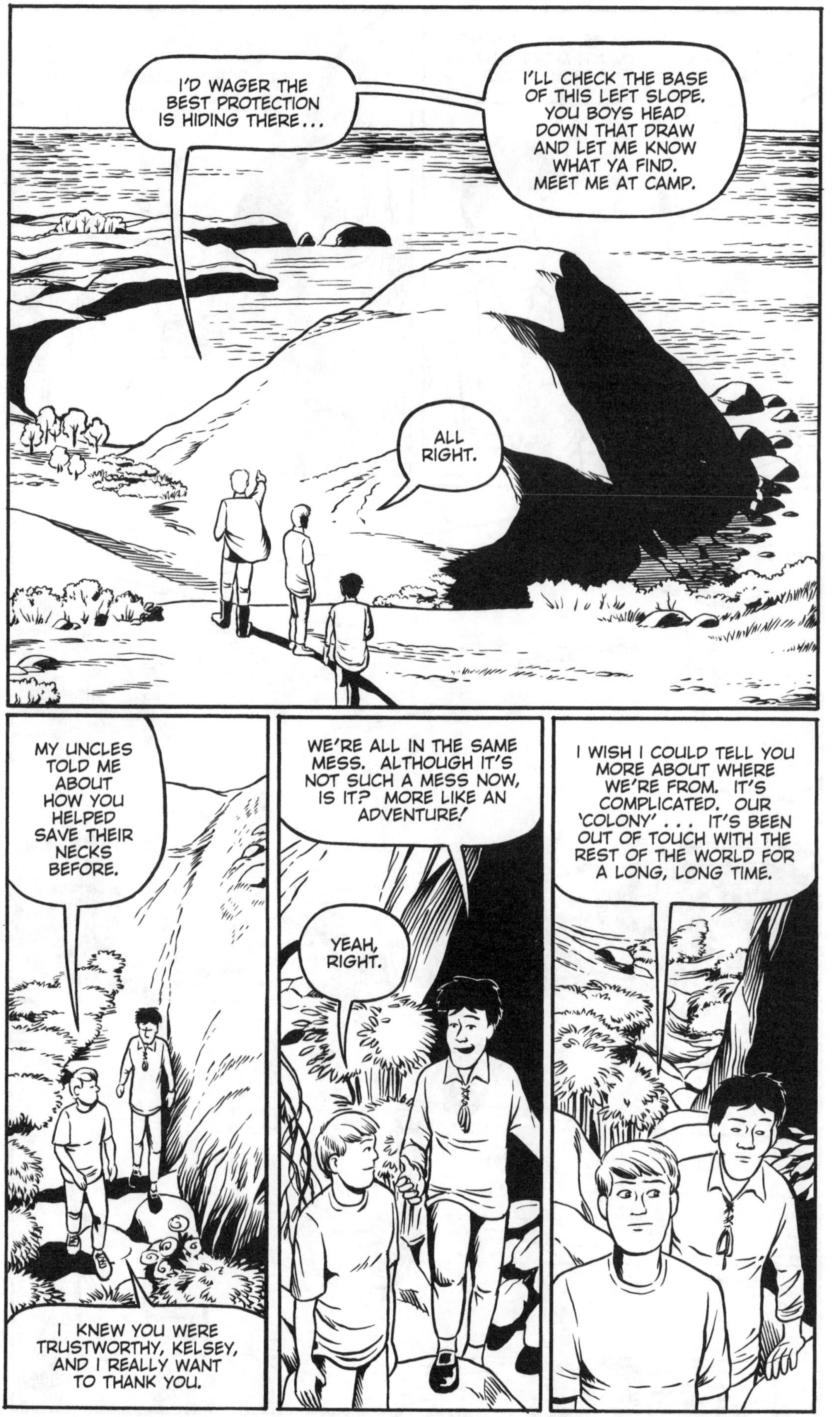
I'D WAGER THE BEST PROTECTION IS HIDING THERE...
I'LL CHECK THE BASE OF THIS LEFT SLOPE. YOU BOYS HEAD DOWN THAT DRAW AND LET ME KNOW WHAT YA FIND. MEET ME AT CAMP.
ALL RIGHT.
MY UNCLES TOLD ME ABOUT HOW YOU HELPED SAVE THEIR NECKS BEFORE.
I KNEW YOU WERE TRUSTWORTHY, KELSEY, AND I REALLY WANT TO THANK YOU.
WE'RE ALL IN THE SAME MESS. ALTHOUGH IT'S NOT SUCH A MESS NOW, IS IT? MORE LIKE AN ADVENTURE!
YEAH, RIGHT.
I WISH I COULD TELL YOU MORE ABOUT WHERE WE'RE FROM. IT'S COMPLICATED. OUR 'COLONY' . . . IT'S BEEN OUT OF TOUCH WITH THE REST OF THE WORLD FOR A LONG, LONG TIME.

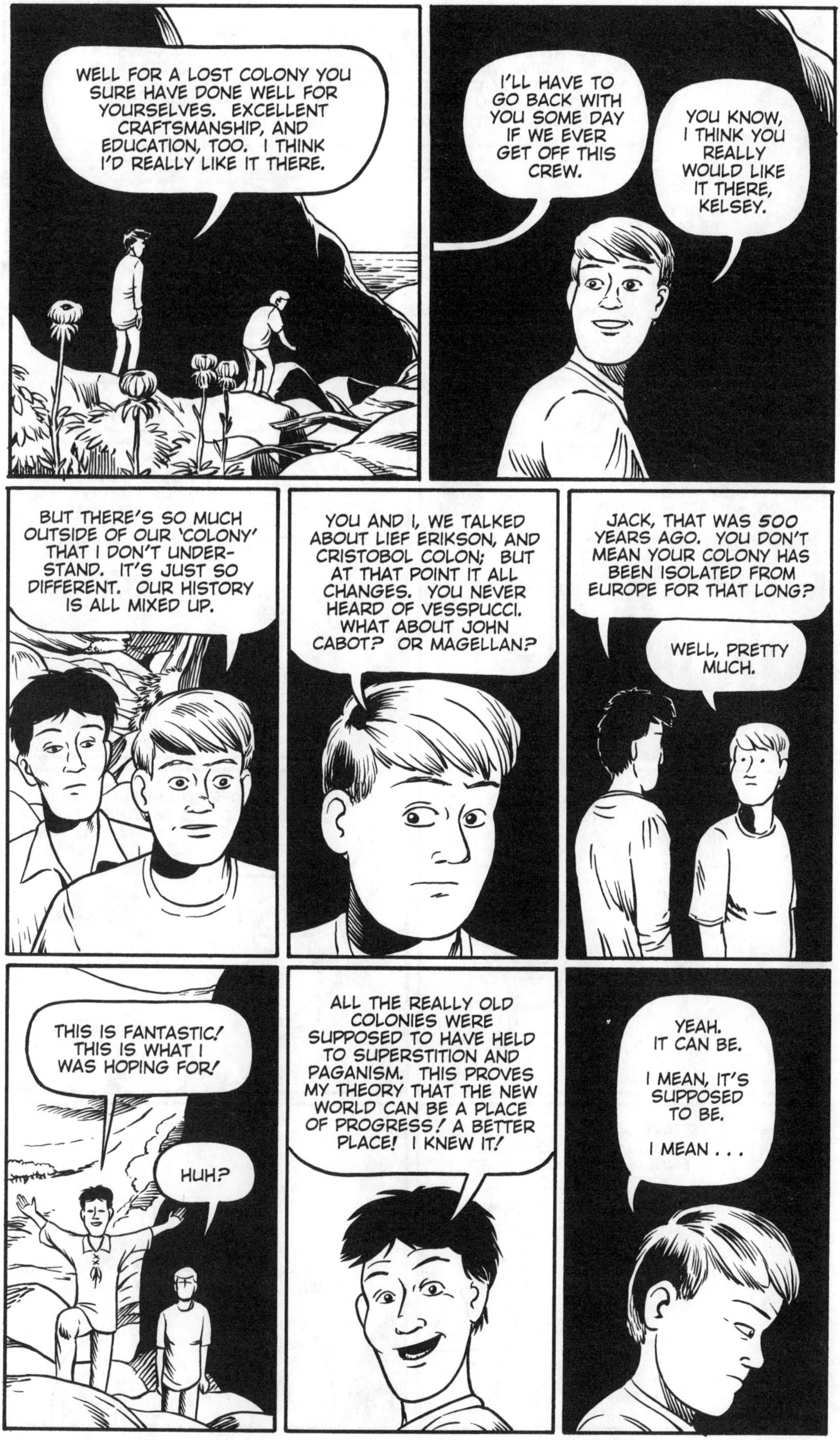
WELL FOR A LOST COLONY YOU SURE HAVE DONE WELL FOR YOURSELVES. EXCELLENT CRAFTSMANSHIP, AND EDUCATION, TOO. I THINK I'D REALLY LIKE IT THERE.
I'LL HAVE TO GO BACK WITH YOU SOME DAY IF WE EVER GET OFF THIS CREW.
YOU KNOW, I THINK YOU REALLY WOULD LIKE IT THERE, KELSEY.
BUT THERE'S SO MUCH OUTSIDE OF OUR 'COLONY' THAT I DON'T UNDER-STAND. IT'S JUST SO DIFFERENT. OUR HISTORY IS ALL MIXED UP.
YOU AND I, WE TALKED ABOUT LIEF ERIKSON, AND CRISTOBOL COLON; BUT AT THAT POINT IT ALL CHANGES. YOU NEVER HEARD OF VESSPUCCI. WHAT ABOUT JOHN CABOT? OR MAGELLAN?
JACK, THAT WAS 500 YEARS AGO. YOU DON'T MEAN YOUR COLONY HAS BEEN ISOLATED FROM EUROPE FOR THAT LONG?
WELL, PRETTY MUCH.
THIS IS FANTASTIC! THIS IS WHAT I WAS HOPING FOR!
HUH?
ALL THE REALLY OLD COLONIES WERE SUPPOSED TO HAVE HELD TO SUPERSTITION AND PAGANISM. THIS PROVES MY THEORY THAT THE NEW WORLD CAN BE A PLACE OF PROGRESS! A BETTER PLACE! I KNEW IT!
YEAH. IT CAN BE.
I MEAN, IT'S SUPPOSED TO BE.
I MEAN . . .

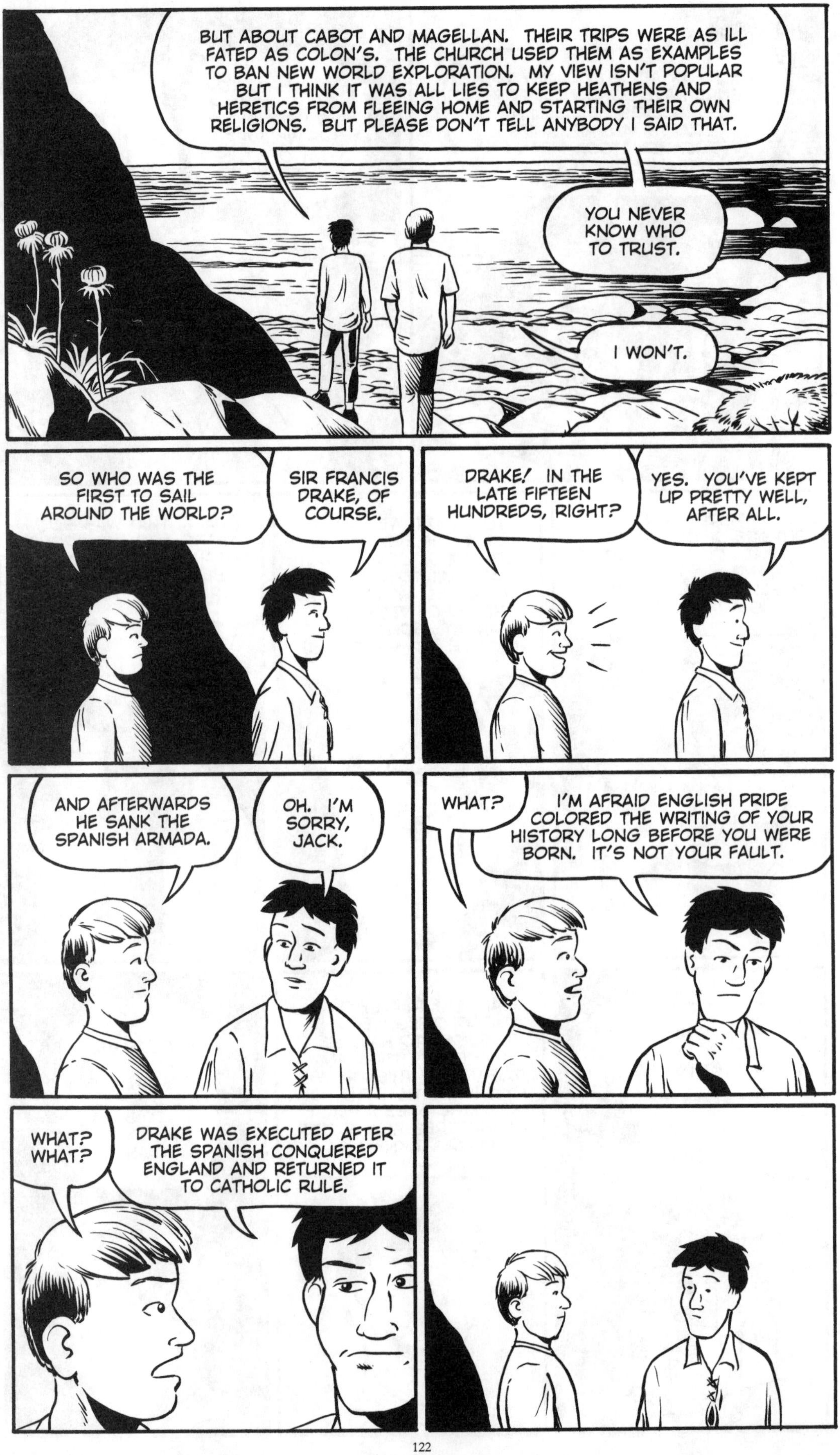

BUT ABOUT CABOT AND MAGELLAN. THEIR TRIPS WERE AS ILL FATED AS COLON'S. THE CHURCH USED THEM AS EXAMPLES TO BAN NEW WORLD EXPLORATION. MY VIEW ISN'T POPULAR BUT I THINK IT WAS ALL LIES TO KEEP HEATHENS AND HERETICS FROM FLEEING HOME AND STARTING THEIR OWN RELIGIONS. BUT PLEASE DON'T TELL ANYBODY I SAID THAT.
YOU NEVER KNOW WHO TO TRUST.
I WON'T.
SO WHO WAS THE FIRST TO SAIL AROUND THE WORLD?
SIR FRANCIS DRAKE, OF COURSE.
DRAKE! IN THE LATE FIFTEEN HUNDREDS, RIGHT?
YES. YOU'VE KEPT UP PRETTY WELL, AFTER ALL.
AND AFTERWARDS HE SANK THE SPANISH ARMADA.
OH. I'M SORRY, JACK.
WHAT?
I'M AFRAID ENGLISH PRIDE COLORED THE WRITING OF YOUR HISTORY LONG BEFORE YOU WERE BORN. IT'S NOT YOUR FAULT.
WHAT? WHAT?
DRAKE WAS EXECUTED AFTER THE SPANISH CONQUERED ENGLAND AND RETURNED IT TO CATHOLIC RULE.

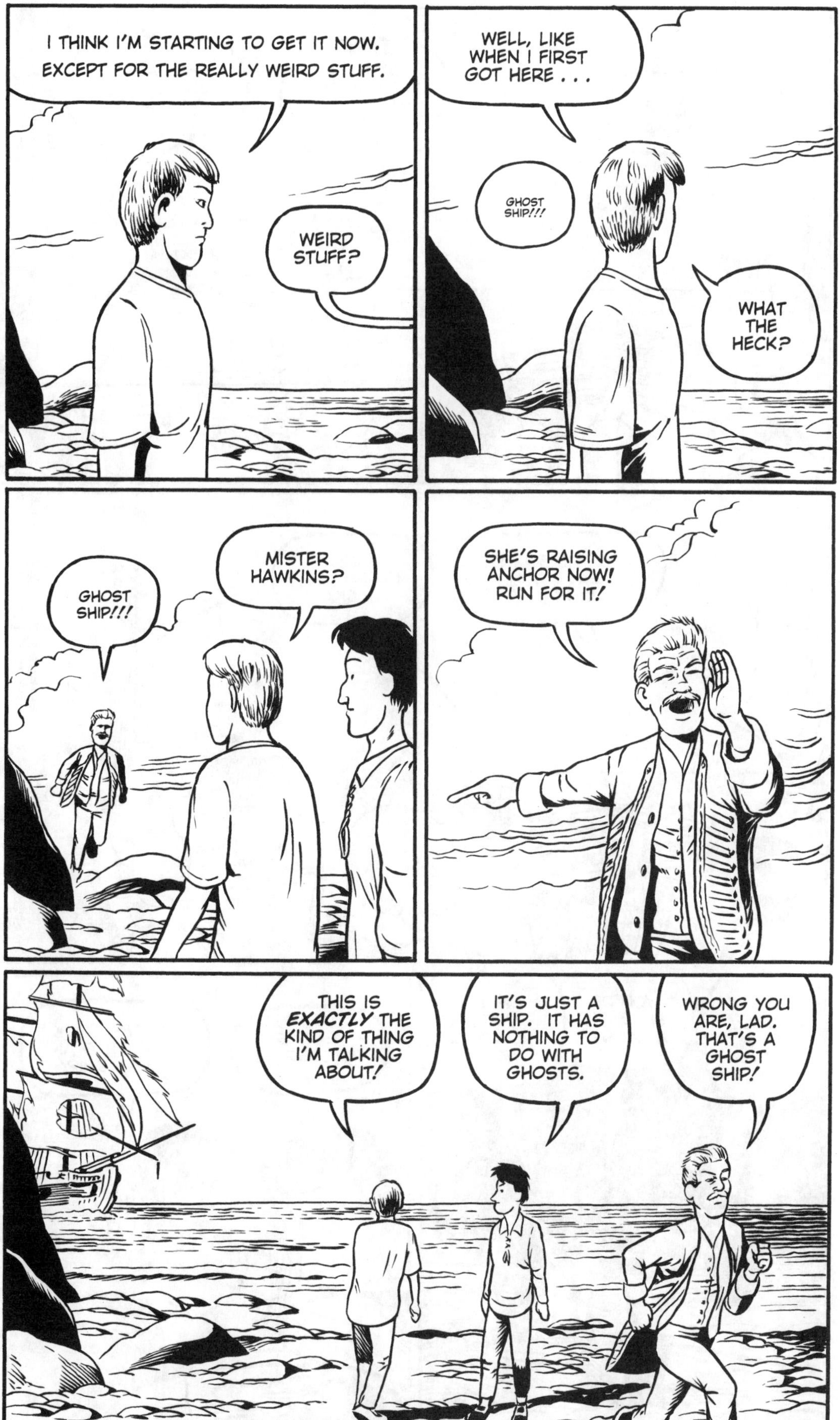
I THINK I'M STARTING TO GET IT NOW. EXCEPT FOR THE REALLY WEIRD STUFF.
WEIRD STUFF?
WELL, LIKE WHEN I FIRST GOT HERE . . .
GHOST SHIP!!!
WHAT THE HECK?
GHOST SHIP!!!
MISTER HAWKINS?
SHE'S RAISING ANCHOR NOW! RUN FOR IT!
THIS IS EXACTLY THE KIND OF THING I'M TALKING ABOUT!
IT'S JUST A SHIP. IT HAS NOTHING TO DO WITH GHOSTS.
WRONG YOU ARE, LAD. THAT'S A GHOST SHIP!

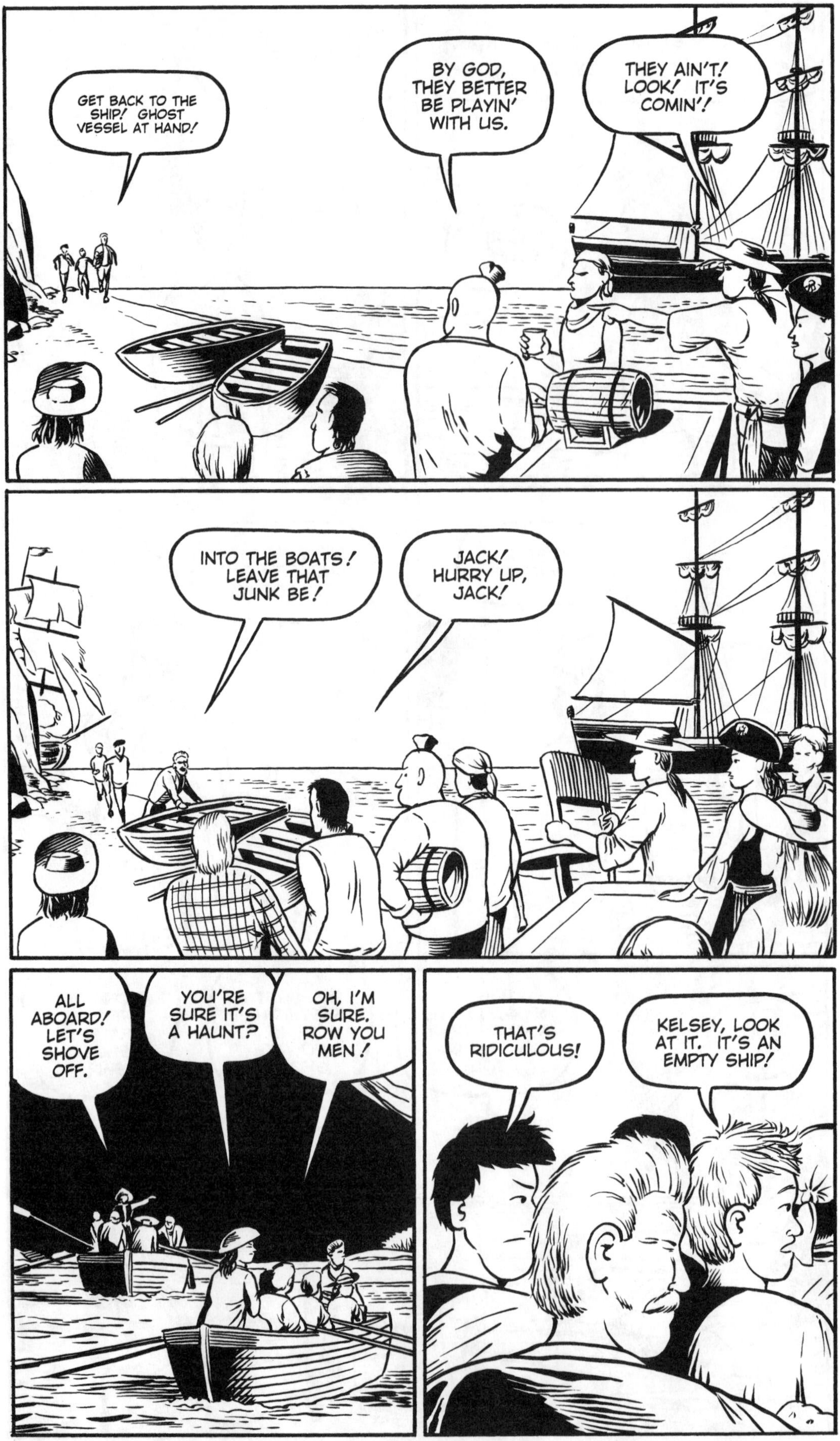
GET BACK TO THE SHIP! GHOST VESSEL AT HAND!
BY GOD, THEY BETTER BE PLAYIN' WITH US.
THEY AIN'T! LOOK! IT'S COMIN'!
INTO THE BOATS! LEAVE THAT JUNK BE!
JACK! HURRY UP, JACK!
ALL ABOARD! LET'S SHOVE OFF.
YOU'RE SURE IT'S A HAUNT?
OH, I'M SURE. ROW YOU MEN!
THAT'S RIDICULOUS!
KELSEY, LOOK AT IT. IT'S AN EMPTY SHIP!

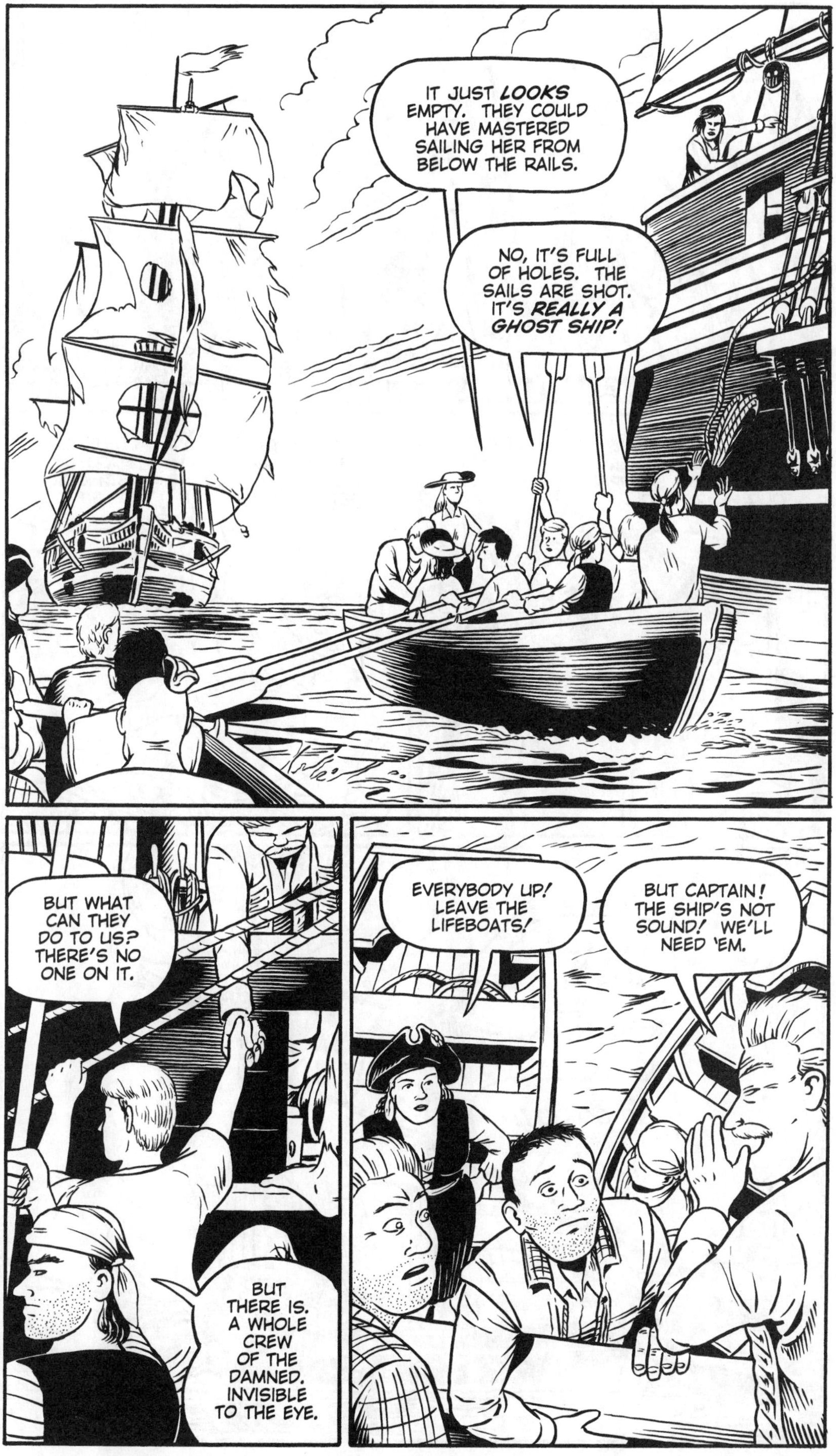

IT JUST LOOKS EMPTY. THEY COULD HAVE MASTERED SAILING HER FROM BELOW THE RAILS.
NO, IT'S FULL OF HOLES. THE SAILS ARE SHOT. IT'S REALLY A GHOST SHIP!
BUT WHAT CAN THEY DO TO US? THERE'S NO ONE ON IT.
BUT THERE IS. A WHOLE CREW OF THE DAMNED. INVISIBLE TO THE EYE.
EVERYBODY UP! LEAVE THE LIFEBOATS!
BUT CAPTAIN! THE SHIP'S NOT SOUND! WE'LL NEED 'EM.

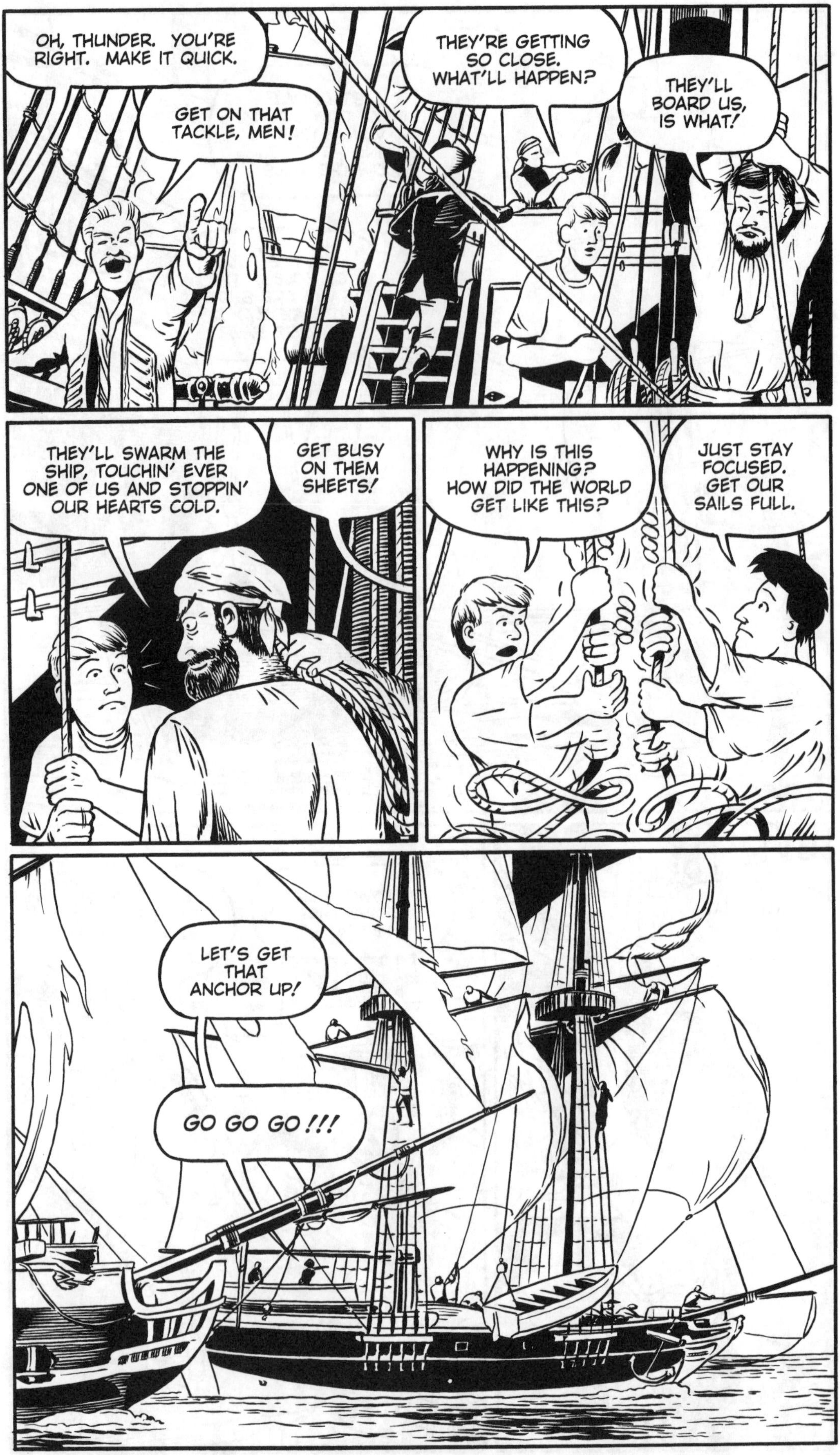
OH, THUNDER. YOU'RE RIGHT. MAKE IT QUICK.
GET ON THAT TACKLE, MEN!
THEY'RE GETTING SO CLOSE. WHAT'LL HAPPEN?
THEY'LL BOARD US, IS WHAT!
THEY'LL SWARM THE SHIP, TOUCHIN' EVER ONE OF US AND STOPPIN' OUR HEARTS COLD.
GET BUSY ON THEM SHEETS!
WHY IS THIS HAPPENING? HOW DID THE WORLD GET LIKE THIS?
JUST STAY FOCUSED. GET OUR SAILS FULL.
LET'S GET THAT ANCHOR UP!
GO GO GO!!!

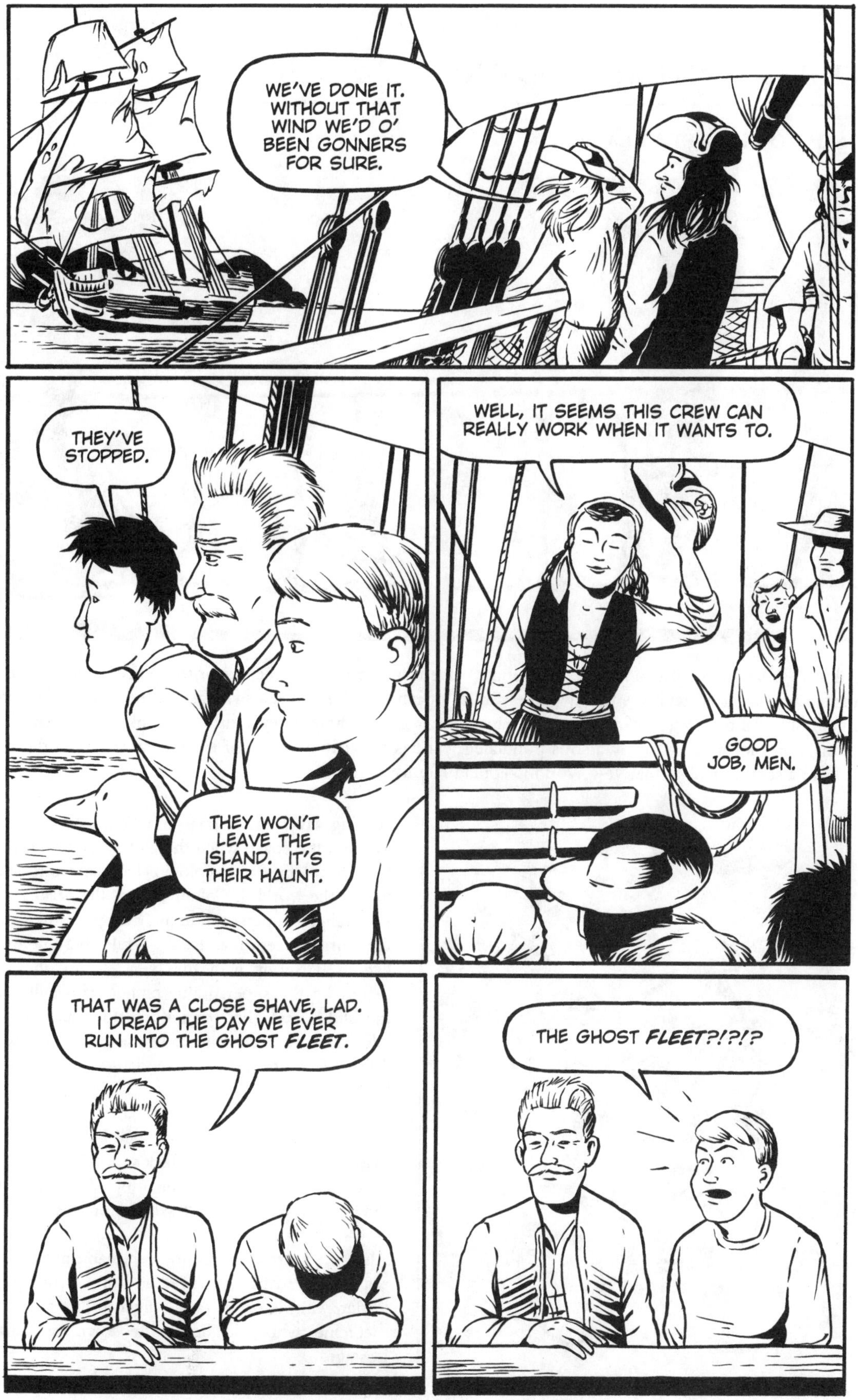
WE'VE DONE IT. WITHOUT THAT WIND WE'D O' BEEN GONNERS FOR SURE.
THEY'VE STOPPED.
THEY WON'T LEAVE THE ISLAND. IT'S THEIR HAUNT.
WELL, IT SEEMS THIS CREW CAN REALLY WORK WHEN IT WANTS TO.
GOOD JOB, MEN.
THAT WAS A CLOSE SHAVE, LAD. I DREAD THE DAY WE EVER RUN INTO THE GHOST *FLEET*.
THE GHOST *FLEET?!?!?*

NEXT: NOT THE GHOST FLEET

THE ADVENTURE CONTINUES...

ON INTO THE GREAT LANDS

Colonia #6 begins a fresh story arc. After many adventures in the Caribbean, our troop heads inland after a mishap at sea. Faced with seemingly endless miles of inhospitable Florida swampland, they are victims of a cruel irony. All of the water is tainted, perhaps by magic, and there is not a drop to drink. Their trek takes them to an old Spanish fort, which is populated, yet has no visible means of entry. The secret to the fort unlocks a secret to all of the New World Colonian Hemisphere.

Seeking civilization, Jack and company press on towards the coast, when they meet Sally, who hails from a nearby Pagan colony. Jack comes to learn that in the world of Colonia, it was the pagans who fled religious persecution in Europe rather than the Puritans centuries later. While these colonies live in harmony with the New World, they are feared by the superstitious pirates who hail from the Old World. Far from a dull ride, this two-part tales continues in issue 8, where Sally's ability to "slip-slide" are given a sudden and dangerous boost.

Further down the road, there will be a quest for a man, supposedly from Jack's world, with the ominous name of "Rip Van Winkle." Prepare for the greatest plot twist of the series on this one.

Also, the search to procure a ship and put back to sea is delayed by an injured and murderous pirate leader, who demands Jack deliver to him a chest of medicine while he holds the town of Cartier hostage.

THE INFORMAL BOOK REVIEW

The Conquest of Paradise
Christopher Columbus
and the Columbian Legacy
Kirkpatrick Sale
Knopf (No ISBN)

This is the book that really planted the seed for Colonia. I read it in 1993 and was completely captivated with it. After deciding I wanted to do a fantasy series set in the New World, com-plete with New World folklore, I remembered a legend about Spanish Ghosts who had been driven mad looking for gold (and tipped their heads along with their hats) and just had to read it again.

Although there are a few anecdotal legends like this in *Conquest*, the essence of the book is that it debunks all of the history we learned in school about the discovery. It's amazing how much of it is just flat-out wrong. I won't give anything away, because the surprise is half the fun, but I will tease you with one of the more intriguing questions: Did Columbus die never knowing he had discovered the New World? Well, he did and he didn't. Find out why for yourself if you have a chance to read it. There's some clever maps that help illustrate this paradox, too.

Also of interest is the portrait of Columbus as Colonial Governor in the decades following the voyages. These truly tragic colonies are something we hear little about in school. In fact, we seem to jump all the way from the discovery to Jamestown in history class, don't we? I think this is why I find that period of history in between so interesting, because it is so obscure. As this book's title suggests, it chronicles Columbus' legacy beyond his natural years on into the next few centuries.

Do beware the author's bias towards Native Americans as a superior culture. I think he paints much too utopian a picture of native society and much too grim a picture of medieval Europe. He inserts this agenda of his into the book so continuously that it really become tiresome after a while. I think you could find a few pitfalls about living in a stone age society but he seems to find none.

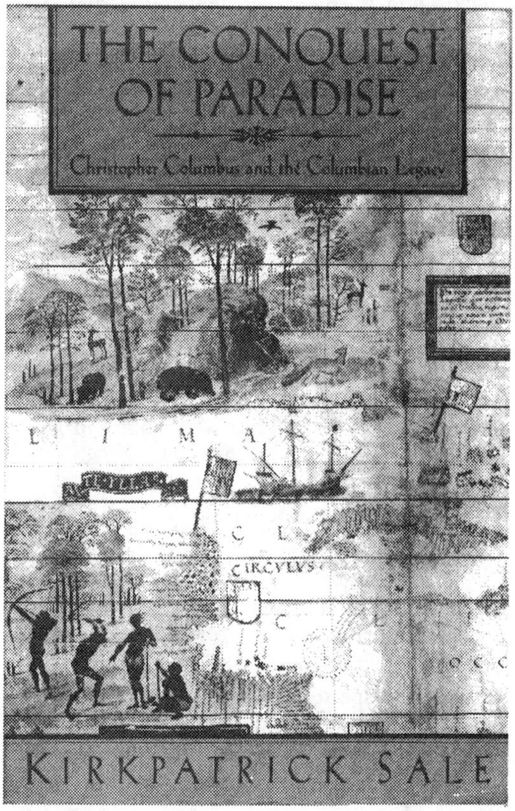
THE CONQUEST OF PARADISE
Christopher Columbus and the Columbian Legacy
KIRKPATRICK SALE

A big part of the attraction in reading about the Columbian discovery (aside from the fact that it began the greatest cultural migration in world history) is that the historical evidence is almost in our hands but not quite. The event is not completely lost to history, but not fully documented either. Columbus kept a log which survived the journeys, something I never knew. His own bias and personal agendas shaped the facts within them, and they were recopied and translated more than once before reaching us (the originals are long gone), and so the whole subject is rife with controversy among historians. Once you get pulled in you will start making your own speculations.

Graphic ©1990 Knopf

For your amusement . . . Which ship is Cinnabar's vessel modeled after?

FROM THE REFERENCE LIBRARY

Once upon a time I had the notion that if you could draw "good enough" you didn't need to look at the world around you anymore. I used reference occasionally but for the most part it was just me and the pencil. I started to realize just how much I wasn't truly drawing any-more. I was just repeating my inner bag of tricks rather than looking, translating, exploring, erasing(!), all the things drawing should be. My artwork started to go downhill when it should have been getting better with age. I think this happens to a lot of artists, unfortunately. So when I started *Colonia* I decided it was time to get back to basics. Soon after, I discovered the joy of collecting reference and building a little library as a hobby in and of itself.

Dover Coloring Book Series

Those of you familiar with these know what a great historical reference tool they are. They seem quite accurate, especially in their por-trayal of costumes. Sometimes the drawings are sub-par, but the sparse line style is more informative than old engraving reproductions found in other reference volumes. *Early American Crafts and Occupations*, *Knights and Armor*, *Old Fashioned Farm Life* . . . there's quite a variety to be had. I picked up *Shipwrecks and Sunken Treasures* and *North American Ducks Geese and Swans* for this series for three bucks apiece new.

Concise Illustrator's Reference Series

These figure drawing books are among my favorites because they have several figures per page, all multiple angles of the same pose. It's in color, but the saturation is muted, letting the grey tones of the photographs portray the contours. I found this and many others at Half Price Books so happy hunting.

For your amusement . . .
Does the "set" look familiar in the scenes at Captain Reed's table? Which famous movie co-starring a rather young John Carradine is it taken from?

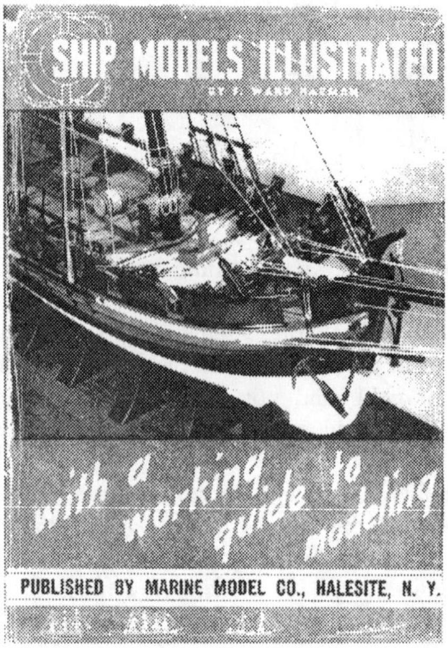
SHIP MODELS ILLUSTRATED
with a working guide to modeling
PUBLISHED BY MARINE MODEL CO., HALESITE, N. Y.

Ship Models Illustrated
F. Ward Harman
Marine Model Company (no ISBN) 1943

While looking for books on ships I stumbled on this book of ship models. What a perfect reference! Written and illustrated by a little chap who loves to build little ships (not in bottles). One of them was even presented to President Roosevelt. So now I know what the heck a windlass is (I think). My copy is a 7th printing so it was obviously loved by many.

Graphic ©1943 Marine Model Company.

Western Garden Book
ISBN: 0-376-03851-9

This is pricey at $30 but I had already picked up a copy for work when I was a gardener. If you ever get stuck on variation in flora, crack open this and you will have more than enough to get you going. Out of date volumes can be had for cheap at used book stores, but they lack the extensive color photo section and the front of the new edition.

A tip A tip o' the hat to the Orkney Web Site at Stowrie.demon.co.uk

Log of the Centurion
Based on the original papers of Captain Philip Saumarez on board HMS Centurion, Lord Anson's flagship during his circumnavigation 1740-1744
Leo Heaps, Macmillan (No ISBN) 1974

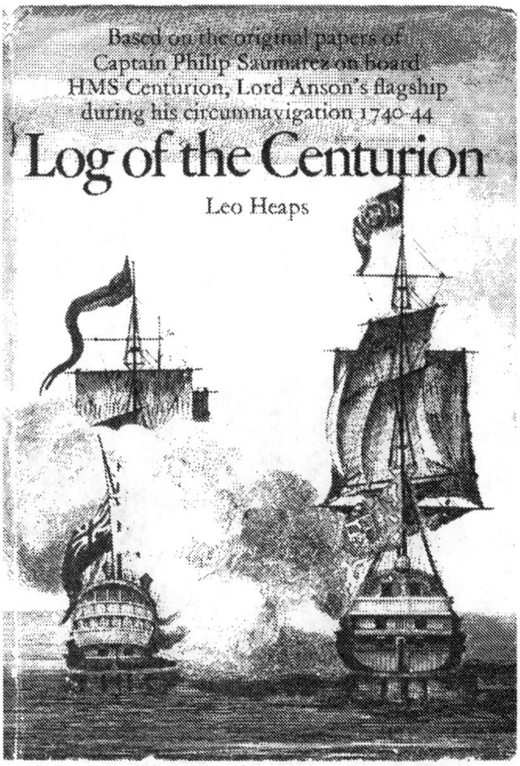
Based on the original papers of
Captain Philip Saumarez on board
HMS Centurion, Lord Anson's flagship
during his circumnavigation 1740-44
Log of the Centurion
Leo Heaps

It was with very happy luck that I discovered this book. Back when I was just daydreaming about what Colonia was going to be I was taken with the idea of building my own little reference library. The hunt for used book stores led me to a local public library outlet store where old books are put out to pasture. This one was sitting right out front and center beaming with joy that a cartoonist who wanted to make a pirate comic had just walked in.

I wanted a feel for life at sea and this is the real thing. The first thing you notice is the regular-ity and casual nature of deaths reported in the log. One entry reads, "George Ramsey seaman, Francis Sullivan and George Ruth soldiers departed this life." And four men had died the day before and two died the day after.

The Centurion was a military ship commis-sioned by the crown of England to go out and harass vulnerable Pacific Spanish ports (whom England was once again at war with), so perhaps it was even an optimal engagement for a seaman at the time. Which only makes it clear that even as late as the 1740's, life at sea was still a completely dreadful and often fatal experience for the rank and file.

Although the ship was run with military discipline, its adventures were in many ways pirate-like. The officers were given freedom to seek and sack what targets they chose, so long as they were Spanish, and the spoils were to be divided up between crew and crown (with very tiny percentages going to the crew, naturally, and the majority of that going to the officers).

The filling of the ranks had parallels with the pirate world as well. Like Captain Kidd populating his crew with prisoners, these officers took aboard 259 old naval hospital pensioners. They didn't stand a chance and the majority died off throughout the voyage.

The voyage of the Centurion ended the era of the lone raider as an effective wartime tool, as the massive and heavily gunned fleets of the European powers matured. It also pre-staged the cure for scurvy and the ability to measure longitude, making it the most modern and detailed account of a closing era, and excellent reference for Colonia.

Finally, the most incredible part of the story. They captured the galleon Acapulco and went home with over $100,000,000 in today's currency. Reportedly the biggest haul in all the golden age of piracy, yet I've never heard it mentioned in my books or documentaries. Sadly, the heroic and dutiful young officer who kept the log, Philip Saumarez, did not get to enjoy his wealth long, as he suffered a direct hit by cannonball shortly after this adventure.

SHIPS IN YOUR OWN HOME PORT

Even though I live ashore of the San Francisco Bay, I had no idea there were any real period ships to be seen in the area. One day when work was painfully slow, I took a half day off and went hiking in the City. I went up Nob Hill, then up Russian Hill, where I spied the masts of a square-rigged sailing ship. I felt as though I had been stranded on an island and had just spied my rescue waiting in the sheltered cove below. Hooray!

Of course this was Hyde Street Pier, and the ship was on permanent display, but it still felt like an adventure. I trotted down to the dock and was faced with an admission gate and a turnstyle blocking my path. Arr! I though to myself I would have to come back some time with a camera. Then I regained my senses and realized "I'm here! I must go in now!" and paid the toll keeper his ransom and went aboard. It was off-season and a week-day, which gave me almost free reign of the ship.

The ship's name is Balclutha, by the way. She's a bit new for my reference purposes, being built in the 1880's and having a steel hull, but there are still many characteristics I absorbed with euphoria. I felt the sway of the deck, and got a real feel for the dimensions of a ship. Touching cannons and rope makes for drawing better cannons and rope, I think. I learned how block and tackle worked, and even went below to lie in a bunk for a while and pretended I was a crewman.

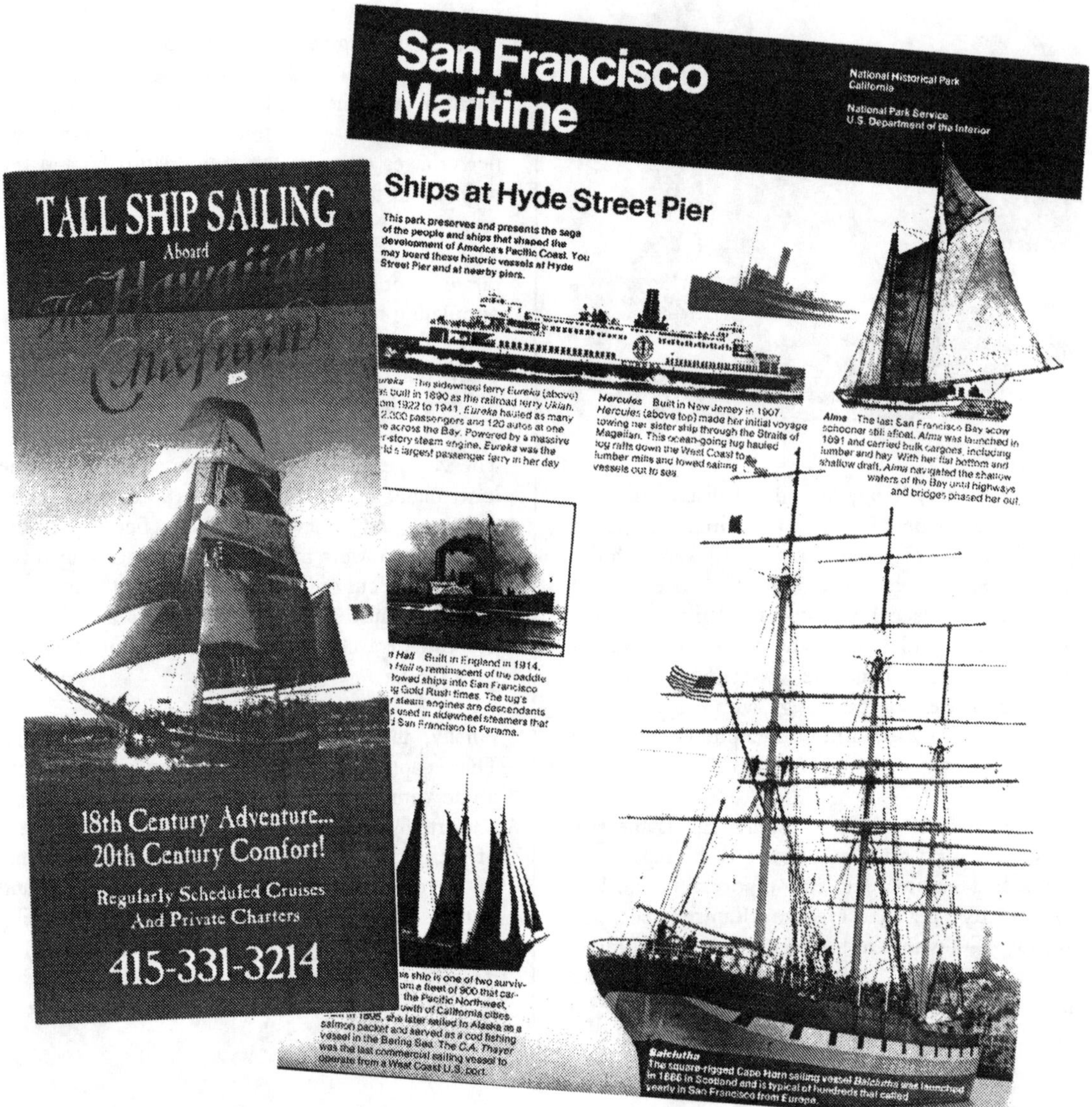

San Francisco Maritime
National Historical Park California
National Park Service U.S. Department of the Interior
Ships at Hyde Street Pier
This park preserves and presents the saga of the people and ships that shaped the development of America's Pacific Coast. You may board these historic vessels at Hyde Street Pier and at nearby piers.
Hercules Built in New Jersey in 1907, Hercules (above top) made her initial voyage towing her sister ship through the Straits of Magellan. This ocean-going tug hauled log rafts down the West Coast to lumber mills and towed sailing vessels out to sea.
Alma The last San Francisco Bay scow schooner still afloat. Alma was launched in 1891 and carried bulk cargoes, including lumber and hay. With her flat bottom and shallow draft, Alma navigated the shallow waters of the Bay until highways and bridges phased her out.
Balclutha The square-rigged Cape Horn sailing vessel Balclutha was launched in 1886 in Scotland and is typical of hundreds that called yearly in San Francisco from Europe.
TALL SHIP SAILING
Aboard
18th Century Adventure...
20th Century Comfort!
Regularly Scheduled Cruises
And Private Charters
415-331-3214

SHIPS IN YOUR OWN HOME PORT

This was back when I was working on issue #2. Then more recently, after discovering the No Quarter Given website (see letters column), I learned that there are working, sailing tallships all over the world. The more vintage models being reproductions. They are also the very ships seen in the many documentaries I have taped for reference. The Lady Washington, a partial model for Captain Reed's "Lady Jain," resides in Seattle. Her sister ship, the Hawaiian Chieftain, was found to dock right in my own backyard, in the town of Sausalito. The next thing I knew I was out taking pictures of her and chatting up the crew. If you live near a major port, chances are you've got a tallship anchored nearby. If not, they may visit your port on the many special event journeys they embark upon.

Naturally each ship has her own website. A trip to www.californian.org/ will link you to them all.

FROM THE REFERENCE LIBRARY

American Folklore and Legend
Reader's Digest (0-89577-045-8) 1978

Visiting Our Past
America's Historylands
National Geographic (No ISBN) 1977

The Commanding Sea
Six Voyages of Discovery
Clare Francis
BBC / Pelham Books, Ltd. (0-7207-1307-2) 1981

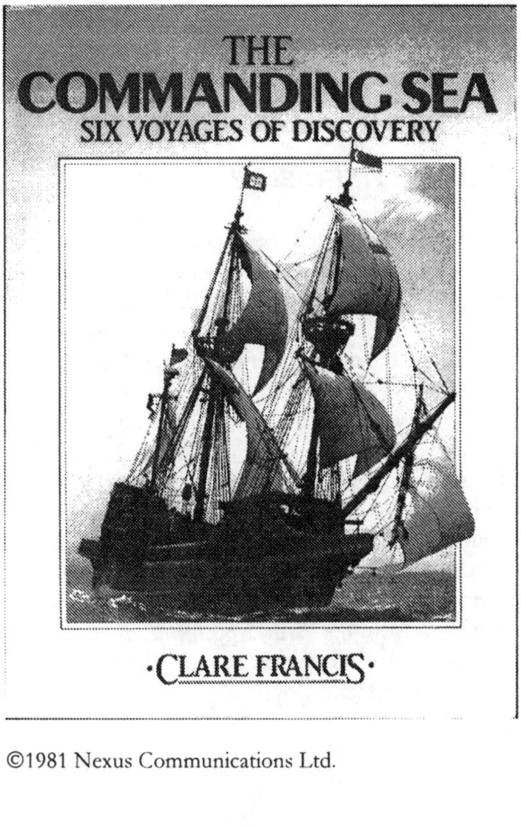
THE
COMMANDING SEA
SIX VOYAGES OF DISCOVERY
·CLARE FRANCIS·

©1981 Nexus Communications Ltd.

Just a brief visit to the library this time folks, as I devote a lot of space to the bi-monthly hub-bub.

As you may have discovered, looking for reference at a Border's or similar high-end chain store can be daunting. Very expensive coffee table books seem to dominate over the encyclopedic, and it's easy to walk away empty handed. Here's where the used bookstore can lift your spirits. What may at fist look like "crummy dated books from the Seventies" can, once you get past this prejudice, turn out to be a treasure trove of text and visuals.

They do lack a modern approach to history, which is better found in a new and critical release, but they cover very large historical and cultural periods, are packed with illustrations and photographs, and the combined price for all three sturdy well-kept hardcovers was under thirty dollars.

HORATIO HORNBLOWER on A&E

I missed this sea faring series when it first ran, but managed to tape it later when it appeared on A&E Classroom in the wee hours of the morning. It's a bit historically new for my reference (Napoleonic Era) but it's great entertainment. You can purchase this six hour program directly from A&E at www.aetv.com/scenes/horatio/index.html

And get this . . . not long after finishing the scene in this issue where Jack gets tossed overboard, I watched a boarding scene on Horatio, in which an invader grabs the ship's boy and tosses him over in just the same way!

FROM THE REFERENCE LIBRARY

Anchor Atlas of World History
Volume 1, From the Stone Age to the Eve of the French Revolution
ISBN: 0-385-06178
Volume 2, From the French Revolution to the American Bi-Centennial.
ISBN: 0-385-13355-3
Anchor/Doubleday

If you're as big a political geography geek as I am you will love these books. It's like having snapshots of the world as its boundaries lay during hundreds of different periods in time, from broad eras to brief battle lines. All left hand pages are maps and all right hand pages are text, packed with encapsulated history and dates for pivotal events. They are technically reference books but I sat and read them like little novels. The original editions are German made and the map designs are so much more clear, communicative, and downright hand-some than most.

130 The First World War/The End of the War (1918)
NORWAY
SWEDEN
DENMARK
GREAT BRITAIN
FRANCE
SWITZERLAND
AUSTRIA HUNGARY
RUSSIA
ALBANIA
OTTOMAN EMPIRE
DENMARK
NETHERLANDS
BELGIUM
FRANCE
RUSSIA
SWITZERLAND
AUSTRIA (HUNGARY)
The war year of 1918
The revolution in Germany

Pirate Tales
A&E Documentary

In addition to collecting books I've also been amassing a video collection for props, locales, costumes, etc., which is often more effective than print as reference. There is an abundance of programs floating around out there on cable (especially the History Channel) that recruit living history buffs in their production.

Great Ships - The Pirate Ships
History Channel Documentary

This issue owes a lot to this excellent program. Seeing these beautiful old ships out and on the water is so different than any book reference can provide. Strangely enough, I had designed the Anne Reed and Bonnie O'Malley characters long before seeing this. But the actress who plays the real Mary Read looks kind of like Bonnie, and the actress who plays the real Ann Bonnie looks exactly like Colonia's Anne Reed.

**Answers: (1) The Golden Hind
(2) Captain Kidd (starring John Laughton)**

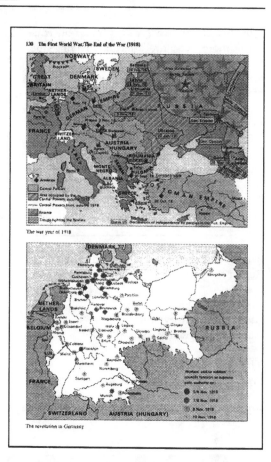

Special thanks to Todd Klein and Chad Woody for feedback on preliminary copies of Colonia #1

WHAT'S A HAUG-BOY?

Curious as Jack was by Lucy's reference to a Haug-Boy? To English speaking peoples this creature would be called a "Hogboy," "Hog-boon," or "Brownie." A sort of benevolent cousin to the more infernal Trows (Trolls) and Fairy-folk. A Hogboy might have friendly relations with both man-folk and magical creatures, hence Lucy's assumption. Tracing the Hogboy's origins further back into Norse mythology, we find it stems from "Haug-bui," or Mound-Dweller, as all of these Troll and Fairy-like creatures seemed to be inhabitants of hills and mounds. To avoid confusion with a hog as we know him from the farm, I prefer the Norse Haug over hog. And there you have it. In the land of Colonia, it's a Haug-Boy.

Here are some sketches from the Fall of 1997, when I was getting ready to start the first issue. I remember doing some of these in a laundromat. I obviously hadn't picked up any reference on ducks for this first page. Soon after I got an animal book and used the Shelduck as a model. Pete and Richard sure do look different.

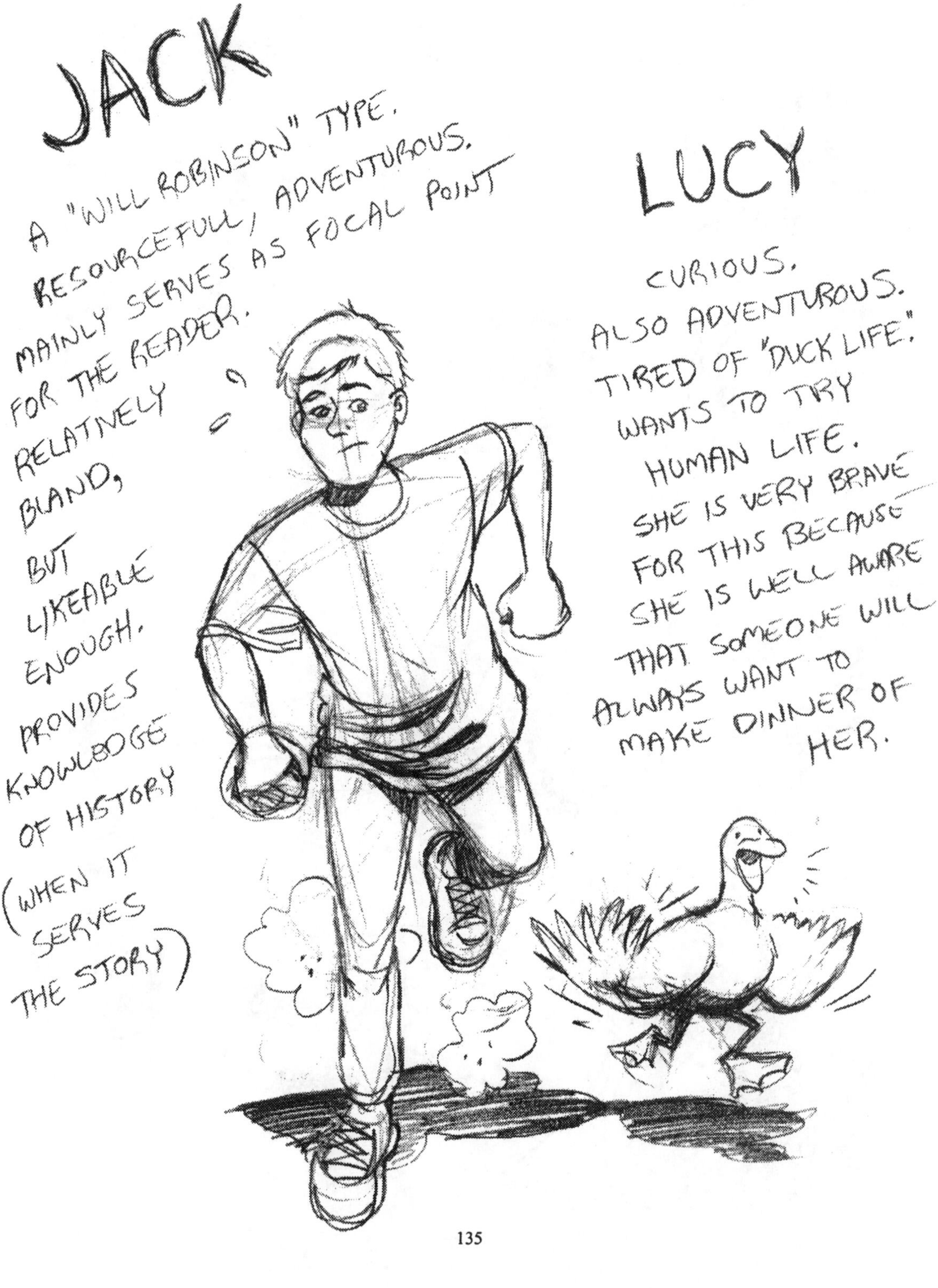
JACK
A "WILL ROBINSON" TYPE.
RESOURCEFULL, ADVENTUROUS.
MAINLY SERVES AS FOCAL POINT
FOR THE READER.
RELATIVELY
BLAND,
BUT
LIKEABLE
ENOUGH.
PROVIDES
KNOWLEDGE
OF HISTORY
(WHEN IT
SERVES
THE STORY)
LUCY
CURIOUS.
ALSO ADVENTUROUS.
TIRED OF "DUCK LIFE."
WANTS TO TRY
HUMAN LIFE.
SHE IS VERY BRAVE
FOR THIS BECAUSE
SHE IS WELL AWARE
THAT SOMEONE WILL
ALWAYS WANT TO
MAKE DINNER OF
HER.

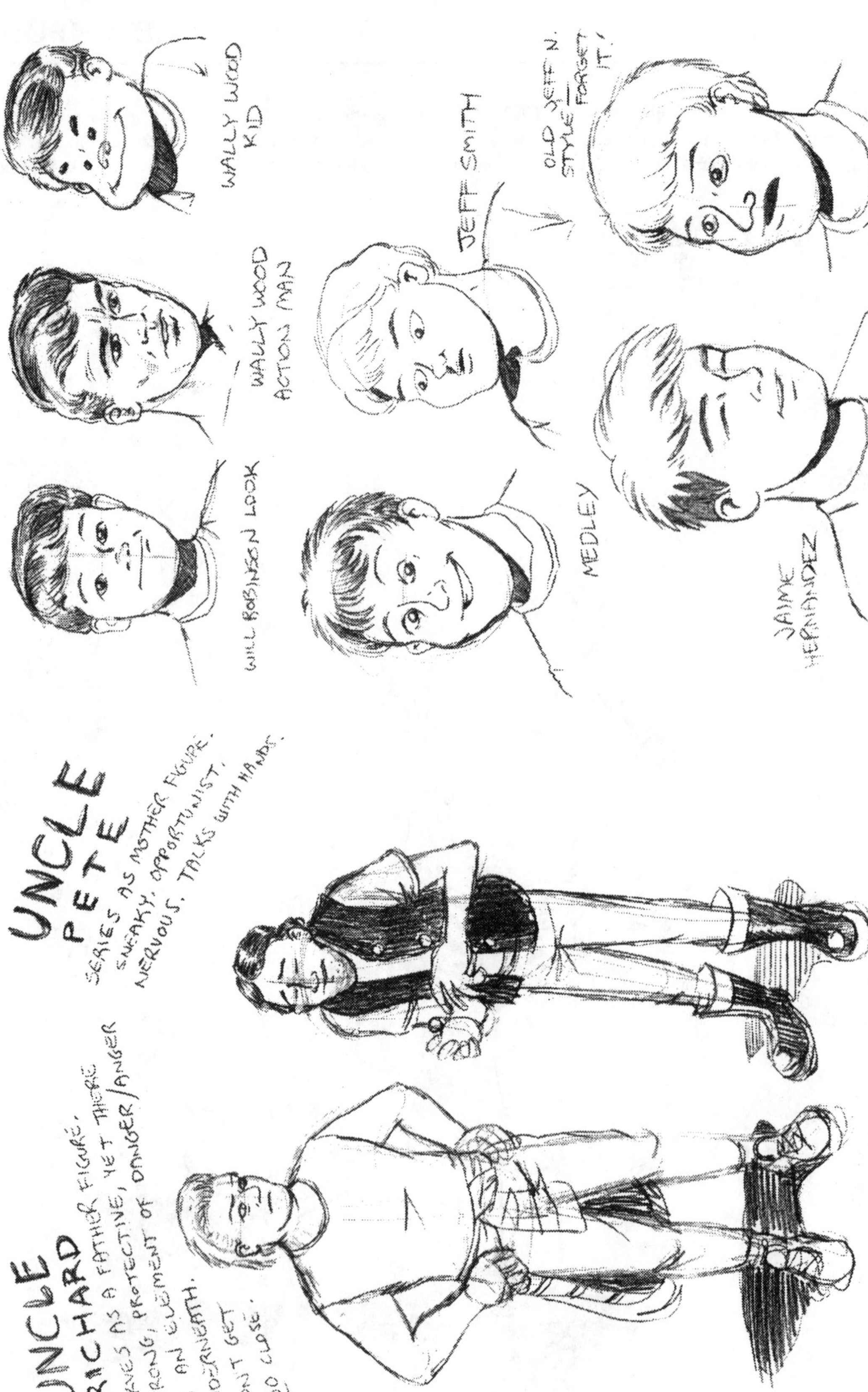
UNCLE RICHARD
SERVES AS A FATHER FIGURE. STRONG, PROTECTIVE, YET THERE IS AN ELEMENT OF DANGER/ANGER UNDERNEATH.
DON'T GET TOO CLOSE.
UNCLE PETE
SERIES AS MOTHER FIGURE. SNEAKY, OPPORTUNIST. NERVOUS. TALKS WITH HANDS.
WILL ROBINSON LOOK
WALLY WOOD ACTION MAN
WALLY WOOD KID
JEFF SMITH
MEDLEY
OLD JEFF N. STYLE — FORGET IT!
JAIME HERNANDEZ

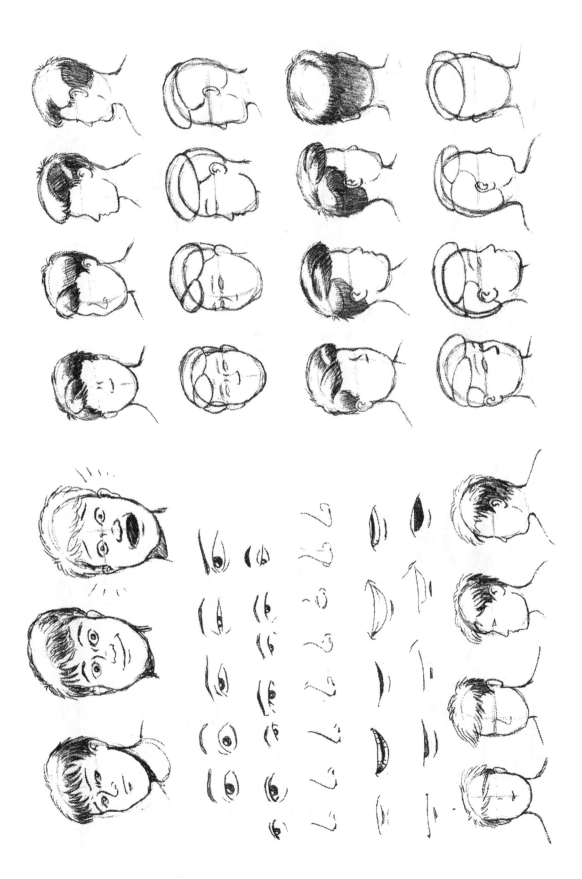

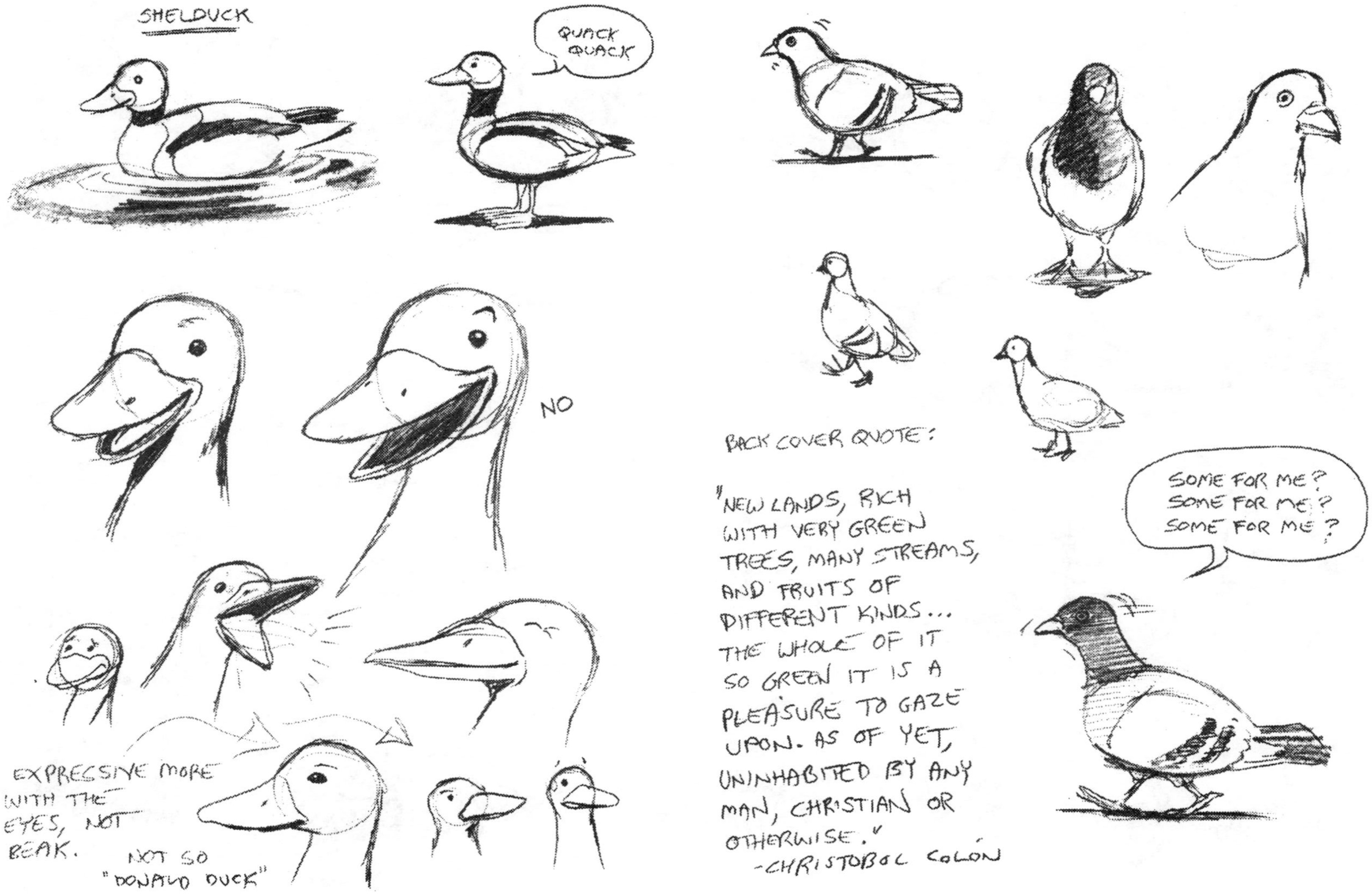
SHELDUCK
QUACK QUACK
NO
EXPRESSIVE MORE WITH THE EYES, NOT BEAK.
NOT SO "DONALD DUCK"
BACK COVER QUOTE:
"NEW LANDS, RICH WITH VERY GREEN TREES, MANY STREAMS, AND FRUITS OF DIFFERENT KINDS... THE WHOLE OF IT SO GREEN IT IS A PLEASURE TO GAZE UPON. AS OF YET, UNINHABITED BY ANY MAN, CHRISTIAN OR OTHERWISE."
-CHRISTOBOL COLÓN
SOME FOR ME? SOME FOR ME? SOME FOR ME?

CAPT. CINNABAR

OBSESSED
UNPREDICTABLE —
SOMEHOW LOVEABLE
KIND OF BEING
THE UNEXPOSE
A LOT.
NAMON'C
RELIEF.
HE LIKES
CINNABAR,
of COURSE.

THE OLD
MAN-OF-FISH

139

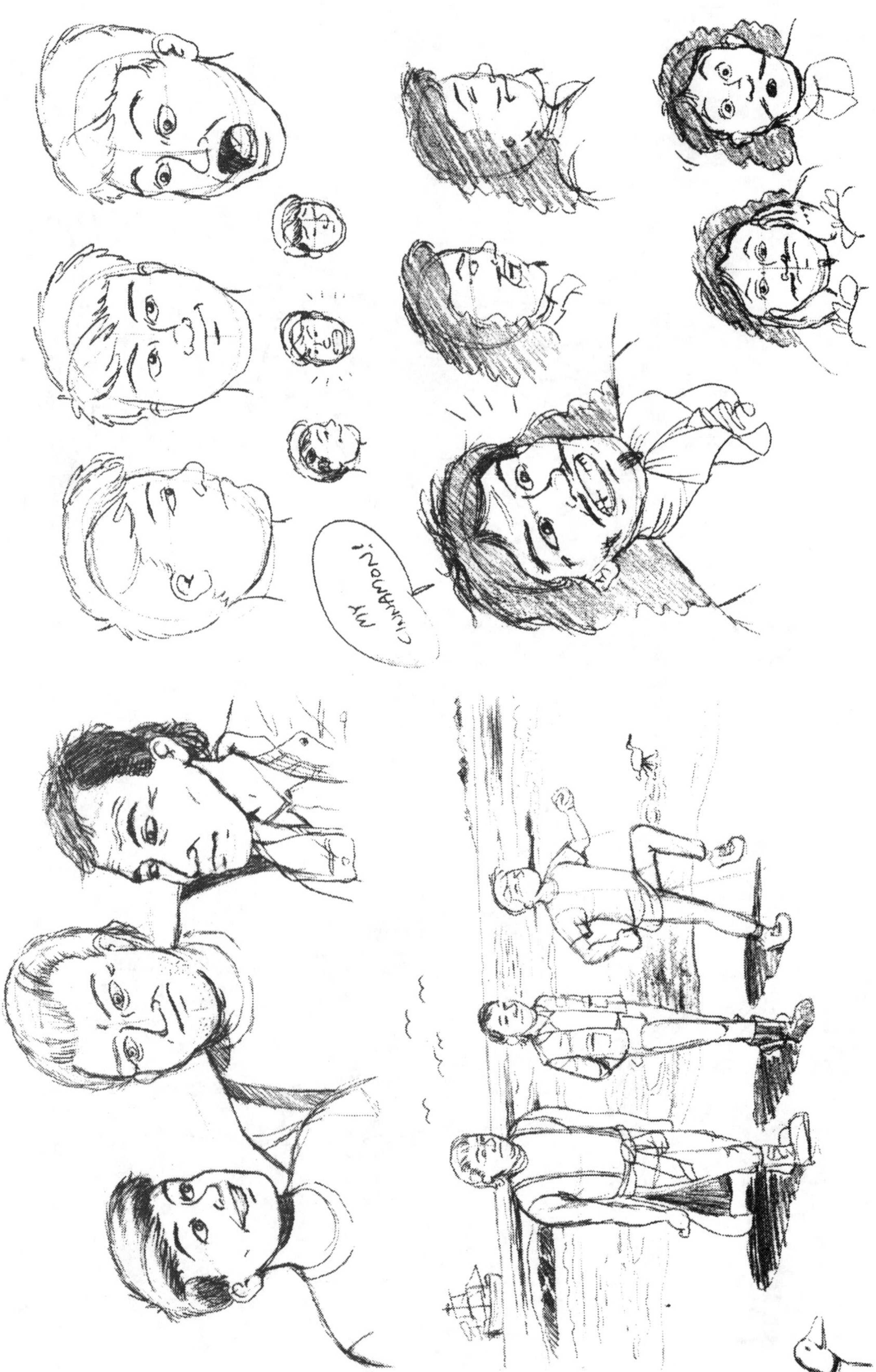
MY CINNAMON!

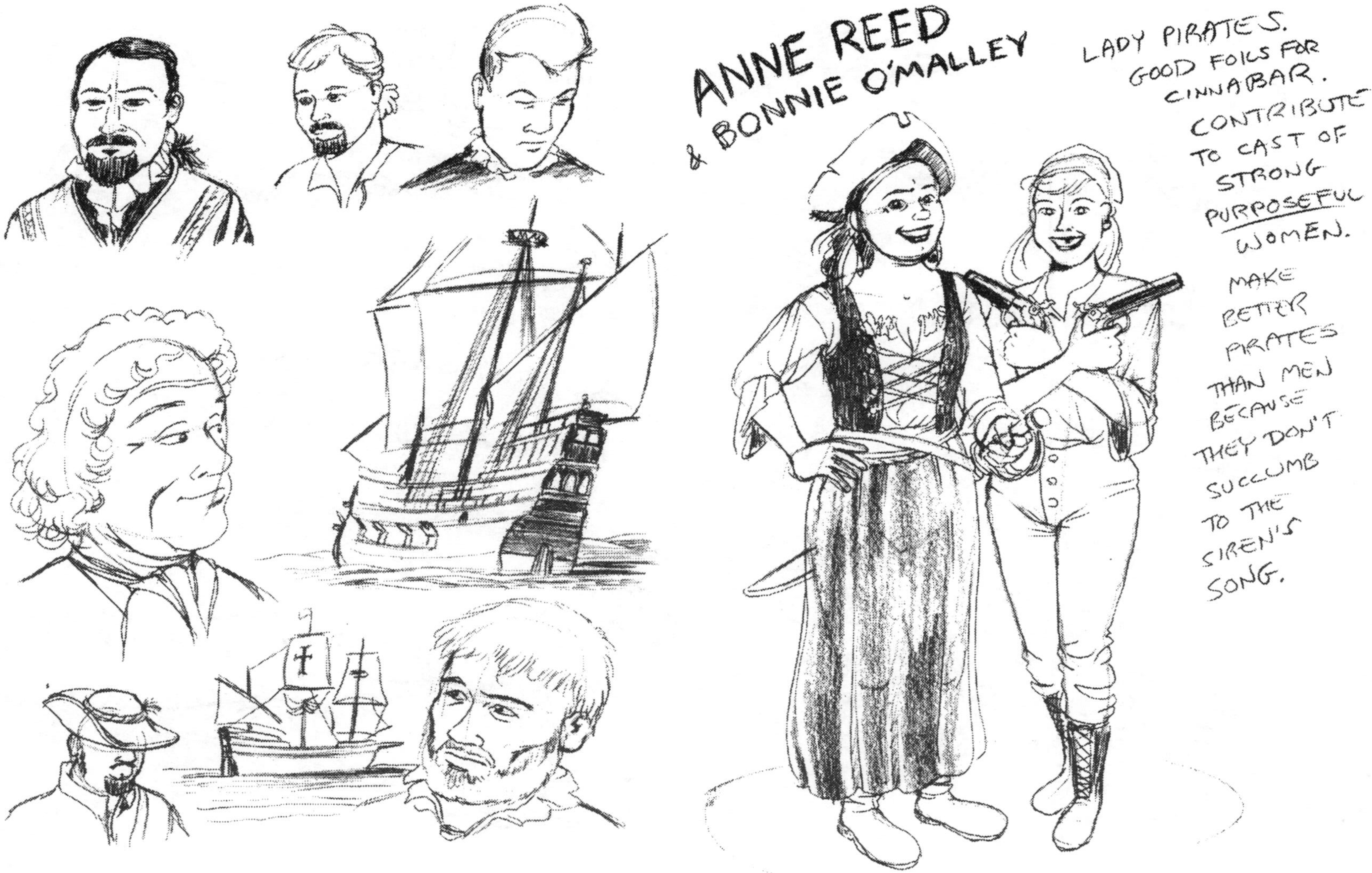
ANNE REED
& BONNIE O'MALLEY
LADY PIRATES.
GOOD FOILS FOR
CINNABAR.
CONTRIBUTE
TO CAST OF
STRONG
PURPOSEFUL
WOMEN.
MAKE
BETTER
PIRATES
THAN MEN
BECAUSE
THEY DON'T
SUCCUMB
TO THE
SIREN'S
SONG.

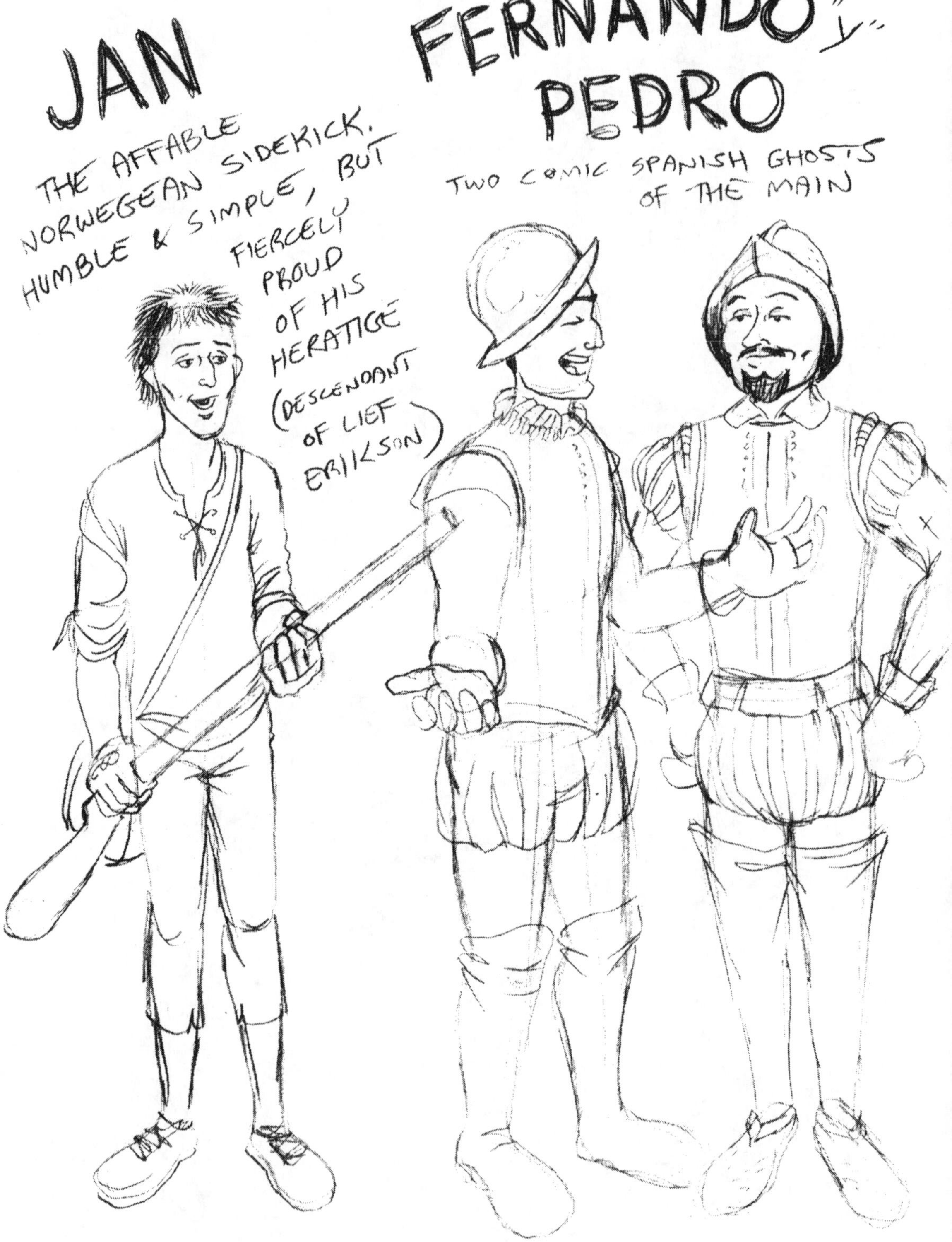
JAN
THE AFFABLE NORWEGEAN SIDEKICK. HUMBLE & SIMPLE, BUT FIERCELY PROUD OF HIS HERATIGE (DESCENDANT OF LIEF ERIKSON)
FERNANDO "y" PEDRO
TWO COMIC SPANISH GHOSTS OF THE MAIN

COLONIA ORIGINAL ART FOR SALE

I'm still too sentimental about the first issue to sell those pages, but I do have original art from the rest of this collection for sale. Some have already been sold by mail or at conventions, but here is a list of what remains.

COLONIA #2: pages 6, 8, 10, 12, 18, 19, 22, 23
COLONIA #3: pages 4, 6, 7, 15, 16, 17, 18, 19, 21, 22
COLONIA #4: all pages except 10 and 22
COLONIA #5: all pages except 11 and 21

The price per page is $40, including shipping. Please give a few alternate choices if possible, and make check or money order out to: Jeff Nicholson, P.O. Box 193681, San Francisco, CA 94119. You can also e-mail me for the most current list of what is available (including issues after this collection) at: jeff@coloniapress.com

OTHER COMICS SERIES

ULTRA KLUTZ was my obsession from the 1980's. It's been recognized as the closest thing to COLONIA that I've done, even though it is my oldest body of work. The sense of wonder, the open ended scope, and the way absurdities clash with carefully constructed worlds; it's all there in Ultra Klutz. Originally one of the longest running creator-owned self published comics, the series ran monthly for two years and weighs in at 730 pages. ULTRA KLUTZ BOOK ONE collects the first 23 issues plus unpublished material, and folks, there's just a handful left! ULTRA KLUTZ DREAMS collects the short stories created for anthologies in one 32 page comic.

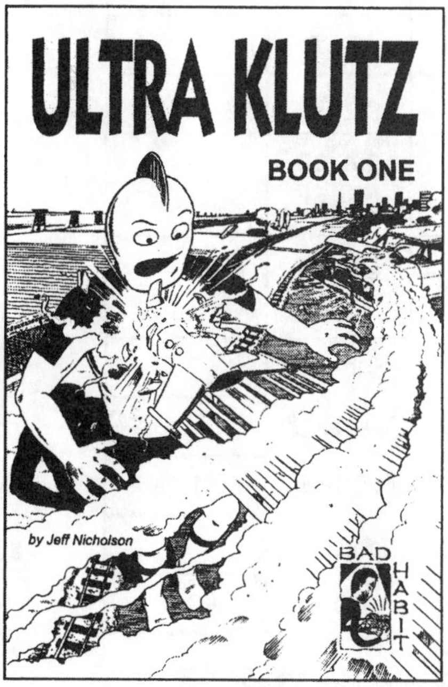
ULTRA KLUTZ
BOOK ONE
by Jeff Nicholson
BAD HABIT

FATHER & SON personified the generation gap of the early 90's: Generation X versus the Baby Boomers. As win-win dad Richard Schultz marched off to the silicon valley trenches each day, lose-lose son Chris Schultz shambled through life trying to piece together a band, a relationship, or whatever. The most "commercial" of my work, yet still populated with absurdist characters and confounding plot directions. After the original four issues were released by Kitchen Sink Press, I decided to step further away from "commercial" and follow my instincts on a revised, updated Father & Son. Now the KSP issues are collected into the EVERYBODY'S FAVORITE SELL-OUT collection, and the newer work is in the LIKE, SPECIAL #1.

THROUGH THE HABITRAILS is a collection of dark humored short stories about life on-the-job. and beyond. A nameless protagonist tackles inter-office romance, is bemused over his fellow workers and banal tasks, and tries to leave the company behind entirely in search for that elusive something more. As you progress THROUGH THE HABITRAILS, the short stories combine to form a larger novella which spirals towards a dramatic conclusion. Most people are surprised the same person created this series and COLONIA, and I even have a hard time relating to it as something I wrote. Despite its grim outlook, it is still the most well received of my work before COLONIA. Fans of HABITRAILS will also be curious to know that I did an issue of **THE DREAMING** for Vertigo in 1996 (issue 15, later collected in "The Gates of Horn and Ivory").

Order online with PayPal at *www.coloniapress.com*
or mail a copy of this form (or your own hand-drawn version) to:
COLONIA PRESS, P.O. BOX 193681 SAN FRANCISCO, CA 94119

Name and address: _____

_____

_____

Please send me the following books:

Quantity	Title	Price each	Total
	Colonia: Islands & Anomalies	$12.95	
	Colonia #1 (second printing)	$2.95	
	Colonia #2	$2.95	
	Colonia #3	$2.95	
	Colonia #4	$2.95	
	Colonia #5	$2.95	
	Colonia #6	$3.50	
	Colonia #7 (shipping May '02)	$2.95	
	"Not Colonia " set (all 5 books below)	$29.95	
	Father & Son: Sell Out	$9.95	
	Father & Son, Like, Special #1	$3.95	
	Ultra Klutz Dreams	$2.95	
	Ultra Klutz: Book One (Remaindered)	~~$29.95~~ **$14.95**	
	Through the Habitrails (Remaindered)	~~$14.95~~ **$9.95**	
		Sub-total	
		CA residents please add 8 % sales tax	
		Domestic Shipping	$1.35
		Int'l Shipping (see left)	
		TOTAL	

E-mail me (jeff@coloniapress.com) for an exact rate at Economy (Surface) Letter-Post. All foriegn checks/MOs must be drawn from a US affiliated bank or will require an additional $5 depositing fee.

Make check or money order payable to **COLONIA PRESS**

To be informed of new releases or other Colonia events, sign up for the e-mail newsletter via Jeff@coloniapress.com